MONGOLIAN FILM MUSIC

Mongolian Film Music
Tradition, Revolution and Propaganda

LUCY M. REES

LONDON AND NEW YORK

First published 2015 by Ashgate Publishing

2 Park Square, Milton Park, Abingdon, Oxfordshire OX14 4RN
52 Vanderbilt Avenue, New York, NY 10017

Routledge is an imprint of the Taylor & Francis Group, an informa business

First issued in paperback 2020

Copyright © 2015 Lucy M. Rees

Lucy M. Rees has asserted her right under the Copyright, Designs and Patents Act, 1988, to be identified as the author of this work.

All rights reserved. No part of this book may be reprinted or reproduced or utilised in any form or by any electronic, mechanical, or other means, now known or hereafter invented, including photocopying and recording, or in any information storage or retrieval system, without permission in writing from the publishers.

Notice:
Product or corporate names may be trademarks or registered trademarks, and are used only for identification and explanation without intent to infringe.

British Library Cataloguing in Publication Data
A catalogue record for this book is available from the British Library

The Library of Congress has cataloged the printed edition as follows:
Rees, Lucy M.
 Mongolian film music : tradition, revolution and propaganda / by Lucy M. Rees.
  pages cm
 Includes bibliographical references and index.
 ISBN 978-1-4724-4623-7 (hardcover : alk. paper)
1. Motion picture music–Political aspects–Mongolia–
History–20th century. 2. Motion picture music–Mongolia–20th century–History and criticism. 3. Socialism and motion pictures–Mongolia. I. Title.
 ML3917.M66R44 2015
 781.5'42095173–dc23

2015010981

ISBN 978-1-4724-4623-7 (hbk)
ISBN 978-0-367-59789-4 (pbk)

Contents

List of Figures and Tables	*vii*
List of Music Examples	*ix*
Acknowledgements	*xi*
List of Abbreviations	*xiii*
A Note on Mongolian Transliteration	*xv*
A Note on Mongolian Names	*xvii*

1	Tradition, Politics and Film Music	1
2	Tradition and Transition in Mongolian Music	13
3	New Beginnings: Patriotism, Propaganda and Professional Music	33
4	Socialist Cinema from Conception to Dissemination	55
5	A Standard of Socialist Cinema: *The Clear River Tamir* (*Tungalag Tamir*, 1970–1973)	75
6	Perestroika, a Wise Queen and a Delinquent Rock Star	95
7	New Directions: The Democratic Revolution and the Aftermath of the Socialist Era	115
8	Tradition, Revolution, Propaganda and Consolidation: A Brief Conclusion	139
Appendix A	Feature Films Produced by the State Film Studio, 1938–1990	149
Appendix B	Glossary of Mongolian Words	159
Appendix C	Glossary of Film and Film Music Terminology	163
Appendix D	Timeline	165

Bibliography	*169*
Interviews	*175*
Filmography	*179*
Index	*183*

List of Figures and Tables

Figures

2.1 Horse-head fiddles, Egshiglen musical instrument factory, Ulaanbaatar   17

3.1 Musicians play as Tsogt Taij leaves his palace for Lhasa. Tsagaany Tsegmed as Tsogt Taij. *Tsogt Taij*, Film Factory (Mongol Kino), 1945   40

4.1 Dari's happy expression on hearing the harmonica at the end of the film. Myatavyn Badamgarav as Dari, *The Harmonica* (*Aman Khuur*), Film Factory (Mongol Kino), 1963   69

5.1 Tömör is stabbed by Tügjil, accompanied by a cymbal crash. Togtokhyn Sanduijav as Tömör, *The Clear River Tamir* (*Tungalag Tamir*), Film Factory (Mongol Kino), 1970–1973   85

5.2 Erdene and Itgelt at a party in a wealthy family's house. Norovyn Baatar as Erdene and Ayuurzanyn Ochirbat as Itgelt, *The Clear River Tamir* (*Tungalag Tamir*), Film Factory (Mongol Kino), 1970–1973   89

6.1 Mandukhai becomes queen on her wedding day. Namsrain Suvd as Mandukhai, *Mandukhai the Wise Queen* (*Mandukhai Tsetsen Khatan*), State Film Head Office (Mongol Kino), 1988   103

7.1 Chinggis Khaan statue (built in 2006), Sükhbaatar Square, Ulaanbaatar   123

7.2 A *dombra* on a hand-woven Kazakh rug, Töv province, Mongolia   135

Tables

3.1 The most prolific Mongolian film composers of the Socialist era   50

3.2 The most prolific film directors and their collaborations with composers   51

List of Music Examples

3.1 The opening phrase of the melody played when Tsogt Taij talks to
his mother, *Tsogt Taij*   39

5.1 The first statement of the melody of the opening cue to Part 3,
The Clear River Tamir   93

6.1 The melody of Mandukhai and Önöbold's theme, *Mandukhai the
Wise Queen*   105
6.2 Fanfare figure, *Mandukhai the Wise Queen*   105

Acknowledgements

I am very grateful to everyone who helped me throughout my research into Mongolian film music and during the production of this book. First, I would like to thank my PhD supervisors, Professor Kevin Dawe and Dr Judith Nordby for unremitting support and valuable insight; Professor David Cooper and Dr David Sneath for their encouragement when this project was at the PhD thesis stage; the Leeds University Research Scholarship for funding the bulk of my research, and Nicki Sapiro for help with the funding application. I would like to thank everyone at Ashgate who helped with the production of this book, particularly Heidi Bishop for believing in my project and for continuously offering helpful advice and guidance, and to Emma Gallon, Barbara Pretty, Michael Bourne and Tania Whiting for all their support. I would also like to thank Martin Thomas, Kelly Knight and Graham Howells for help with computers, photographs and film stills; Geoffrey Humble for proofreading the very early stages of this book and Sara Peacock for proofreading the final version; and to Kelly Knight, Christine Bennett and Hilary Knight for baby-sitting, thereby giving me valuable time to work on the book. Finally, I would like to thank the numerous Mongolians who helped me throughout my fieldwork, in particular Tümenjiin Bekhbat for excellent interpreting and valued frienship, Zandan Bilegt and Uuganaa Urjinbadam for valued friendship and for putting me in touch with many of my interviewees, and to Almagul Karagaz, Amara Dorjsüren, Askar and Risgul, and especially Jambyn Solongo and the staff at the University of Film Arts in Ulaanbaatar.

List of Abbreviations

The following abbreviations and acronyms will be used in this book:

B&W	Black and white
CD	Compact disc
COMECON	Council for Mutual Economic Assistance
CPSU	Communist Party of the Soviet Union
DVD	Digital versatile disc
INT	Interview
Lit.	Literally
MIDI	Musical instrument digital interface
MNB	Mongolian National Broadcaster (television channel)
MPR	Mongolian People's Republic
MPRP	Mongolian People's Revolutionary Party
SATB	Soprano, alto, tenor, bass
UNESCO	United Nations Educational, Scientific and Cultural Organization
USA	United States of America

A Note on Mongolian Transliteration

My transliterations of Mongolian names and terms are intended to correspond as closely as possible to the Cyrillic orthography. Since there are more letters in the Cyrillic alphabet than the Latin alphabet, I have used more than one Latin letter to represent certain single Cyrillic letters, for example 'ch' to represent 'Ч/ч'. Unstressed final vowels, for example Халха (*Khalkha*), retain their final 'a' even though they are not pronounced. I have adopted established orthographic conventions, such as using *kh* to represent the Mongolian x, as in Khaan (Хаан). Therefore, Халха is spelled *Khalkha*, rather than the more recently preferred *Halh* or *Halha*. Both 'И/и' and 'Й/й' are transliterated as 'i', as 'Й/й' appears only with another vowel as a diphthong or long (double) vowel.

A Note on Mongolian Names

Mongolians have one given name and one *ovog*: their father's name with a genitive suffix, transliterated 'in', 'iin', 'en', 'yn' or 'ny'. The *ovog* comes before the given name and is often initialised. For example, the composer Jantsannorov's father was called Natsag, so his 'full name' is Natsagiin Jantsannorov or N. Jantsannorov. Mongolians are usually called only by their given names, so quite often a person's *ovog* is unknown. Within the following chapters, I will use the *ovog* or initial when known on the first mention of a person's name and only the given name thereafter.[1] Recently, many Mongolians prefer to drop the genitive suffix, so there can be some confusion as to which name is the given and which the *ovog*. Occasionally, a Mongolian's name will not follow the conventions described here, such as the cinema projectionist Tsagaan Nokhoi (lit. White Dog) referred to in Chapter 4.

---

[1] In Appendix A and the Filmography, only the given name is used.

Chapter 1
Tradition, Politics and Film Music

The Mongolian socialist government decreed the establishment of a film industry in the mid-1930s with the principal aim of disseminating propaganda to the populace. The state film studio was founded in 1936, and it remained the sole film studio until 1990, when a democratic revolution brought the Mongolian Socialist era (1921–90) to an end. In the 1930s and 1940s, experts from the Soviet Union came to Mongolia to train people in the art of filmmaking, and later, Mongolians studied formally at film schools in Moscow and other Eastern Bloc cities, where they also spent years absorbing Eastern European socialist culture and society. On returning to Mongolia, these graduates utilised their new skills and knowledge to produce films at the state film studio on topics prescribed by the government, which were subsequently disseminated to every citizen. These films celebrated socialist progress, diffused Marxist–Leninist ideology, denounced those deemed a threat to the authority of the state, and instated the 1921 socialist revolution as the starting point of modern Mongolian history. The new political system had a wide-reaching influence in Mongolia, from the economy to societal structures, from the capital city to the most remote localities, and amongst citizens of all ages from the newborn to the elderly. Mongolian filmmakers were therefore immersed in socialism not only in a professional capacity but also during daily life, whether or not they truly sympathised with the ideology.

The film industry needed new composers to provide the music for the films, so Mongolian musicians who showed potential as composers went to the Soviet Union for periods of up to eight years to study music formally at conservatoires. Many of these had been born into nomadic families from rural areas, where they had learned traditional Mongolian instrumental and vocal music orally from elder family members. This dual musical background, in addition to the political context of the Mongolian film industry, made a profound impression on Mongolian film composers and the film scores they composed. As a result, a rich mosaic of music can be heard in Mongolian film soundtracks[1] of the Socialist era, incorporating the genres learned informally at home, those taught formally at Soviet conservatoires, and music genres supported by the government, financially and ideologically. With very few exceptions, Mongolian film scores before 1990 were played by a symphony orchestra, although additional genres and ensembles were sometimes heard, including military brass bands, Russian accordion tunes, revolutionary

---

[1]   A film soundtrack includes three main elements: the dialogue, the music (the score) and the sound effects.

songs, popular music based on Anglo-American models and versions of traditional Mongolian melodies.

One of the most significant musical developments was the creation of *mergejliin khögjim* (lit. professional music), a genre that was heard throughout the Socialist era played by the symphony orchestra and clearly influenced by the music composers learned in Soviet conservatoires but with a distinctly Mongolian flavour. Potentially this music could appeal to the entire socialist nation: it promoted the symphonic music prevalent in Soviet cinema, with which the Mongolian public was familiar, whilst maintaining a strong, albeit modified, element of traditional Mongolian music.

The motive behind establishing a film industry and training a new cohort of Mongolian film composers to score the films with appropriate music was largely political. The messages the films and their soundtracks were intended to convey were also political, although they had to appeal to a nation steeped in centuries of nomadic culture and tradition, so political content had to be handled appropriately. The reasons for this political impulse are clear, given that Mongolia had adopted a completely new ideology and political system that would take time and effort on the part of the government to administer fully across a large, sparsely populated country. The question addressed in this book is how film music developed throughout the Mongolian Socialist era in the context of the new political system and within the constantly evolving film industry. To answer this question, we must first look at the context in which the film composers lived and worked from their background and training to the culture of the new film industry and their status within the new socialist society. This book then explores how composers reconciled what they had learned at Soviet conservatoires with their traditional musical backgrounds, and investigates why and how composers combined these dual musical influences in their scores. We also look into how composers met their obligations to complement the political messages of the films through their music whilst appealing to a sparsely populated and largely rural nation.

During my research into Mongolian film music, I spent a year living in Mongolia between 2008 and 2009, where I conducted over forty formal interviews with a variety of informants. These ranged from film and music professionals to film viewers, city dwellers to nomads, and from those who had lived and worked during the Socialist era to those who were too young to remember life before 1990. Although some informants spoke about their work during the Socialist era with a hint of nostalgia, they provided first-hand accounts of what it was like to work within the music and film industries during the regime and its aftermath, including information that is wholly unavailable outside Mongolia and that has not been documented in any other way.

There is very little information about the working lives of filmmakers and composers during the Socialist era in the form of documents, memoirs or personal correspondence, and so on, with the exception of a few editorials in the party newspaper *Ünen*, which was in itself a form of propaganda. These interviews were therefore a crucial part of this research. All informants were free during the interviews to impart information that may have been sensitive during the Socialist era without any obligation to promote or sympathise with the socialist regime. A sizable portion of the information in this book comes directly from these interviews, which cover a broad range of expertise and points of view, and helps tell the story of Mongolian film music from a distinctly Mongolian perspective. In addition to the interviews, I spent time living in nomadic communities as well as the capital city, observed film and music editing sessions at Mongolia's first and largest film studio, viewed statistical information, accessed archives,[2] and viewed over eighty films.[3]

After 1990, the film and music industries were no longer subject to strict governmental controls and anyone who wished to become a musician, composer, filmmaker or actor could do so. New filmmakers and composers, however, had not received the training, funding or governmental support of the Socialist era, so numerous low-budget films were produced by inexperienced personnel on outdated equipment. When Mongolia began to recover from its post-1990 economic nadir, a sense of pride in pre-Socialist-era traditions emerged in tandem with the embracing of new cultural influences from countries to which Mongolians now had access. As the Mongolian borders opened, foreign filmmakers arrived and produced films to appeal to the audiences of their homelands, although many of these met with a mixed reception in Mongolia. From around 2006, the Mongolian film industry, which by then constituted numerous independent studios, started to produce films that were comparable to those of wealthier nations regarding sound and picture quality. By the time I left Mongolia in 2009, film scores featuring hip-hop and heavy metal were commonplace. Following the Democratic Revolution in 1990, governmental guidelines to produce propaganda films disappeared. The variety of genres, styles and situations within the music and film industries in the aftermath of the Socialist era mirrored the political and cultural influences to which contemporary Mongolian film composers were subject.

---

[2]   Although the Mongolian film archive holds a copy of each film of the Socialist era, there is no such archive for film scores. All scores of the era were handwritten, no copies were made, and many were destroyed shortly after the music was recorded (see Chapter 4). Furthermore, during politically charged riots in Ulaanbaatar in July 2008 – shortly before I arrived for fieldwork – the building of the Mongolian Philharmony was badly damaged and looted. This building had housed the entire music instrument collection of the Mongolian State Symphony Orchestra and the only copies of hundreds of handwritten scores by Mongolian composers.

[3]   Films, particularly those of the Socialist era, are not widely available in formats such as video or DVD. I therefore viewed many of these films only once, although I viewed the films presented in this book as case studies more than once. I watched the majority of films of the Socialist era at the library of the University of Film Arts (Kino Urlagiin Deed Surguuli) in Ulaanbaatar, or by watching them when they were broadcast on television.

Tradition: A Very Brief Overview of Mongolia

Mongolia is a landlocked country in northeast Asia comprising vast steppe lands, desert and mountainous regions. It has a population of approximately three million, over a third of which lives in the capital city, Ulaanbaatar. The rural population herds livestock and lives in round felt tents called *gers*, also known as yurts. In 2010, 42.5 per cent of the population was rural, although this proportion dropped to 30.7 per cent by January 2012 (World Bank, 2012a) and is likely to decrease over coming years. Urban populations expanded rapidly during the Socialist era and today a drastic contrast in lifestyle can be seen between rural areas and central Ulaanbaatar. The current living conditions in the countryside, which constitutes the majority of Mongolia's land mass, are similar to those of the thirteenth century with the addition of modern commodities such as television sets and motorbikes. Meanwhile, residents of Ulaanbaatar and other cities live in a rapidly developing urban environment, where expensive cars and designer labels are becoming commonplace. The currency is the tugrik (*tögrög*) and the economy has been one of the fastest growing in the world since 2011, largely on account of the recent boom in mining (World Bank, 2012b). It has an extreme continental climate, with temperatures during the winter plummeting regularly below minus 30 degrees Celsius in contrast to hot, dry and relatively short summers.

Mongolia borders on the Russian Federation, including the Buryat Republic, Tuva and the Altai Republic in the north, and the People's Republic of China, including the Inner Mongolian Autonomous Region in the south. The country is divided into 21 provinces (*aimag*) and the population comprises around 20 ethnic groups.[4] The largest ethnic group at 86 per cent is the Khalkha Mongols, whilst the Kazakhs, a Turkic people living mainly in the far-western province of Bayan Ölgii, are the largest ethnic minority at around 4 per cent.[5] Many other Mongol peoples live outside Mongolia, mainly in Russia and China. The traditional music practices of Mongolia's ethnic minorities were largely discouraged during the Socialist era, and Khalkha music was used as the basis for new genres of folk music that were developed at this time.

One of the main events in the Mongolian calendar is *Naadam*, an annual three-day festival that takes place in July. The festival involves the 'three manly sports' (*eriin gurvan naadam*) of archery, wrestling and horse racing, in addition to music, traditional food and the opportunity for nomads from different localities to socialise. *Naadam* was included in the UNESCO list of Intangible Cultural Heritage for the country in 2010 (UNESCO, n.d.). Another important event is the Mongolian lunar New Year, *Tsagaan Sar* (lit. white month or white moon), which usually takes place in February. A version of *Tsagaan Sar* known as Herdsmen's

---

[4] Sources vary widely regarding the number of ethnic groups in Mongolia. B. Suvd states there are 16 ethnic groups (Suvd, 2006, p. 51) whereas Carole Pegg lists 36 groups (Pegg, 2001, p. xiv), although doesn't state that these are specifically ethnic groups.

[5] National Statistical Office of Mongolia, 2011.

Day or Collective New Year was celebrated by some Mongolians during the Socialist era, whilst others celebrated *Tsagaan Sar* in secret during this time, since they were forbidden to do so publicly. The Kazakh population celebrates their New Year (*Nauryz*) in March, and other ethnic groups have their own celebrations and festivals at various times of year, although these would certainly have been discouraged during the Socialist era.

An important concept for Mongolians is that of *nutag*, which is often translated as 'homeland' and refers to the locality where individuals were born and raised. The concept of *nutag* is the subject of numerous folks songs, both pre-1921 traditional songs and songs newly composed during the Socialist era. The majority of Mongolians claim to feel an affinity with the countryside, whether or not they were born in a rural area. Horses have played an integral role in Mongolian life for centuries and feature widely in poetry, songs, legends, art, decorations, music and films. Horse racing is one of the three manly sports of *Naadam* and the horse-head fiddle (*morin khuur*) is one of Mongolia's most iconic musical instruments. The ability to ride a horse well is considered second nature to most Mongolians, especially in the countryside, and people who dislike horses or even those who ride badly are often considered something of an oddity.

The *ger* has been at the centre of nomadic life for some eight centuries, and it is the setting for many film scenes. *Gers* can be dismantled and reassembled easily, although nomadic Mongolians tend to move between the same summer and winter pastures annually rather than moving from place to place on a whim. Many Mongolians observe the traditional positioning, layout and décor of their *gers*. The door faces the south, women sit on the west, where cooking equipment is kept, men sit on the east, where hunting equipment may be stored, and there is a sacred area to the north that may house a shrine or family photographs. Whilst the *ger* is the standard dwelling in the countryside, it is more associated with poverty in urban areas. The *ger* districts on the outskirts of Ulaanbaatar are areas where people live in *gers* rather than permanent buildings and are roughly equivalent to shanty towns in other countries.

Each ethnic group in Mongolia has its traditional costume, which can signify not only a person's ethnic origin but also their gender, status, rank or age. Costumes are linked to seasons and occasions, and are often imbued with symbolism, such as the red and blue fabric favoured by Khalkha Mongols being used to symbolise fire and sky (Suvd, 2006, p. 55). The fundamental garment is the *deel*, a robe worn by both men and women, although nowadays most people in Ulaanbaatar and many in the countryside wear Western clothes and save traditional costume for special occasions. Historically, the most widely practised religions in Mongolia have been Buddhism and shamanism, although religion was suppressed during the Socialist era. After 1990, Buddhism and to a lesser extent shamanism have seen a revival, and a sizeable portion of the population is now secular.

Mongolia has a rich heritage of oral narrative and verse, including proverbs and sayings, riddles, incantations, songs, tales, epics, raillery and a genre peculiar to Mongolia called triads of the universe. A triad of the universe is similar to

6 *Mongolian Film Music*

the proverb or riddle: three statements are made to display the most idiosyncratic characteristics of an object, using parallelism and alliteration, although the object in question is not mentioned (Hangin, 1998, pp. 89–90). There are numerous other traditions and customs in Mongolia ranging from art to food to etiquette and many of these appear in film scenes.

Revolution: A Very Brief History of Mongolia

Chinggis Khaan (Genghis Khan), founder of the Mongol Empire (1206–1368), is undoubtedly the most famous Mongolian worldwide.[6] He was largely ignored by the Mongolian film industry during the Socialist era, since his feudalistic rule was incompatible with socialist ideology, although numerous films about his story have been produced since 1990. The Mongol Empire was the largest land-based empire the world has ever witnessed, and although Chinggis Khaan has gained notoriety around the world for his tyranny, Mongolians revere him as their most celebrated historical figure and national symbol. His story is chronicled in *The Secret History of the Mongols*, written shortly after his death in 1227 by an anonymous author, and remains an important source of Mongolian and medieval history.[7]

From the mid-fourteenth century, power was fragmented in Mongolia as a succession of leaders claiming to be descendants of the imperial khans struggled for political ascendancy. In the sixteenth century, there was a major conversion to Tibetan Buddhism, and many Buddhist leaders gained political power. Tibetan Buddhism consequently replaced shamanism as the principal religion in Mongolia, although both systems of belief remained powerful forces in the country until the Socialist era. In the seventeenth century, the Mongols recognised the Manchu (Qing) emperor as their khan, and they remained under Manchu rule until the end of the Qing Dynasty (1644–1911). In December 1911, Outer Mongolia declared independence from China, and the Bogd Khan – the eighth incarnation of the Javzandamba Khutagt, the Buddhist leader of Mongolia – was proclaimed head of state.

Much of northeast Asia was in turmoil during these first decades of the twentieth century, and it was in this context that the Mongolian People's Party was founded. In 1918, two progressive groups of nationalists formed; one included a military leader named Damdiny Sükhbaatar and the other included Khorloogiin Choibalsan, who had contacts in Russia and later became the Mongolian Prime Minister.[8] After several meetings with the Russian contacts, the two groups joined forces and on 25 June 1920 became the Mongolian People's Party (Isono, 2010, pp. 913–14).

---

[6] I use this spelling (Chinggis Khaan) as opposed to the more widely used 'Genghis Khan' since it corresponds more closely to the spelling in the Classical Mongol script.

[7] For further information about early and surviving copies of this chronicle, see Cleaves' Introduction in Anon., 1982, pp. xx–lxv.

[8] Choibalsan was Prime Minister of Mongolia 1939–52.

Tradition, Politics and Film Music 7

In October 1920, the Russian warlord Ungern-Sternberg attempted to take over the Mongolian capital city, then named Niislel Khüree (lit. capital camp or capital monastery). Ungern-Sternberg was supported by several Mongol princes and the Russian White Army, also known as the White Movement or White Guard, which was the opposing force to the Bolshevist movement, the Russian Red Army. He tried to overtake Niislel Khüree again in February 1921 and this time he was successful. On 27 June 1921, a revolutionary movement consisting of the Russian Red Army and the Mongolian People's Army led by Sükhbaatar subdued Ungern-Sternberg and took control of the capital, which was renamed Ulaanbaatar (lit. red hero) in 1924 in Sükhbaatar's honour. The 1921 Revolution paved the way for Mongolia to become a socialist nation under the guidance of the Soviet Union.

Sükhbaatar is portrayed as the ultimate Mongolian socialist hero in the numerous films about the 1921 Revolution, whilst the Chinese, the Russian White Army, Mongolian noblemen and Buddhist leaders are portrayed as the enemy. Following the Bogd Khan's death in 1924, the Mongolian People's Republic (MPR) was created. The ruling party, renamed the Mongolian People's Revolutionary Party (MPRP), was the only permitted party in Mongolia until 1990. Instigated by the 1921 Revolution, Mongolia became the first of the Soviet satellite states and remained a socialist country for almost 70 years.

In 1986, Mikhail Gorbachev, General Secretary of the Communist Party of the Soviet Union,[9] introduced the policies of glasnost and perestroika.[10] These policies acted as a catalyst for a series of largely peaceful protests in Mongolia against the socialist government starting in December 1989. The protests gained momentum and led to the Democratic Revolution in 1990, culminating in a democratic election in July, which introduced a transition to democracy and a market economy. The MPRP won the majority in the July 1990 election and remained in power, although Mongolia ceased to be a socialist country influenced by the Soviet Union.

Propaganda: Cultural Policy in Mongolia

The establishment of the Mongolian film industry and the drastic changes made to Mongolian music making during the twentieth century were a direct result of cultural policy. Although Mongolia never became part of the Soviet Union, the two nations shared an elder-brother / younger-brother relationship, and Mongolia's cultural policies were modelled on those of its elder brother nation. The Mongolian–Soviet friendship was publicised widely in the party newspapers of both Mongolia (*Ünen*) and the Soviet Union (*Pravda*). The Mongolian government was populated by Mongolian figureheads throughout the Socialist

---

[9] Nikita Khrushchev was the first General Secretary of the Communist Party of the Soviet Union (CPSU) from 1953, after Lenin and Stalin's administrations.

[10] Glasnost (openness) and perestroika (restructuring) were policies inaugurated by Gorbachev in the Soviet Union in the 1980s. For further information, please see Chapter 6.

era, but it was to all intents and purposes guided by Moscow. As a result, Soviet policy makers largely formed the basis of the ideas behind Mongolian cultural policy. Yet whilst Mongolian society became infused with Soviet ideology and culture, film music as well as other aspects of twentieth-century Mongolian life developed in different directions from that of its elder brother nation.

Cultural policies regarding music and film from the early years of the Soviet Union were later replicated in Mongolia. In 1918, music critic and member of the Moscow Conservatoire Nadezhda Bryusova, in a report to the First All-Russian Conference of Proletarian Culture Organisations, announced the need to discard the musical traditions of the component nations of the Soviet Union and to replace them with a new proletarian music created and championed by the Proletkult (Bryusova 1918, pp. 252–55). Proletkult, a portmanteau word deriving from the Russian for proletarian culture, was a movement to promote proletarian art forms and to denounce any art hitherto created by the bourgeoisie. Similarly in Mongolia, the government suppressed many pre-1921 musical traditions, such as those of ethnic minorities, and instead provided generous state funding and support to promote new music deemed suitable for the proletariat.

Leon Trotsky wrote in the Soviet party newspaper *Pravda* that cinema was an excellent method of propaganda and, given that a proletarian's day should be divided into three eight-hour slots of work, sleep and leisure, watching films was the most industrious way citizens could spend their allotted leisure time (1923, pp. 106–9). The Mongolian government likewise emphasised the importance of cinema as a tool for propaganda, not only through articles in *Ünen* but also through initiatives to build cinemas in every province. In the mid-1920s, the Soviet government made plans to bring cinema to the Russian countryside, a move echoed in Mongolia with the use of mobile cinemas. In 1927, cultural critic N. Malkov published an article in Soviet newspaper *Zhizn Iskusstva* (*Life of Art*) that emphasised the glory of mass music – that is, music that prioritises the collective over the individual (Malkov, 1927, pp. 264–8). Choirs, symphony orchestras and brass bands were consequently favoured over soloists and small ensembles such as trios or quartets. The symphony orchestra was used in almost every Soviet and Mongolian film score of the Socialist era, and in many cases, choirs, brass bands and other large-scale ensembles were also employed.

Starting from 1921, Mongolia went through three stages of implementing socialism. These stages, and indeed the political system itself, are referred to as socialism rather than communism. Pure communism is an ideal towards which all socialist countries should aspire, and not one socialist state, including the Soviet Union, achieved this goal before the socialist regimes of the Eastern Bloc fell in the early 1990s. Until 1940, Mongolia was in its first stage of socialism, referred to as its 'democratic stage' in a document entitled *Cultural Policy in the Mongolian People's Republic* (UNESCO, 1982). This stage was devoted to ensuring every citizen embraced socialist ideology through access to culture, which included music and film (UNESCO, 1982, p. 12). The darker side of this stage, and one not publicised by the MPRP, was the purges of the 1930s. Choibalsan was Minister of

Internal Affairs from 1936 to 1939, and during this time, guided by the leader of the Soviet Union, Joseph Stalin, he led measures to imprison, exile or assassinate anyone deemed counter-revolutionary, including intellectuals, noblemen, shamans and Buddhist lamas. Choibalsan's actions culminated in the Great Purge of 10 September 1937 to 22 April 1939, throughout which 29,198 people were sentenced for counter-revolutionary activity (Baabar, 1999, pp. 359–61). During this time, 20,356 lamas were killed and several thousand more were exiled, imprisoned or forced into other professions (Buyandelger, 2008, p. 54). The true fate of lamas, shamans and the nobility was not presented publicly; instead, these groups were portrayed in a universally negative light in the films of the Socialist era.

The second stage of Mongolian socialism fell between 1940 and 1961, and focused on economic and political objectives (UNESCO, 1982, pp. 15–16). This stage coincided with the deaths of Choibalsan (who was then Prime Minister) in 1952 and Stalin in 1953, and the subsequent relaxation of their hard-line politics. This was known as the Khrushchev Thaw in the Soviet Union, which began officially in February 1956 with a speech Stalin's successor Nikita Khrushchev delivered at the Twentieth Congress of the Communist Party of the Soviet Union (CPSU). From 1961, Mongolia was deemed to have established socialism fully (UNESCO, 1982, p. 17).

Economic and societal development during these stages incorporated everything from industry, construction, infrastructure and collectivisation to film production and the arts. Such developments were outlined in a series of government action plans known as the five-year plan(s), the first of which covered the period 1947–52 and laid out strategies to develop the national economy and culture. There were numerous policies relating to propaganda and censorship, and the state employed professional propagandists and censors to implement the policies. The MPRP established cinema, radio and television in addition to concert halls, music ensembles and newspapers to achieve the aim of disseminating socialist ideology throughout Mongolia. Films, posters and literature glorified the proletariat and encouraged unconditional loyalty to the state. Additionally, groups of people deemed undesirable were denounced, particularly during the purges of the 1930s. The government utilised censorship to ensure no subversive materials could be distributed, and introduced mass initiatives to disseminate films, radio and cultural performances to rural areas.

In 1962, Mongolia became a full member of the Council for Mutual Economic Assistance (COMECON), although it had been an observer since the 1950s. COMECON was an organisation for economic development, whose member states were mostly those of the Eastern Bloc, and it became the source of much of Mongolia's policy and legislation, which was channelled through the MPRP.[11] Given the influence of the Soviet Union and Mongolia's obligations to COMECON,

---

[11] COMECON was established in 1949 and dissolved in 1991. The Soviet Union, Bulgaria, Czechoslovakia, Hungary, Poland, Romania, East Germany, Albania, Cuba, Vietnam and Mongolia were members at various points between these two dates.

10   *Mongolian Film Music*

it is unlikely that the MPRP made many independent decisions from this time until the mid-1980s, when Gorbachev's policies of glasnost and perestroika led to the loosening of Moscow's control over the member states of COMECON.

Mongolian cultural policy during the Socialist era had a profound effect on society and culture and prompted the eradication of many Mongolian traditions and systems of belief that had been customary before 1921. Yet despite efforts on the part of the state to create a homogeneous socialist society, traditional Mongolian culture was still a strong force amongst the population. Nonetheless, many Mongolians practised the cultural traditions of their forebears in secret in order to avoid political persecution. After 1990, it was no longer necessary to do this clandestinely, and so the horse-head fiddle, Chinggis Khaan and Buddhism, amongst other traditions and cultural icons, became notably present once again. Simultaneously, Mongolian film composers had unprecedented access to musical influences that had previously been restricted, such as Anglo-American and East Asian popular music. Throughout Mongolia's film music history, film composers utilised traditional Mongolian music in their soundtracks, often combined or in tandem with the music of nations with which Mongolia had close political or cultural relations.

Preview

This book is an overview of Mongolian film music, specifically from the Mongolian perspective, from the founding of the state film studio in 1936 to the aftermath of the Socialist era. We discuss the political motives and initiatives that drove the music and film industries in the twentieth century, the process of filmmaking and film composition in the Mongolian context and the cultural environment in which the film composers lived and worked. We also discuss certain key composers, films and film scores, presented here as case studies.

Mongolian film soundtracks of the Socialist era contain a rich variety of music genres, including traditional Mongolian music and modified versions thereof, and genres that were popular in the Soviet Union. To facilitate an understanding of their usage in film soundtracks, a survey of these genres is presented in Chapter 2 in addition to a short discussion on tradition.

Chapter 3 is about the establishment and early development of Mongolian cinema and film music. We discuss the background and training of new film composers, which led to the creation of a new style of symphonic music in Mongolia known as professional music (*mergejliin khögjim*). We also look at the social status of film composers within the context of the Socialist era. Since these early film scores were the start of the 'golden age' of Mongolian film scoring, discussions of the concept of a golden age and key Mongolian composers are also presented.

In Chapter 4 we discuss the process of Mongolian filmmaking, from the governmental plans that dictated what topics films should cover to the dissemination of the films to the entire population. This is followed by a summary of the main themes and issues presented in films in the 1950s–1970s and a case study of one of Mongolia's most prolific and respected film composers, Dagvyn Luvsansharav.

Chapter 5 is an in-depth discussion of one film score of the 1970s: *The Clear River Tamir* (*Tungalag Tamir*, 1970–73), which typifies Mongolian film scoring of this decade. The film is a three-part epic about the 1921 Revolution with a score that showcases the music genres prevalent throughout the Socialist era.

In Chapter 6 we analyse the influence of glasnost and perestroika on Mongolian film composers in the 1980s. This chapter includes case studies of two contrasting film scores, one which glorified the past and furthered developments in professional music, and the other which looked to the future and contained electronic and popular music. Both films echoed the sentiments of a large proportion of the population in the 1980s, who had tired of socialism and desired change.

Chapter 7 begins with a summary of the downfall of socialism in Mongolia and the dissolution of the Soviet Union, which paved the way for radical developments in film music after 1990. The remainder of the chapter is a survey of the various and diverse trends in Mongolian film music from 1990. The final chapter is a brief conclusion and provides answers to the questions raised about the development of film music in Mongolia.

Chapter 2
Tradition and Transition in Mongolian Music

> Mongolian music has been developing for over a thousand years. It develops year
> by year, it is always changing. The traditions do not change completely but they
> are developed.
>
> Ariunbold, INT[1]

Throughout the twentieth century, Mongolian music developed significantly.
Many changes to musical genres, instruments and performance contexts occurred
as the direct result of governmental edicts. Developments also came about due
to the introduction of music genres new to Mongolia, predominantly from the
Soviet Union. This chapter provides an overview of the principal government-
approved music genres practised in Mongolia throughout the twentieth century
that appeared in film soundtracks. This will facilitate an understanding of their
function and significance as a tool for propaganda within the films, as discussed
in subsequent chapters.

As was the case in the Soviet Union, the scores for Mongolian films throughout
the Socialist era were predominantly symphonic, although traditional Mongolian
musical styles and genres were also utilised. The traditional genres in question,
however, were modified versions developed with the aid of Soviet experts at the
behest of the socialist government rather than those performed and heard before
1921. When traditional Mongolian music appeared in films, it was sometimes used
to showcase these newly developed genres, whilst at other times it was presented
in scenes portraying outmoded pre-revolutionary life. This often gave traditional
Mongolian music somewhat negative connotations in the context of the grand
symphonic film scores that usually accompanied scenes of socialist progress
and prosperity.

Folk Music, Traditional Music and Musical Traditions

The terms folk music, traditional music and musical traditions are often used
interchangeably, and there are certainly overlaps between these phrases.
Ts. Ariunbold (INT) of the State College of Music and Dance in Ulaanbaatar says
that Mongolian traditional and folk music 'are two sides of the same coin … They
cannot be separated.' The term folk music has been applied to such a wide variety

---

[1] INT denotes a reference to an interview.

of music worldwide that a simple definition is virtually impossible. Mark Slobin acknowledges how difficult the term is to define, since it has been used to describe everything from Romanian funeral laments to the songs of Afghan tea houses, and because of the colonial connotations the term (in translation) can carry when applied to non-Western music (Slobin, 2011, pp. 1–2).

In the Mongolian context, the folk music the socialist government chose to modify during the twentieth century included a variety of vocal and instrumental styles associated with Khalkha nomadic communities that was originally transmitted orally, mostly performed on home-made traditional instruments, and originated long before 1921. Characteristics of Khalkha folk music include the use of pentatonic scales, melodies performed solo or in unison, music that is improvised or of an improvisatory nature, the absence of harmonies and, particularly in western Mongolia, the use of overtones. The MPRP adapted, standardised and professionalised Khalkha folk music to create new genres, which were then used for purposes of propaganda, whilst the folk music of other ethnic groups was mostly disregarded or even outlawed.

Traditional music – and this can include folk music – can be defined as music that is peculiar to a specific country or region, or to a group of people, for example an ethnic group. One feature that can make music peculiar to a location or group is instrumentation. Certain instruments are associated closely with one country or region, even though they may be present worldwide, for example the sitar and India, whereas other instruments, such as the guitar, are not readily associated with one specific location. In the latter case, the performing style of the instrument can be linked to certain traditional music genres. There are significant differences, for example, in the way a Western classical musician plays the clarinet compared to a member of a klezmer band. Another important factor is the subject matter of the lyrics of traditional vocal music, the sentiments of which may not be easily understood by people outside the culture in question.

Although a specific community may perform various genres of music from around the world, there are genres that are embedded into their history and therefore part of their traditional heritage, whilst other genres are 'loaned' or have been assimilated into their society. Musical genres, musical history, instrumentation and performance styles can be as important to a society as its language, customs, costume, folklore or cuisine, although this is of course a somewhat romantic or even essentialist idea. Mongolian traditional music includes the folk music of the various ethnic groups, the court music of the pre-1921 ruling classes, and the religious music of Mongolia's Buddhists and shamans, in addition to the genres developed during the twentieth century.

Although folk music and traditional music are often associated with history and cultural heritage, it is possible for musical traditions to be created anew. Theoretically, anything can become a tradition provided it is repeated in a similar context. A group of friends may have a 'tradition' of meeting in a particular café for coffee every Friday morning at 11 o'clock, for example. Whereas one-off musical events often take place, a musical event must be repeated in a similar manner and context for it to earn the status of a tradition. An orchestral concert in itself is not a tradition, whereas the British Proms season is. Musical traditions include specific repertoire that is performed customarily on special occasions and music that is used habitually to perform certain functions. The song 'Happy Birthday to You' is an example of the former; a lullaby, an example of the latter. Music for ritual and ceremony also falls under this category. The musical traditions of a society may also include the way music is created or composed, how it is disseminated amongst the society and the wider community, and the way the music is preserved, be it by means of written scores, audio recordings or memory.

The new folk music genres the socialist government developed from Khalkha traditional music and the genres that were introduced from outside Mongolia (principally the Soviet Union) in the twentieth century became new Mongolian traditions in their own right. Yet does the fact that these genres were introduced within the last century make them any less traditional? The answer could be a firm yes depending on whom is asked, and there are traditionalists amongst performers and listeners alike who assert that if drastic changes have been made to music, then it has contravened tradition and is therefore no longer traditional. Music contains, at least partially, enduring norms that will be utilised by those who consider themselves traditional musicians, and who believe a line should be drawn between traditional music and more innovative music, regardless of how ill-defined that line may be. On the other hand, traditional music and musical traditions are not static, and develop as time progresses in tandem with culture and society. The pace of musical change is likely to accelerate the more rapidly a culture develops. Furthermore, adding a modern element to a long-standing tradition, such as adding machine heads to a traditional stringed instrument to help keep it in tune, can make the tradition more relevant to the time in which it is presented. Symphonic music and certain other musical genres introduced to Mongolia from the Soviet Union after 1921 were, from the Mongolian perspective, new and modern to Mongolians at the time. The combination of musical elements of these newly introduced genres with traditional Mongolian music led to the creation and development of new musical traditions in their own right as the Socialist era progressed.

Traditional Mongolian Instrumental and Vocal Music

Traditional musical instruments associated with the Khalkha Mongols can be divided into two categories: those for domestic music (*geriin khögjim*), which includes music played during herding or in the *ger* or camp, and those for palace music (*ordony khögjim*), or formal celebrations associated with the ruling classes. There is a certain amount of overlap between these categories, particularly in light of the Socialist era, when herding practices and domestic music making changed considerably and the ruling classes ceased to exist. Instruments for religious purposes, including shamans' drums and Buddhist temple instruments, form a third category. Before the Socialist era, the shape, size and design of musical instruments varied between regions depending on the skills and preferences of individual instrument makers and on what natural resources were available to use as materials. During the Socialist era, the design and materials of many instruments were standardised, and nowadays instruments are often made in factories in Ulaanbaatar.

The domestic musical instrument category includes lutes, fiddles, woodwind, and the jaw harp (*aman khuur*).[2] The most popular lute is the two-stringed *tovshuur*, which was used widely to accompany epics and dances before 1921. The most notable of the strings and the traditional instrument featured most widely in film soundtracks is the horse-head fiddle (*morin khuur*), a two-stringed bowed spike fiddle decorated with a carved horse's head at the top of the neck (Figure 2.1). The horse-head fiddle occupies a special place within past and current Mongolian culture, and Ulaanbaatar-based horse-head fiddle maker Doljinsürengiin Ulambayar (INT) describes it as 'the father of all bowed stringed instruments'. Peter Marsh's research has focused on the horse-head fiddle; he has analysed the instrument from a variety of standpoints including its history, its development during the Socialist era, and its metamorphosis from a national symbol to a (reimagined) cultural icon after 1990 (Marsh, 2009). The reverence Mongolians have for the horse-head fiddle may be connected to the deep love and respect for horses inherent in Mongolian culture. There is an abundance of songs, poems and legends about horses, praise songs are sung to horses that win races, and the terms for distinct musical tempi correspond with the seven words to describe the gait of a horse.

The wind instruments used for domestic music include the *limbe*, a side-blown flute; the *tsuur*, an end-blown overtone flute from western Mongolia; and the *ever büree*, a curly tube with finger holes, originally made from animal horns, with a sound similar to the lower register of the clarinet. The *limbe* is often referred to as the shepherd's flute and is played by herders to entertain themselves during their daily work. It can also be used with the horse-head fiddle to accompany songs and dances.

Amongst the palace instruments are the *khuuchir*, a two- or four-stringed bowed instrument similar to the Chinese *erhu*; the *shanz* or *shudraga*, a three-stringed banjo often played with a large plectrum, similar to the Japanese *shamisen*; the *yoochin*, similar to the hammer dulcimer; and the *yatga*, a zither similar to the Korean *gayageum*, Chinese *guzheng* or Japanese *koto*. When palace instruments appeared on screen, they were played invariably by wealthy characters or at lavish ceremonies in scenes set before the Socialist era.

The *bishgüür*, a non-valved wind instrument similar to a Tibetan temple instrument called the *gyaling*, was used originally within Buddhist ceremonies, although nowadays it can be heard within other musical genres. Percussion instruments are generally limited to religious and ritual music, such as the

---

[2] The jaw harp, a traditional herders' instrument popular throughout central Asia, is also known as the Jew's harp, although there is no evidence to suggest any links with Judaism.

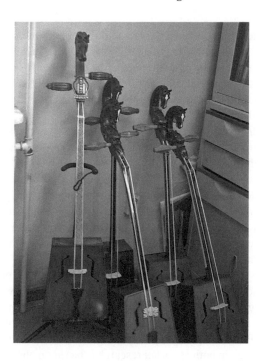

Figure 2.1　Horse-head fiddles, Egshiglen musical instrument factory, Ulaanbaatar

shaman's drum or Buddhist cymbals. Shamanic and Buddhist music, vocal styles and instruments appear frequently in film scenes that portray shamans and Buddhist lamas in a negative light, as was customary within socialist propaganda.

There is considerable debate in Mongolia as to the origin of some traditional instruments, and determining their origin would require extensive knowledge of the history of all Asian instruments. Whilst certain nations lay claim to the origin of particular instruments such as the Chinese to the *khuuchir*, *shanz* and *yoochin* and the Koreans to the *yatga* there are no countries other than Mongolia that claim the horse-head fiddle or the *tsuur*. Traditional-instrument orchestras have existed since the Mongol Empire so it is likely that many of the instruments listed above originated in the steppe and were introduced to a large part of the Asian continent during the expansion of the Empire. It is equally plausible that Mongolian invaders assimilated the instruments of conquered lands into their musical armoury.

Singing and vocal music are extremely popular in Mongolia amongst professional musicians and the general population, and have been used widely in Mongolian film soundtracks, both during and after the Socialist era. Of the many and varied Mongolian vocal traditions, the style Westerners most readily associate with Mongolia is *khöömii*, also known as overtone singing or throat singing. When I interviewed *khöömii* teacher Odsüren at the Mongolian University of Arts and Culture in 2009, he told me he objects to the term throat singing. The word *khöömii* refers to the whole space between the jaw and the collarbone, so this translation is inaccurate and gives non-Mongolian speakers a false idea of the techniques involved. There are a number of theories as to the origins of *khöömii*, and Odsüren believes it arose as a survival mechanism for nomads, who imitated animal sounds when hunting and used it for herding and breeding to form good relationships with their livestock (Odsüren, INT).

Within nomadic communities, women have usually undertaken tasks such as cooking and milking animals whilst men have been largely responsible for hunting and animal husbandry. This may explain why *khöömii* was traditionally sung by men, and is sung only by men in film soundtracks of the Socialist era, although girls have been able to learn *khöömii* in educational establishments in Ulaanbaatar since 1990. The *khöömii* heard in film soundtracks, including the Mongolian–foreign co-productions of the post-Socialist era, generally accompanies pastoral scenes and is often mixed with other music, thereby hinting at some of its original functions and connections with herding practices.

Carole Pegg's research into Mongolian performance incorporates music, poetry, dance and ritual. Pegg (1992) provides an overview of Mongolian *khöömii*, covering aspects such as theories of origin, performance practice, classification of *khöömii* styles, and possible connections with nature and the spirit world. Pegg's paper complements the information given in her book (Pegg, 2001) although in both cases her research is based on one *khöömiich* (singer of *khöömii*), Tserendavaa, and it should be noted that different *khöömiich* would offer alternative viewpoints. Whereas Tserendavaa and Mongolian musicologist Badraa have classified *khöömii* into 6 styles (Pegg, 1992, pp. 44–5), Odsüren (INT) has divided it into 12, although he says beginners should think of it as two styles: high or whistling (*isgeree*) and low (*kharkhiraa*).

Whilst *khöömii* is widely regarded the quintessential Mongolian vocal sound worldwide, Mongolians tend to view the long-song (*urtyn duu*) as the pinnacle of Mongolian vocal art. Along with the horse-head fiddle, the long-song was included in UNESCO's list of worldwide Masterpieces of the Oral and Intangible Heritage of Humanity (see UNESCO, n.d.). The long-song is so called due to the length of the syllables, which are extended to incorporate melisma, ornamentation, falsetto and leaping between wide intervals, and the name bears no relation to the length of the song itself. The lyrics are of secondary importance to the vocal technique, and unintelligibility of the text is not seen as problematic. I have observed horsemen in the countryside singing long-song for their own entertainment as they herded their animals, and it is often sung as the opening number of theatre performances by professional folk music troupes and at the *Naadam* festival. Mongolian musicologists Enkhtüvshin and Enebish argue that the long-song developed from *uukhai*, a traditional vocal piece sung in praise of winners of traditional sporting competitions such as archery (Enkhtüvshin and Enebish, 2007, pp. 10–11). The technique and style of *uukhai* are very similar to those of long-song, although the latter is more melodic and structured. Long-song and *uukhai* appear frequently in films of the Socialist era, especially during scenes depicting the original performance contexts of these styles, namely celebrations, traditional sporting competitions and festivals.

Other vocal genres heard in film soundtracks, although to a lesser extent than long-song, *uukhai* and *khöömii*, include the short-song (*bogino duu*), a syllabic song with intelligible lyrics, and the epic (*tuuli*), a lengthy poetic tale of heroes and battles often accompanied by the horse-head fiddle. Further traditional vocal genres include praise songs (*magtaal*), wish songs (*yerööl*), legends (*domog*) and curses (*kharaal*), although very little use has been made of them in film soundtracks except for occasional appearances during scenes of *Naadam* festivals or other traditional celebrations.

Professionalising and Recontextualising Music

After 1921, the Mongolian government sought to replace pre-revolutionary principles with socialist ideology and believed that developing new art and media was an expedient method of doing so. Media that had not existed in Mongolia before the Socialist era, such as cinema and radio, could be used to circulate socialist ideology from the outset. In contrast, music, which had been practised in Mongolia for centuries, required significant adaptation before it became a suitable vehicle for socialist propaganda. Changes were made to existing music genres to dissociate them from pre-revolutionary music practices, and genres new to Mongolia were created or introduced. It was the music of the most populous ethnic group, the Khalkha Mongols, that was adapted to serve the purposes of the socialist government, whereas musical traditions of other ethnic groups were largely neglected or suppressed. In turn, this new standardised music was used to score the new films, which helped promote socialist ideology, diffuse propaganda and destabilise the feudal structures, religious orders and ethnic diversity that posed a threat to the ideals of socialism. The traditional music heard in film soundtracks of the Socialist era was the new, modified variety, since the state would not have encouraged filmmakers to promote pre-1921 traditional musical practices.

Whether the manoeuvres on the part of the socialist government that changed music were welcomed or viewed as oppressive is a debatable point. Many of the Mongolian music professionals I interviewed believe the musical innovations brought about by the socialist regime were not only part of the continuous development of music but also enriched Mongolians' musical lives. The MPRP provided extensive support for the arts and media in terms of funding, training, job opportunities, and establishing new performance and broadcasting spaces. On the other hand, the government supported only selected musical genres, and the musical traditions of ethnic minorities and religious groups were suppressed.

Politically enforced musical change was not unique to Mongolia during the twentieth century; the country's musical developments were similar to those of the Central Asian Republics of the Soviet Union (Kazakhstan, Kyrgyzstan,

20 *Mongolian Film Music*

Uzbekistan, Tajikistan and Turkmenistan), which began in the 1920s.[3] Some of the transformations that began in the Soviet Union at this time included institutionalising music by establishing schools and theatres, censoring pre-Socialist-era culture, standardising music practices and destabilising communities whose ideology differed from socialism, such as Sufi orders (Djumaev, 1993).

Mongolia followed its elder brother the Soviet Union when the MPRP introduced a cultural revolution known as the Great Leap Forward between 1929 and 1932, whereby practices considered 'old' or 'backward' were replaced with socialist ideology.[4] During this time, Mongolian musicologist Duragjav expressed the need for musicians to be trained professionally, which led to formal training for musicians and composers in both Mongolia and the Soviet Union and the establishment of musical institutions in Ulaanbaatar. Furthermore, like the elimination of Sufi orders in the Soviet Central Asian Republics, Buddhism and shamanism were suppressed in Mongolia in a bid to centralise power, and this resulted in the loss of associated religious musical practices in their original performance contexts.

In 1934, on page three of the January edition of *Sovetskaya Muzika* (*Soviet Music*), the journal of the Composers' Union of the Soviet Union, Joseph Stalin stated that music should be 'national in form and socialist in content'. Stalin's vision was implemented throughout the twentieth century in both the Soviet Union and Mongolia, although it was continuously open to the interpretation of various members of the MPRP and the heads of music committees and unions. Pegg discusses in detail cultural changes implemented by the MPRP in order to advance Stalin's objective and implies that musical developments in the twentieth century were imposed on Mongolia (Pegg, 2001, pp. 253–83). Marsh has also assessed the overhaul of Mongolian traditional music as politically driven, and his findings are consistent with my research in that many of these musical developments were welcomed by Mongolian musicians (Marsh, 2006; 2009, pp. 47–72). Pegg began her research in the late 1980s, when socialism was crumbling and being replaced with a market economy; strong anti-Soviet sentiments would have been prevalent at this time. Marsh, however, began his research in 1998, and I conducted mine mainly between 2008 and 2010, when socialism was no longer seen as an adverse institution from which Mongolia should have decamped.

The Mongolian Composers' Union was established in 1957 and was modelled on the Soviet Composers' Union, which had been set up in 1932. This body was largely responsible for overseeing musical development and innovation over the next three and a half decades. In 1959, alongside the process of collectivisation, the MPRP officially launched a Cultural Leap Forward, which included motions to improve literacy, sanitation and health, and establish libraries, bath-houses, schools and nurseries, barber shops and recreation rooms, in addition to developing music

---

[3] See Djumaev (1993), Levin (1996) and Frolova-Walker (1998).
[4] There was a cultural revolution in the Soviet Union between 1928 and 1931.

and cinema. Throughout the Socialist era, the MPRP put various cultural policies in place in accordance with the series of five-year plans.

During the Socialist era, the principal performance space of music in Mongolia was relocated from the *ger* to the newly created schools and theatres. Before 1921, the *ger* or camp (*ail*) was the centre of almost all music making, in addition to monasteries. At home, children learned music from their parents, impromptu and ritual performances were held amongst family members and neighbours, travelling bards visited *gers* to perform epics, and herders sang or played music for their own entertainment within the grazing radius of their *gers*. Traditionally, Mongolians learned music by copying elder family members, so music was learned without being taught formally. During the Socialist era, formal training began to replace traditional learning, thus the idiosyncrasies of family oral traditions gave way to standardisation. This situation was not unique to Mongolia, and the trend of replacing informal music learning with formal music teaching occurred in other Eastern Bloc states.

A School of Culture was established in Ulaanbaatar in 1937, which at first offered two-year courses in playing traditional instruments and acting. The school expanded in 1945 and henceforth provided training for dancers and conductors. In 1959, the year of the Cultural Leap Forward, it was renamed the State College of Music and Dance, and classes in European classical music were added to the curriculum. It was in this institution that the majority of Mongolian film composers began their musical training. In the early decades of the college, students and teachers were expected to play both European symphonic and traditional Mongolian instruments, but during the 1980s it became more common for students to specialise. Since 1990 it has been the policy within the college that students must choose to play either traditional Mongolian or European symphonic instruments and never mix the two disciplines (Chinbat, INT).

One of the consequences of teachers and students being trained in both symphonic and traditional music during the 1960s and 1970s was that European instrumental techniques began to be adopted when playing traditional Mongolian instruments, for example violoncello bowing techniques being used on the horse-head fiddle (Marsh, 2009, pp. 55–6). Mongolian film composers studied both European symphonic and traditional Mongolian music during their formative years of music training in Ulaanbaatar, which, at least in part, influenced subsequent compositions that combined musical elements of both.

Another significant development in music education, which began in the 1940s, was that of musicians and composers being sent for training in the Soviet Union and other Eastern Bloc countries, as part of the elder-brother / younger-brother relationship. It was not only musicians who received formal Soviet training, but also numerous other professionals including journalists, engineers and construction workers, not to mention members of the MPRP. Ninety per cent of the teachers at the State College of Music and Dance and the majority of working composers, conductors and performers studied for up to eight years at conservatoires in Moscow, Kiev, Yekaterinburg and other major Eastern Bloc cities.

Whilst abroad, not only did they receive an Eastern European classical musical education but they also learned the Russian language and spent their time immersed in Soviet culture, politics and daily life. On return to Mongolia, what these musicians had learned both in the Eastern Bloc and during their nomadic upbringings would be passed on to Mongolian concert audiences and students in the form of their compositions and performances, and through their teaching at the State College of Music and Dance. Within time, all these factors led composers to combine symphonic and traditional musical elements in their compositions, which they used both on the concert platform and within film soundtracks.

When conducting interviews with teachers at the State College of Music and Dance, I asked whether being trained in the Soviet Union had had any negative effects. The unanimous response was that being trained abroad had been predominantly a positive experience. Professor Chuluuny Chinbat, who was educated in Armenia and Bulgaria as a conductor, believes there were only advantages to be gained from studying in the Eastern Bloc, since their conservatoires were better equipped than Mongolian schools and it gave him the opportunity of living in a 'culturally bounteous environment'. To explain that it is preferable to go abroad to learn new techniques, repertoire and methodologies, Chinbat refers to the Mongolian saying, 'it is better to see something once than to hear about it a thousand times' (Chinbat, INT). The college director of administration, Ariunbold, likewise sees the benefits of studying abroad and was, at the time of research, trying to forge links between music schools in the USA and Western Europe in the hope that Mongolian students can study there in the future.

For those children who did not receive a musical education at the State College of Music and Dance, there were other ways that socialist ideology and new music could be brought to them. The Revolutionary League of Youth was set up in 1921, followed by its subsidiary for younger children in 1925, the Pioneers, where children would learn revolutionary songs (*khuvsgalyn duu*) and have access to the newly developed genres of folk music. In this way, children would learn revolutionary songs *en masse* in a formalised setting rather than informally at home, thereby keeping children closely aligned with socialist ideals. Revolutionary songs appeared regularly in film soundtracks, so when people who had been members of the Revolutionary League of Youth or the Pioneers watched films, the songs were already familiar to them, thereby reinforcing their message. The policy of music education for all was supplemented by music lessons at school, in which children learned about European orchestral instruments and both Soviet and new Mongolian composers. In addition to musical education, the MPRP ensured that general education focused on socialist ideology, and nothing was taught in schools of the years prior to the revolution, which would have led young Mongolians to see 1921 as the beginning of their cultural heritage.

Soon after the 1921 Revolution, the state sent cadres to the countryside to sing revolutionary songs to herders. 'Red *gers*' were constructed to house the cadres and as a venue for public meetings, and by 1940 there was a red *ger* in every province. The idea of having a fixed location developed and soon permanent buildings known as red corners (*ulaan bulan*), otherwise known as clubs, cultural clubs or cultural centres, were built. The MPRP not only decreed the establishment of such cultural centres but also stipulated how many should be built and where. The ultimate aim was for the cultural centres to be easily accessible to every citizen. Herders could learn and perform music at these rural cultural centres, and those showing promise were often sent to Ulaanbaatar for further training. Those deemed the most talented in Ulaanbaatar were subsequently sent to the Soviet Union or other socialist countries to complete their musical education. On their return, they would compose, perform, conduct or teach music in Mongolia, thereby continuing the cycle of propagating socialist ideology through music.

As early as 1920, party-controlled institutions were created to further the dissemination of ideology through culture. The party newspaper *Ünen* (*Truth*), comparable to the Soviet broadsheet *Pravda*, was first circulated in November 1920, and was initially printed in Irkutsk, Siberia. Mongolian state radio was founded in 1931, which at first broadcast only in Ulaanbaatar, but broadcast countrywide from 1934. The radio music department was introduced in 1950 and at first musicians would come into the studio and perform live. From 1957 music was recorded and stored in a newly established radio music archive, which was supplemented by exchanging recorded music with other socialist countries. From the 1960s, extracts from Mongolian film scores were used as background music for radio programmes, which were then broadcast in rural villages through new loudspeakers that were placed there in the same decade. In addition, Mongolia's first theatre of the Socialist era, the Bömbögör Nogoon, was established in 1931, a military music ensemble in 1932, the state film studio in 1936, the state circus in 1940, a puppet theatre in 1948, a children's theatre and State Opera and Ballet Theatre in the 1940s, the national library in 1951, the National Academic Drama Theatre in 1963, and state television in 1967. The Central Palace of Culture in Ulaanbaatar's main square, Sükhbaatar Square, has also housed numerous ensembles over the last few decades under the umbrella name the Mongolian Philharmony. Ensembles include the State Symphony Orchestra, established in 1956; Mongolia's first state rock band Soyol Erdene (lit. Cultural Treasure), created in 1971; a jazz big band; and the Horse-Head Fiddle Ensemble, created in 1989 and established officially in 1992. Each of these ensembles has participated in the recording of film soundtracks. Similar institutions, including opera houses and national philharmonic organisations, were also set up in the Soviet Central Asian Republics in the early half of the twentieth century.

The Mongolian National Song and Dance Academic Ensemble was established in 1945 to perform traditional Mongolian music and dance, albeit in a form approved by the MPRP.[5] This ensemble consisted of a traditional-instrument orchestra, various solo instrumentalists, vocalists, contortionists and a dance troupe. Before the Socialist era, performers would often sit or dance in a circle

---

[5] The ensemble was originally called the Mongolian People's Song and Dance Ensemble.

24 *Mongolian Film Music*

facing each other inside the *ger*. During the Socialist era, the creation of Western-style theatres and cultural clubs with a stage, proscenium and auditorium meant that performers had to change their positioning. Dancers were rearranged into lines facing the audience, and the positioning of the traditional-instrument orchestra became akin to a Western orchestra, although Marsh points out this positioning was similar to Chinese music ensembles in pre-Socialist era Mongolia (Marsh, 2009, p. 59). The horse-head fiddles were placed where the violoncellos would be, the *khuuchir* replaced the violins, the *limbe* and *bishgüür* were positioned as an orchestral woodwind section, and a conductor stood on a podium at the front facing the ensemble. Performing traditional Mongolian music in Western-style layouts and venues was another way in which Mongolian music met European classical traditions.

Musicians and dancers of the Mongolian National Song and Dance Academic Ensemble – as was the case with the military ensemble, circus, children's theatre, the State Opera and Ballet Theatre, and the Mongolian Philharmony – were full-time professionals. For many, music making became a paid job rather than an unpaid hobby, as was the case in other Eastern Bloc countries, and so they played music approved of by the authorities. The formally trained professional performers and widely disseminated performances of the National Song and Dance Academic Ensemble were therefore able to satisfy governmental demands to promote socialist ideology in a manner accessible to twentieth-century Mongolian audiences. Professionalising folk music not only allowed the MPRP to standardise, monitor and disseminate music, but also to fulfil socialist policies of providing gainful employment to every citizen. Since 1990, a number of private folk music ensembles of full-time professionals have been established in Mongolia, particularly in Ulaanbaatar and *ger* camps (campsites for tourists with *ger*s provided). Many of these ensembles tailor their repertoire to cater to the perceived tastes of their mainly foreign audiences.

The establishment of state musical institutions and theatres, the professional training of musicians, and the musical provision for children meant that music became recontextualised. Music learning was taken from the *ger* to the school and even to the Soviet Union, and music performance was taken from the *ger* to the cultural club or theatre. In this way, the state replaced the head of the family as the overseer of music making, and much of the traditional subject matter of performances, such as pre-revolutionary or mythical heroes, was replaced with socialist ideology. As a result, music became more formalised and rehearsed, and the idiosyncrasies of individual musicians and improvisatory nature of much music became a thing of the past.

Standardising Musical Instruments and Tunings

Whilst musicians were being trained formally to cope with the demands made on them by the new music and performance contexts of the Socialist era, instruments likewise had to be improved. Given that musicians were performing to paying audiences and officials rather than family members, and were being recorded for film soundtracks and radio broadcasts, the sound quality had to meet expected standards. The sounds musical instruments produced also had to fill the new performance spaces. Furthermore, instrumental tunings had to be standardised to make all instruments aurally compatible within the new professional folk music ensembles. Aside from any ideological reasons for creating homogenised tunings and instrumental constructions, these practical issues had to be addressed.

Before the Socialist era, the body of the horse-head fiddle was round and the face made of animal skin. The strings of the instrument and the bow were made with the tail hairs of stallions rather than mares because, due to a horse's physiological makeup, urine often falls on the tail hairs of mares and reduces the quality. Rounder hairs were preferable to angular ones, so tail hairs were chosen with care. Following the practice of Soviet experts training Mongolians, Russian violin maker Denis Yarovoi visited Mongolia in the 1960s and created a new horse-head fiddle using European instrument-making techniques. From this time, the body of the new horse-head fiddle was made with birch wood, the face with pine, and the strings with nylon. Nylon and wood stayed in tune better than the former animal-skin and horse's tail-hair construction. F-holes, like those of the European violin family, were added to the soundboard and bridges were affixed in order to improve the instrument's acoustic properties. In addition to improving the construction of the instrument, new instruments in the horse-head fiddle family were created: the *ikh khuur*, which corresponds in pitch range and size to the double bass, and the *dund khuur*, which corresponds to the violoncello. The whole range of pitches was therefore available for the new repertoire that was being composed for the instrument.

It was not only instruments that were subject to modification but also vocal techniques and performance practices. Whilst the sounds produced by *khöömiich* formerly led to success in herding and animal breeding, they may not have been perceived as pleasing to the ear within the contexts of theatre performance or film score recordings. Odsüren (INT) explains that the *khöömii* sung by trained professionals in theatres and on film soundtracks is 'significantly more polished' than that of herders.

Russian musicologist and orchestrator Boris F. Smirnov (1912–71) was appointed to the role of state music educator in Mongolia between 1940 and 1946. He instigated the process of retuning Mongolian instruments to correspond with pitches of the diatonic scale, and ensuring the new tunings of each instrument became standard. The strings of the horse-head fiddle, for example, were henceforth tuned to F and B flat. There is little evidence as to the tunings of instruments before Smirnov and these were likely to have been at the discretion of individual musicians. Standardising the tunings of musical instruments meant that the regional and individual tunings used before the Socialist era were eradicated, and this was in keeping with socialist ideology that aimed to replace multiple pre-revolutionary identities with a pan-socialist identity. European tuning systems were adopted throughout the Soviet Union and in other Eastern Bloc countries in the first half of the twentieth century, including Uzbekistan (Levin, 1996, p. 62), Azerbaijan (Frolova-Walker, 1998, pp. 355–6) and Bulgaria (Rice, 1994, p. 192).

The practice of harmonising and orchestrating folk melodies began in the Soviet Central Asian Republics in the 1930s, at first by visiting Russian composers and later by local composers. Mongolia followed suit in the early 1940s, notably with the first Mongolian national opera *Three Dramatic Characters* (*Uchirtai Gurvan Tolgoi*). It was composed in 1942 by Bilegiin Damdinsüren (1919–92) for symphony orchestra with *bel canto* singing, orchestrated by Smirnov. The 'arias' share similar characteristics with many pre-1921 Mongolian folk songs in that they are driven melodically rather than rhythmically or harmonically, are structured by the repetition of verses, and are based on the pentatonic scale, albeit one that corresponded to five pitches of the diatonic scale. Characters sing in unison rather than in harmony and there is an extended long-song in the final scene. The costumed staging of the story in three acts, *bel canto* singing style and use of a symphony orchestra to harmonise the melodies, however, are typical of European opera. Harmonising monophonic Khalkha folk melodies was therefore the first step in the fusing of traditional Mongolian musical traditions with Western symphonic music. Approximately twenty Mongolian national operas have been composed since 1942 and many of these composers also composed film scores.

The Cyrillic alphabet replaced the classical Mongol script as the official alphabet in Mongolia on 15 March 1941 (Grivelet, 1995, p. 49).[6] In this decade, Western musical notation was introduced to Mongolia with the intention of replacing the few and varied regional methods of notating music and the more usual practice of learning music orally. Film composers had to compose diatonic music so they could notate it in the form of a score and, consequently, musicians had to tune instruments diatonically in order to play from the scores. The combined factors of music being documented in the form of handwritten scores and music being professionalised made it possible for members of the Mongolian Composers' Union to monitor music making and ensure modifications in tuning were being maintained.

The developments in instrumental construction and tuning during the Socialist era made traditional Mongolian instruments closer to Western orchestral instruments in terms of appearance, sound and technical capabilities. Mongolian film composers were therefore able to combine traditional Mongolian and Western music in their compositions readily, since the instrumental sounds of both genres had become more compatible. Since film was as important a platform for the dissemination of music as the new theatres and music ensembles, the MPRP would certainly have encouraged this practice.

---

[6] The Mongolian Cyrillic alphabet includes a small number of extra symbols to incorporate sounds in the Mongolian language that do not exist in standard Russian.

Music of the People

During the Socialist era, it was not only instruments, tunings and performance contexts that were altered significantly but also song lyrics and performance techniques. This led to new song genres being developed from existing Khalkha traditions and these appeared in film soundtracks alongside the *de rigueur* symphonic music. Ideological changes to music in the twentieth century meant that within existing songs, references to Buddhism, shamanism, feudal practices, or folk heroes and legends were removed, and new lyrics were composed with socialist ideology firmly in mind. Many of the new song genres employed the *bel canto* singing technique, borrowed directly from European opera, thereby further removing folk songs from pre-revolutionary performance practices and reinforcing links between traditional music and European classical music. The Mongolian Composers' Union had the power to decide which pieces could be performed or published, and it was difficult for a composer who was not a member of the union to get his pieces performed or published at all.

The new and adapted forms of folk music in the Socialist era, with diatonic harmonies and lyrics approved by the state, became known as music of the people (*ardyn khögjim*) or public song (*ardyn duu*). Many Mongolian musicians and musicologists, including Danzangiin Enkhtsetseg (a *khuuchir* teacher and musicologist) and Nyamsüren (*yoochin* player of the Tümen Ekh new folk ensemble), further divide this new folk music. Music of the people (*ardyn khögjim*) is the folk music played by ordinary people, whilst music of the ancestors (*yazguur khögjim*) is the music performed by professional folk ensembles in theatres. Both Enkhtsetseg (INT) and Nyamsüren (INT) told me that there is very little difference between the two other than the instrumentation, in that music of the people is played on instruments for domestic music and music of the ancestors is played on the instruments of palace music.

Another popular genre is the composed song (*zokhiolyn duu*), a new folk-type song with a simple structure, sung by a soloist accompanied by a small instrumental ensemble, but newly composed rather than being a modified version of an existing song. The composed song and public songs were used frequently as the film song – that is, the song played at the end of a film during the credits, which was also broadcast regularly on the radio to advertise the film before it was released. People throughout Mongolia eventually had access to the radio, and were therefore already familiar with film songs before they saw the film in question.

Numerous other song genres came into existence during the Socialist era, although they were less prevalent than the composed song or public song. Marsh mentions the common song (*niitiin duu*), which was similar to the composed song and performed by professionals in theatres and cultural clubs (Marsh, 2009, p. 52). Pegg outlines numerous other song genres that emerged during the Socialist era, as catalogued by writer and scholar Byambyn Rinchen (1905–1977), including lyrical songs (*utga uyangatai duu*), songs of everyday life (*aj baidlyn uyangatai duu*), work songs (*khödölmöriin duu*), saddle songs (*emeeliin duu*) and satirical songs (*khoshin shog duu*) (Pegg, 2001, pp. 273–4). The revolutionary song (*khuvsgalyn duu*), a new genre developed in the Soviet Union, also made frequent appearances in films, particularly in scenes depicting these songs being sung by companies of soldiers.

The Traditional Music of Ethnic Minorities

The fact that musical practices of the Khalkha Mongols were standardised, professionalised and widely disseminated during the Socialist era demonstrates the level of attention and support the MPRP conferred on these traditions. Conversely, the music of Mongolia's ethnic minorities – that is the ethnic groups other than the Khalkha – was to all intents and purposes proscribed. During the Socialist era, the musical instruments of ethnic minorities were confiscated, their rituals and celebrations suppressed, and their music was neither encouraged nor performed publicly. Ethnic homogeneity was facilitated by policies of resettling and scattering ethnic groups, thereby weakening social infrastructures and reducing the opportunities for these groups to participate in their traditions communally. This process was carried out to a far greater degree in the Soviet Central Asian Republics, where 'ethnic dilution' took place – that is, the settling of numerous ethnic Russians within Central Asian communities.

With the exception of one musical film produced in 1956, *Our Melody* (*Manai Ayalguu*), very little music from ethnic minority groups appeared in film soundtracks before 1990. This is largely due to the suppression of these musical traditions under the socialist regime and the government's focus on promoting Soviet and modified Khalkha musical practices. Of the 29 film composers of the Socialist era, only one, the Kazakh Khusayany Musaif (b. 1941), came from an ethnic minority group, although he only ever composed one film score. Given the government's focus on developing Khalkha musical practices, musicians and composers from ethnic minorities were generally not chosen to receive formal musical training. As a result, their music was not subject to Soviet or European musical influence as was the case with professionalised Khalkha music. Consequently, after 1990, when ethnic minorities had greater freedom to practise their musical traditions once more, their surviving music remained relatively unchanged in comparison to Khalkha music, which had been modified significantly throughout the Socialist era. The examples of music from ethnic minorities in film scores after 1990, therefore, are likely to be more representative of pre-revolutionary music in comparison to Khalkha music. The music of ethnic minorities in post-1990 films is generally limited to that of the Kazakhs.

Music and Systems of Belief

Mongolia followed two main systems of belief before the Socialist era: Buddhism and shamanism. Before 1921, many Mongolians relied on shamans not only for spiritual guidance but also for medicine, healing and economic advice. Concurrently, Buddhism thrived and it was usual for herders to send at least one son to live at a monastery to become a monk. Additionally, there are numerous Mongolian customs and beliefs that stem from neither shamanism nor Buddhism, and were adhered to by religious followers and the non-religious alike, such as the singing of epics by bards.

Propaganda was used to help expunge religious belief, and the portrayal of Buddhists and shamans in Mongolian films was altogether negative. Film scenes of cunning, degenerate lamas and incompetent shamans are plentiful and these scenes were often scored with religious music. Ironically, it was these scenes that helped preserve Buddhist and shamanic musical traditions throughout the Socialist era, since practising the music in temples or during ceremonies was strongly discouraged.

The main instruments used by shamans are drums and the jaw harp, and musicians performing *khöömii* or the horse-head fiddle sometimes echo the vocal sounds the shaman produces whilst in trance during ceremonies. Instruments and vocal sounds, however, are not considered music within these contexts but an essential part of the ceremony. The most important part of Buddhist ceremonies is chanting, and the languages used include Tibetan, Sanskrit and Mongolian. Instruments are performed in monasteries and temples for ceremonial use rather than enjoyment, although Buddhists are more inclined to refer to this as music. The instruments used daily in Buddhist ceremonies include the conch shell, cymbals, *damaru*, a large drum called the *khingereg*, and the bell and *vajra*.[7] Additional instruments are used for special occasions, such as the bull trumpet or telescope trumpet (*ikh büree*) and *gyaling*, a flute traditionally made from the thighbone of a virgin. There are other instruments used only in closed ceremonies, and the monks who play them are chosen specially for this task and are not allowed to talk about them. When I interviewed Ulaanbaatar-based Buddhist abbot Tsorj Buyandelger, he told me that the Buddhist music used in Mongolia originated in Tibetan and Indian traditions but over time it developed into a 'Mongolian sound' (Buyandelger, INT). Although shamanic rituals and Buddhist music have seen something of a revival since 1990, they appear in film soundtracks considerably less frequently than during the Socialist era, since their portrayal no longer serves such an important political function.

---

[7] The bell and *vajra* should always be used together. The *vajra*, a symbolic thunderbolt made of brass, is not a musical instrument and produces no sound.

30   *Mongolian Film Music*

Military Music

Soviet-style military music was a notable presence in Mongolia during the Socialist era, and film soundtracks often featured military band music and military-inspired music played by a symphony orchestra. The Bogd Khan established a military ensemble in Mongolia as early as 1914 following the visit of a Mongolian nobleman to a military base in Russia. Red *gers* and cultural centres were set up in military bases from 1921 and a military music ensemble building was constructed in 1925.[8] The state military ensemble, the Mongolian Military Song and Dance Academic Ensemble, was established officially in 1932.[9] Members of the ensemble were often chosen on account of their musical talent whilst on compulsory military service and were sent to the Soviet Union for formal musical training. The repertoire and line-up of the ensemble, which has remained largely unchanged since its foundation, is based on the Alexandrov Ensemble in Russia, known internationally as the Red Army Choir.[10] The ensemble orchestra is made up of violins, violas, violoncellos, bass guitar, keyboard, flute, saxophones, trombones, trumpets, drum kit and percussion. There is also a wind band, a brass band, a male-voice choir, a female-voice choir, several soloists and a dance troupe. Musical numbers include a mixture of Russian military classics and pieces commissioned from Mongolian composers specifically assigned to the ensemble. Song lyrics, in both Russian and Mongolian, are about patriotism, homeland, military matters, freedom, and protecting Mongolia from invaders. The repertoire is based on Russian models: predominantly 4/4 time with a 'marching' feel, in a minor key, a two- or three-part chorus, diatonic harmonies, and an *accelerando* leading to a rousing perfect cadence at the end of the piece. Mongolian composers were able to put a Mongolian stamp on these pieces with lyrics specific to Mongolian locations and events.

The military ensemble performed regularly across Mongolia throughout the Socialist era, so film composers would have been familiar with their music. Furthermore, film composers would undoubtedly have had access to Russian military ensembles when they were studying music in the Soviet Union. Instrumental pieces and songs in 4/4, a minor key, diatonic harmonies and

---

[8]   The original building of the state military ensemble in Ulaanbaatar is now the building of the University of Film Arts (Kino Urlagiin Deed Surguuli). In 1950 the military ensemble moved to its current building, which had previously been used to house Russian officials.

[9]   The Mongolian Military Song and Dance Academic Ensemble was, at the time of research, still a full-time professional ensemble of 180 members, which performs concerts throughout Mongolia, including celebration concerts for anniversaries of military victories. It is the only professional ensemble that still performs songs in Russian and in a distinctly Russian style. Audiences tend to be the older generations and military personnel.

[10]   The full name of the Russian military music ensemble is the A.V. Alexandrov Russian Army Twice Red Bannered Academic Song and Dance Ensemble, but is usually known as the Alexandrov Ensemble or Red Army Choir.

patriotic lyrics became common in Mongolian film soundtracks from the 1950s, and these songs soon became part of the national consciousness, as was the case with military-style film songs in the Soviet Union.

Music for Films, Music for Propaganda

The manifold music genres and styles of the Socialist era were used in combination with the newly established film industry to help to disseminate socialist ideology. The fact that the socialist government neglected or suppressed the folk music of ethnic minorities and portrayed religious music negatively was as significant as the active promotion of Khalkha traditions and genres imported from the Soviet Union. The creation of a professional music industry and the modification of music under the socialist regime, however, should not be viewed as entirely manipulative or destructive. Many Mongolian music professionals appreciated the role of the MPRP in providing the populace with job opportunities, training, and the experience of living and studying abroad. Furthermore, advocates of socialism recognise the importance of modifying and professionalising music as a suitable means to further the socialist cause.

Formal musical training in the Soviet Union and other socialist countries meant not only that Mongolian composers and musicians learned musical techniques, forms and genres taught at Soviet conservatoires, but also that they spent several years immersed in Soviet life and culture. On these composers' and musicians' return to Mongolia, the combination of their fresh experiences as students in the Soviet Union and their nomadic musical backgrounds led to a syncretism of modern Soviet and traditional Mongolian music in a variety of ways. Mongolia had had a rich musical heritage long before it became a socialist country and became influenced by the Soviet Union, so significant modifications had to be implemented before music could become a suitable vehicle for socialist propaganda. Conversely, Mongolia had never had a film industry before the Socialist era, so a cinematic tradition suitable for disseminating socialist ideology could be established from the onset, and this is what happened from 1936.

Chapter 3

New Beginnings: Patriotism, Propaganda and Professional Music

The Mongolian government established a film industry in the mid-1930s, which operated at first under the close guidance of the Soviet Union. Soviet film and music practitioners trained Mongolians in the arts of filmmaking and composition; meanwhile, the brand new solitary Mongolian film studio produced its first silent films and films scored by Russian composers. The intention behind the establishment of the film industry was to disseminate propaganda to the populace, and by the 1940s, Mongolian filmmakers had gained enough initial experience to produce patriotic films infused with socialist ideology, including films that helped install Sükhbaatar as a new national hero.

The Establishment of the Mongolian Film Industry, 1920s–1930s: A Brief Overview

The Fifth Congress of the MPRP in 1925 identified the importance of cinema in disseminating propaganda, and Soviet films began to be shown in Mongolia the following year. In 1929, film projectionists from the Soviet Union began to train Mongolian apprentices, and a year later, the Soviet film organisation Vostok began to supply films with revolutionary themes to Mongolia. The Mongolian Ministry of Public Education established a cinema department in 1933, and in 1934 the first permanent cinema in Mongolia, the Ard Cinema in Ulaanbaatar, was built and at first screened Soviet films. On 18 October 1935, the Mongolian government issued a decree ordering the establishment of a Mongolian film industry. The state film studio was founded in 1936, operating at first under the name *Kino Üildver*, which translates literally as Film Factory or Film Industry.

By the time the Film Factory was founded, the Soviet Union had already established its dominant position within filmmaking in the socialist world, and Soviet practitioners were in a position to help the younger brother nation set up its new film industry. Seventeen years before the establishment of the Film Factory, Vladimir Lenin signed a decree asserting that all films produced in Russia should become national property. Egorova (1997, p. 3) explains that this decree of 27 August 1919 became accepted as the birth of the Soviet film industry even

34 *Mongolian Film Music*

though numerous films had been produced in Russia before this date.[1] Despite both prolific Russian film production and the campaign to eschew Western culture, American films were very much in demand in Soviet cinemas during the 1920s. Of the films screened in the Soviet Union in 1925, 87 per cent were foreign, and those starring actors such as Charlie Chaplin, Buster Keaton and Harold Lloyd were especially popular (Lovell, 2009, pp. 125–6). By the 1930s, however, very few foreign films were shown publicly in the Soviet Union due to the Cultural Revolution (1928–31) and censorship, although Stalin had a penchant for Western cowboy films, which he viewed in his private cinema (Lovell, 2009, p. 130).

Key players in the Soviet film industry, including its director Boris Shumyatsky and film directors Grigory Alexandrov and Sergei Eisenstein, visited the USA in the early 1930s to observe Hollywood filmmaking. Also in this decade, the method of socialist realism began to be applied officially to Soviet filmmaking, as well as other art forms, and this characterised the style of the majority of Soviet films until the mid-1980s.[2] In comparison to Mongolia's solitary film studio based in Ulaanbaatar, the Soviet film industry was made up of over twenty studios throughout the Soviet Union, including studios in each of the constituent republics. The considerably larger Soviet film industry had had a wealth of experience to draw upon, albeit with an element of Hollywood influence, before its practitioners became mentors for the new Mongolian filmmakers and composers.

The 1928 Russian silent film *Storm over Asia* (*Potomok Chingis Khana*; lit. *The Heir of Genghis Khan*) was the first film to be filmed in Mongolia, although postproduction took place in the Soviet Union, and it has always been considered a Russian film. One of the first Mongolian symphonic scores accredited to specific composers was in the soundtrack to the 1936 film *Son of Mongolia* (*Mongol Khüü*), and the composers in question, I. Rabinovitch and Edouard Grikurov, were from the Soviet Union. *Son of Mongolia* was filmed in Mongolia but by the Russian studio Lenfilm rather than the Film Factory and, in addition to the composers, the film's director, designer and many other crew members were Russian. The lead actors, setting and subject matter, however, were all Mongolian, and many consider it to be Mongolia's first film. It won seventh place on the American National Board of Review Awards list of top 10 foreign films in December 1936.

Son of Mongolia follows Tseveen as he searches for his runaway horse, finds it at a festival, and ends up defeating the festival's champion wrestler. The diverse score includes cues of palace music (*ordony khögjim*), public songs (*ardyn duu*),

---

[1] Two hundred feature films were produced in Russia – then the only producer of feature films in the Russian Empire – in the 1914–17 period alone (Egorova, 1997, p. 3).

[2] Notable early examples in Soviet cinema include the 1934 film *Chapaev*, directed by the Vasiliev brothers and produced by Lenfilm, which tells the story of a commander in the Red Army, and the Maxim Trilogy (1935–39), a three-part story about a factory worker, directed by Kozintsev and Trauberg, also produced by Lenfilm.

New Beginnings: Patriotism, Propaganda and Professional Music   35

military music, orchestral cues and a Russian accordion piece.[3] The film has elements of comedy, fantasy and romance, yet ends with a rousing patriotic speech by Tseveen about his wish for Mongolia to be free from tyrannical lamas and the stark rich–poor divide. The speech cross-fades into triumphant military music accompanied by images of marching soldiers. Whether the film's Soviet composers wrote the traditional-instrument cues or recorded existing Mongolian pieces is not clear. Nonetheless, the brief use of orchestral cues, the military music and even the accordion piece laid the foundations for what were to become new traditions of Mongolian film scoring.

In the same year that *Son of Mongolia* was produced, the Soviet Union donated 12 mobile projectors to Mongolia with the aim of helping the MPRP disseminate films throughout the countryside. It is likely that further Soviet donations contributed to the Film Factory's stock of technical equipment, although the majority of the studio's funding came from the Mongolian state budget. With the Soviet training of Mongolian personnel, donations of equipment and the 1936 production of *Son of Mongolia* by a Soviet studio, the Mongolian film industry was inaugurated under the close guidance of its elder brother, and this set the precedent for the Mongolian films that followed. Since the principal intention to produce films in both Mongolia and the Soviet Union was to disseminate propaganda, this was reflected in the content, tone and imagery of the films, and music was used to highlight key issues and messages.

The Film Factory produced five documentaries between 1936 and 1937 but it was the 1938 silent film *Norjmaa's Way* (*Norjmaagiin Zam*), featuring an entirely Mongolian cast and crew, that was the studio's first feature film. Another silent film, *A Pack of Wolves* (*Süreg Chono*), was produced in 1939, concluding the studio's output of the 1930s. The Film Factory remained the only film studio in Mongolia until 1990, and is still in operation today under the name Mongol Kino.[4] The studio produced 892 documentaries between 1936 and 1990, and 167 feature films between 1938 and 1990, including 6 co-productions with film studios of other socialist nations.[5]

---

[3]   All Mongolian musicians and composers I interviewed who mentioned the accordion stated it was a Russian instrument, although this is not surprising since it was first introduced to Mongolia by Russians. The origins of the accordion, however, are believed to date back 4,500 years with the Chinese aerophone, the *cheng*, and the accordion as we know it today was first patented by a Viennese instrument maker of Armenian descent in Paris in 1829.

[4]   The state film studio was called *Kino Üildver* (Film Factory) until 1986, when its name was changed to *Ulsyn Kinony Yerönkhii Gazar* (State Film Head Office). It was renamed the Mongol Kino Company in 1991, after which it underwent several changes of name until 1997 when it became known as the Mongol Kino Corporation. Nowadays it is more commonly referred to as Mongol Kino.

[5]   *Golden Palace* (*Altan* Örgöö, 1961) and *The Guide* (*Gazarchin*, 1983) were co-produced with DEFA Film (East Germany), *The End* (*Tögsgöl*, 1967), *Attention, Soldiers!* (*Daisny Tsergüüdee*, 1971) and *Battle in Gobi Khyangan* (*Govi Khyangand Tulaldsan Ni*, 1981) were co-produced with Mosfilm (Soviet Union), and *Where are the Khairkhan Öndör*

36 *Mongolian Film Music*

Early Sound Films and a New National Hero: The 1940s

The Film Factory produced a silent film in 1940 called *Bubonic Plague* (*Tarvagan Takhal*) and in the same year, Luvsanjambyn Mördorj (1919–96) became the first Mongolian to be credited as a film composer. This was for his score to *The First Lesson* (*Ankhdugaar Khicheel*, 1940), one of seven Film Factory feature films of the 1940s and one of only two films of this decade to be scored by Mongolian composers.[6] The year 1940 also saw the start of a major governmental initiative to disseminate films to the countryside, and the MPRP made the decision to provide red corners with cinema projectors. The Film Factory produced one more silent film, *Life's Enemy* (*Amidralyn Daisan*), in 1941 and three feature films in 1942 scored by the Soviet composer S. S. Galiperin.

Once the Film Factory started to produce films with music scores, Mongolian filmmakers and composers drew inspiration from their Soviet counterparts regarding the music. Two distinct musical styles became the convention in Soviet cinema before the Soviet Union's involvement in World War II, known as the Great Patriotic War (1941–45): the song for comedies and musicals, and symphonic music for historical, revolutionary and dramatic films (Egorova, 1997, p. 20). Although comedies became popular in Mongolia, musicals did not flourish, the 1956 musical *Our Melody* (*Manai Ayalguu*) being the only example. Historical revolutionary dramas, on the other hand, thrived in Mongolia, particularly films about the 1921 Revolution. Following film-scoring conventions in the Soviet Union, composing scores for full symphony orchestra soon became a tradition in Mongolian film.

A notable absence in Mongolian feature films, not only during the 1940s but throughout the Socialist era, is Mongolia's most prominent historical figure, Chinggis Khaan. The MPRP considered Chinggis Khaan inappropriate as a national hero for the new socialist Mongolia, since his hierarchical system of government and imperialistic rule were incompatible with socialist ideology, and the Soviet Union still remembered the thirteenth-century Mongol invasions of their territory. Chinggis Khaan was so deeply embedded into Mongolian national consciousness that eradicating him from cultural memory would have been an impossible task. Replacing him with a new national hero was the MPRP's best option, and the new hero had to be associated with socialism and revolution. Of the Mongolian personalities involved in the 1921 Revolution, it was the military leader Sükhbaatar who ordinary Mongolians could more readily relate to as a national hero rather than the politicians, who were part of the intellectual elite. The capital city was renamed Ulaanbaatar (lit. red hero) in Sükhbaatar's honour in 1924, and a statue of Sükhbaatar on horseback, sculpted by Sonomyn Choimbol, was erected in 1946 in the main square in Ulaanbaatar, Sükhbaatar Square. Sükhbaatar was further

---

Mountains? (*Khairkhan* Öndör *Khaana Baina*, 1978) was co-produced with Barrandov Studio (Czechoslovakia).

[6] The second was *Tsogt Taij* (*Tsogt Taij*, 1945), discussed below.

etched into national consciousness by the plethora of films about him and the 1921 Revolution produced between 1942 and the mid-1970s, which were supported by generous state funding.

Sükhbaatar (*Sükhbaatar*, 1942), produced by the Soviet studio Lenfilm, is a biopic of the eponymous Mongolian hero of the 1921 Revolution. Although the embellishment of historical facts in the name of artistic licence is to be expected, many events portrayed in this film are of dubious accuracy. One such example is the scene in which Sükhbaatar meets Lenin; there is no conclusive evidence that this meeting took place. Another decision by the filmmakers that caused concern amongst some Mongolians was that the role of Sükhbaatar was not given to a Mongolian, but the Soviet actor L. N. Sverdlin. His dialogue was dubbed in Mongolian, and the dialogue of the Mongolian actors was dubbed in Russian for the simultaneous release of the film in the Soviet Union. It was in 1942 that the MPRP issued its policy of dubbing Soviet films in Mongolian for distribution across the country. *Sükhbaatar* was the first of numerous Mongolian films about the 1921 Revolution that portrayed Sükhbaatar as the new national hero of Mongolia.

The underscoring – that is, the background music – of *Sükhbaatar* by the Russian composers Boris Arapov and Venedikt Pushkov primarily comprises richly textured orchestral cues with diatonic harmonies, utilising the full symphony orchestra. Many of these cues are very short and serve to glue consecutive scenes together, particularly when there is a sudden change of location. Marching-style music in 4/4 played by full orchestra is also used to accompany the numerous scenes featuring soldiers and processions and, most notably, during a scene of the Russian Red Army marching into Mongolia. Traditional Mongolian music genres are represented in *Sükhbaatar* only as diegetic or semidiegetic cues.[7] These cues include palace music to accompany a scene at the Bogd Khan's palace, revolutionary songs (*khuvsgalyn duu*) during scenes of soldiers on parade, and scenes of Sükhbaatar and his men singing public songs. There is also a scene featuring the 'game song' *dembe*, a song for two people that involves guessing how many fingers your opponent will reveal whilst improvising lyrics to match the number. That orchestral music provided the majority of the underscoring whilst Mongolian traditional music appeared only when the scene required it suggests the filmmakers were of the opinion that orchestral music was the most suitable genre for scoring films, even those about Mongolian heroes and battles. It is therefore unsurprising that Mongolia adopted the symphony orchestra for most of its film scores thereafter, particularly since this was standard practice within both Soviet and Hollywood film scoring.

---

[7] Certain pieces of music within films appear on screen as part of the story and both the characters and the audience can see the source of the music, such as an instrumentalist or a record player, and this is termed diegetic music. When the source of the music is present in the story but not seen directly, such as music at a disco when the DJ or loudspeakers are not in shot, this is referred to as semidiegetic music.

By the time the Film Factory produced its final film of the 1940s, *Tsogt Taij* (1945) the MPRP was strongly encouraging countrywide patriotism following the Japanese invasion of Mongolia in 1939 and the start of the Great Patriotic War.[8] At this time, the MPRP was also keen to strengthen its anti-Buddhist propaganda as a means to justify the purges of the late 1930s. Tsogt Taij was a seventeenth-century Mongolian prince who supported the leader of Mongolia and last Great Khan, Ligden Khan, in his politically driven attempt to subdue the Yellow Hat sect of Buddhism in Lhasa in the 1630s. It was the Yellow Hat sect that had developed since the seventeenth century to become the dominant religion in Mongolia. Tsogt Taij could therefore be viewed as a suitable national hero during Choibalsan's attempts to defile the reputation of religious leaders during his time as Prime Minister of Mongolia (1939–52).

Although it was highly unusual for the MPRP to allow a film to be made about a Mongolian national hero other than Sükhbaatar, *Tsogt Taij* served the dual purpose of rejuvenating patriotism through the positive portrayal of national customs and historical battles, and reinforcing the message that Buddhist lamas were a negative influence in Mongolia. Meanwhile, in the Soviet Union, famous historical Russians received similar short-lived attention in the cinema. Stalin commissioned Sergei Eisenstein to direct a film about the notorious sixteenth-century ruler Ivan the Terrible, portraying him as a state-builder, but although Part 1 (1944) won a Stalin Prize, Part 2 (1946) was shelved and Eisenstein reprimanded (Lovell, 2009, p. 29).[9] Tsogt Taij was the only Mongolian historical figure from the pre-1921 era to be granted a starring role in a Mongolian film until 1988, when a film about the fifteenth-century queen Mandukhai was produced.

I interviewed Sürengiin Soronzonbold, who wrote his PhD thesis on the music to *Tsogt Taij*, in 2009. He explained that there was a little-known 1943 play about Tsogt Taij that portrayed him as a violent killer. The writer and scholar Rinchen asked Choibalsan for permission to write a screenplay about Tsogt Taij that would provide people with a more favourable picture of the legendary figure. Choibalsan agreed and Rinchen wrote not only the screenplay but also detailed instructions on the music cues, including mood, instrumentation and spotting – that is, deciding which scenes should have music. The score was composed by Mördorj and Damdinsüren, who at this point had not been educated in Western staff notation. Boris Smirnov orchestrated the music and his name appears on each page of the handwritten score, which is now kept in Moscow. Smirnov was consequently credited as joint composer, even though, according to Soronzonbold, it was Mördorj and Damdinsüren who created the musical ideas (Soronzonbold, INT).

The film features traditional Mongolian customs and costumes. The music includes long-song (*urtyn duu*) with horse-head fiddle accompaniment, *uukhai* and shamanic rituals, as well as Buddhist temple music recorded using the

---

[8] *Tsogt Taij* is the only film of the Socialist era to be released on DVD with English subtitles. It is available only in Mongolia.

[9] *Ivan the Terrible* was scored by Sergei Prokofiev.

instruments from Gandan monastery in Ulaanbaatar, one of the few monasteries and collections of temple instruments to survive the purges. The majority of the cues, however, are played by full symphony orchestra in a late-Romantic style, incorporating diatonic harmonies, rich textures and *rubato*, as was the case in many Soviet films produced at the time. Fast tempo cues accompany the numerous battle scenes and slower cues are used for scenes of soldiers travelling to battle, the love story between Tsogt Taij's son Arslan and the heroine Khulan, and scenes featuring Tsogt Taij's mother.

A notable cue appears in the scene when Tsogt Taij tells his mother he is about to leave the palace in which they live to go to battle in Lhasa. A soft *andante* melody is heard in the flute (Example 3.1) with pedal notes and answering figures in the other wind instruments that suggest harmonies rather than the chords being played fully in a strict rhythmic pattern. Along with *arpeggio* fragments in the *pizzicato* strings, the chords suggested are E minor and A minor. This is an early example of a melody based on the pentatonic scale, that of E, G, A, B and D in this case, being harmonised with very basic harmonies. The gentle music helps portray Tsogt Taij's more tender side in comparison to the fanfares and fast tempo symphonic cues heard when he is in battle.

Example 3.1   The opening phrase of the melody played when Tsogt Taij talks to his mother, *Tsogt Taij*

When Tsogt Taij and his mother finish their conversation, she bids him farewell and he descends the staircase inside the palace, ready to leave for Lhasa. At this point, the cue is heard again but this time we see a group of musicians playing on the landing (Figure 3.1). This changes the perspective of the cue. On its first appearance the music seems to be underscoring, which enhances the emotional impact of the scene. On the second hearing, it is presented as diegetic music, even though the instruments heard are symphonic and those seen are traditional. The filmmakers included musicians in the scene since this would have been usual within a palace during the seventeenth century; however, the composers would have been discouraged from composing a cue of actual palace music (*ordony khögjim*), since this was one of the music genres not backed by the state. Despite the incongruence between the music heard and the instruments seen, this early example of professional music supported the aims of the film: to celebrate patriotism by presenting national customs whilst introducing new music to film audiences.

If the MPRP was to succeed in replacing Chinggis Khaan with a new national hero, steps had to be taken to ingrain the new hero into the consciousness of the populace, and certain films of the 1940s played an important role in this process. Although one film was made about the historical figure Tsogt Taij, which in itself

Figure 3.1   Musicians play as Tsogt Taij leaves his palace for Lhasa. Tsagaany Tsegmed (left) as Tsogt Taij. *Tsogt Taij*, Film Factory (Mongol Kino), 1945

served to divert attention away from Chinggis Khaan, it was Sükhbaatar who was the more suitable figure to represent the new socialist Mongolia. The 1942 film was the first of many to portray Sükhbaatar in a suitably celebratory light, and the rich symphonic cues paved the way for the orchestral scores of the numerous Sükhbaatar films that followed, all of which were ordered, supported and funded by the state. Such orchestral cues became associated closely with Sükhbaatar and socialism, and helped to draw attention away from Mongolia's pre-1921 rich heritage of folk songs in praise of Chinggis Khaan, which were no longer performed in public.

Throughout the 1930s and 1940s, Film Factory personnel gained their initial experience in filmmaking and film scoring, giving them the technical expertise to produce films that would meet state approval and thereby further the socialist cause. After *Tsogt Taij*, the Film Factory had a nine-year hiatus from feature films, although the studio produced 54 documentaries between 1946 and 1953. The Film Factory's next feature film was *New Year* (*Shine Jil*) in 1954, and this saw the beginning of over three decades of prolific filmmaking and considerable developments in film scoring. From this date, each feature film solely produced by the Film Factory was scored by Mongolian composers, who, through their music, contributed to the government's plans to generate and disseminate propaganda in earnest.[10]

---

[10]   The films co-produced with non-Mongolian film studios were all jointly scored by a Mongolian composer and a composer from the country in question. For example, the 1967

Combining Musical Styles and Genres: Prerequisites and Possibilities

The Film Factory employed 29 film composers during the Socialist era, and 21 of these were born and brought up in the countryside. The remaining eight composers were born in Ulaanbaatar, of whom only four composed more than one film score during the Socialist era. The majority of Film Factory composers, therefore, had been raised in a traditional rural Mongolian environment. Of the four Socialist-era film composers I interviewed, three told me they learned folk music orally from their parents and elder siblings in the countryside before they were auditioned and chosen to study music formally.[11] These composers as well as a number of other Mongolians described to me the domestic music-making activities of their childhoods, practising with their families and nearest neighbours almost daily in a variety of contexts, most of which included singing. These activities included horsemen singing long-song and whistling (*isgeree*) whilst working, families singing songs in the *ger* after the evening meal, and travellers entertaining each other with songs during long journeys. They also mentioned herders playing the *limbe* whilst watching their flocks, children singing *giingoo* (a good luck song sung before a horse race), and mothers singing lullabies to their babies.[12]

Following the musical activities of their childhoods, Mongolian composers received formal musical training from Soviet experts. In the early years of the Socialist era, music specialists from the Soviet Union visited Mongolia to share their expertise, as was the case with numerous other professionals from engineers to journalists. From the 1940s Mongolians studied composition formally at conservatoires in the Soviet Union and other Eastern Bloc states.[13] Their tuition included Western staff notation, orchestration, harmony and counterpoint, compositional skills, and the musicological analysis of well-known works by mainly Russian composers of the late-Romantic period and early twentieth century. Influenced by their training in Western music theory and the analysis of works of Russian composers from Tchaikovsky and the 'Mighty Handful' (Borodin, Mussorgsky, Balakirev, Cui and Rimsky-Korsakov) to Prokofiev and

---

film *The End* (*Tögsgöl*), produced in association with Mosfilm, was scored by Mördorj and the Russian composer Nikolai Sidelnikov.

[11] Luvsansharav, Jantsannorov and Sharav learned music from family members in the countryside. The fourth composer, Geserjavyn Pürevdorj, was born in Ulaanbaatar and composed only one film score during the Socialist era.

[12] Such descriptions correspond very closely with the music-making activities I witnessed whilst living in Mongolia between 2008 and 2009, specifically in Töv province, just south of Ulaanbaatar, Övörkhangai province in Central Mongolia, the Gobi and in Bayan Ölgii in far Western Mongolia, although of course my observations would differ from those experienced by composers of the Socialist era.

[13] Sambyn Gonchigsumlaa studied at the Tchaikovsky Conservatoire in Moscow 1943–50. Mördorj and Tsegmediin Namsraijav studied there 1951–56 and 1952–57 respectively. From the 1950s it became the norm for Mongolian composers to study at Soviet conservatoires.

Shostakovich, Mongolian film composers subsequently created similar symphonic sounds and textures within their film scores. Later in the Socialist era, Mongolians who had been trained in the Eastern Bloc subsequently became teachers at the State College of Music and Dance in Ulaanbaatar. These government-organised training programmes were extremely influential for Mongolian film composers and ensured that the Film Factory could benefit from using the best Russian compositional techniques in addition to elements of traditional Mongolian music. Furthermore, it was not just the music tuition that became influential for Mongolian composers but the societal and cultural environment they lived in during their years of training in the Eastern Bloc.

Mongolian composers were influenced by Russian symphonic music not only on account of their formal training but also because they had little access to the orchestral music of other nations. Before 1921, Mongolians, particularly in the countryside, would have had access only to the music they performed at home. As the Socialist era progressed, Ulaanbaatar hosted regular performances of operas, ballets and concert music by Russian and Mongolian composers. Meanwhile, rural Mongolians could access symphonic music via radio broadcasts and film screenings, so the entire population soon became familiar with a broad range of Mongolian and Russian repertoire. The Mongolian State Symphony Orchestra was established in 1956 and after this date became the official orchestra to record scores for the Film Factory. In the latter half of the Socialist era, the State Symphony Orchestra went on tour to the countryside regularly to perform symphonic works and film music to the rural population. Throughout the Socialist era, composers and regular citizens alike had increasing access to Russian and Mongolian symphonic music, yet little or no access to the music of other nations. Film composers therefore had only Mongolian and Russian musical influences at their disposal in order to compose film scores that had to appeal to audiences who were familiar with the same musical repertoire.

The formal musical training Mongolians received was in stark contrast to the informal oral music tuition composers such as Natsagiin Jantsannorov (b. 1948) and Byambasürengiin Sharav (b. 1952) would have experienced during their childhoods, yet both methods of learning music appear to have been hugely influential. When I asked Sharav (INT) whether traditional Mongolian music or European classical music had had a greater influence on his compositions, he answered:

> Both are equal. Exactly equal. Fifty-fifty. My music would not be as it is without those influences. If I didn't have Mongolian nomadic music in my genes then I couldn't write this music. If I hadn't studied the classical style formally then I couldn't write this music. Both are of equal importance.

Mongolian film composers of the Socialist era were working in dichotomous contexts. They were obliged to enhance propagandist images of a modern progressive life to which citizens should aspire, yet they had to do so in a manner that would appeal to a nation founded on traditional nomadic culture. The process of filmmaking involved combining influences from opposite sides of the spectrum: the artistic and political vision of the directors, screenplay writers, designers and actors, and the technical mastery of the cinematographers, cameramen, editors, and lighting and sound engineers. The combining of diverse elements during film production was intended to capture a changing way of life and a shift in values from nomadic tradition to socialism. Composers therefore utilised their dichotomous music-learning experiences when scoring films by composing some cues influenced entirely by Russian symphonic music, other cues wholly incorporating Mongolian traditional music, and cues that combined the two.

The fact that the majority of composers had had a background in both traditional Mongolian music and Russian symphonic music was just one of the manifold reasons some of these composers blended the two. A certain musical compatibility is essential if two genres are to be combined. This syncretism is quite a different matter from one music being appropriated into another, when appropriation means taking one music largely unchanged and possibly without permission and placing it within another.[14] Syncretism requires modification of both types of music in order to for them to be combined, as was the case in Mongolia to which the Soviet Union donated its music willingly. Bruno Nettl has discussed new music genres that emerged in West Africa such as juju and highlife, which came about due to (amongst other things) the compatibility of West African and European music (Nettl, 2006, p. 58). Alan Merriam refers to the lack of syncretism that occurs when two musical styles are incompatible, such as European music and that of the Flathead Indians (Merriam, 1964, p. 314). The fact that folk music in Mongolia became more similar to European classical music following extensive modification resulted in the two genres becoming more musically compatible and therefore easier for composers to combine.

From their different perspectives, both Merriam and Nettl argue the importance of compatibility or at least proximity of cultures to allow syncretism to take place (Merriam, 1964, p. 314; Nettl 1985, pp. 24–5). In the case of Mongolia and the Soviet Union, it was geographical location and to a greater extent socialist politics that created an environment of cultural compatibility. The MPRP had an overt political motive to replace pre-1921 societal divisions with societal equality under the auspices of the Soviet Union, thereby enhancing cultural compatibility between the two nations. Timothy Rice makes the point about music during the Socialist era in Bulgaria that classical music and folk music were modified in order to help blur divisions between pre-Socialist era classes. Rice (1994, p. 181) argues that classical music had formerly been associated with the upper classes and folk with peasant classes. During the Bulgarian Socialist era, classical music had to appeal to the masses in addition to the upper classes, and folk music was adapted and professionalised so it would appeal to the bourgeoisie. In a similar manner to

---

[14]   The practice of sampling is such an example.

Mongolia, classical and folk music in Bulgaria were brought closer together so they would have similar and equal appeal to the whole population.

The relatively rapid introduction of European symphonic music to Mongolia on a large scale through film scores, concert music and new theatres meant that some modification of existing Mongolian music was to be expected. Traditional Mongolian music was modified from the 1940s, bringing it into accordance with European systems of tuning and performance practice. Symphonic music in Mongolia, however, had been introduced only when socialism began to take hold, so it could be moulded to appeal to the masses from the onset. The drive to homogenise the Mongolian population by means of blurring ethnic and social boundaries resulted in the two distinct musical genres – folk and classical – being made more similar. Folk music had been retuned into equal temperament and in many cases harmonised, thereby bringing it in line with European classical music. Similarly, Mongolian symphonic pieces emerged throughout the Socialist era that were based on characteristics of Khalkha traditions, thereby making it more akin to folk music.

Examples of retuned and restyled traditional music are found in the 1959 film *Messenger of the People* (*Ardyn Elch*), scored by Mördorj. The story, set in 1921, follows a woman called Ariunaa, who struggles against adversity to take an important letter to Sükhbaatar. The opening scene depicts a wrestling match at the *Naadam* festival, and the semidiegetic music is the traditional sporting song genre *uukhai* sung in equal temperament with a steady rhythm and a strict repetitive structure, quite unlike the improvisatory *uukhai* that would have been heard before 1921. The film also contains cues of symphonic music imbued with characteristics of traditional Mongolian music. There is a scene in which the writer of the letter to Sükhbaatar is being pursued by White Russian soldiers before he hands the letter to Ariunaa. The underscoring is an extended orchestral cue featuring a string ostinato with a rhythm similar to that of a galloping horse, a characteristic common in horse-head fiddle repertoire. An orchestral cue with a similar string ostinato also appears during a horse-chase scene in *Tsogt Taij*, and this became a popular characteristic within Mongolian film scoring.

According to Buyankhesheg, former music theory teacher at the State College of Music and Dance, the rudiments of Western classical music and Mongolian music theory share the same fundamental principles but with one notable exception: Western music theory is based on the heptatonic scale whereas Mongolian music is based on the pentatonic scale. The pentatonic scale in question, however, is not the pentatonic scale that existed in pre-revolutionary Mongolia, which was not compatible with Western music theory. The new pentatonic scale of the Socialist era consisted of a five-pitch subset of the Western seven-note scale, making it more compatible with European symphonic music. Although Mongolian symphonic music originated in European orchestral music in terms of instrumentation, textures and harmonies, the fact that it retained its pentatonic scale is a significant factor in how Mongolian composers managed to retain an idiosyncratic Mongolian sound. There are numerous examples of melodies based on pentatonic scales in film soundtracks, including melodies performed solo or in unison and harmonised melodies. An example of the former occurs in *Messenger of the People*, when the folk song *Dörvön Uul* (*Four Mountains*) is sung and played in unison by the oboe to accompany a scene of men from Sükhbaatar's army riding home to their *ger*s in the countryside. An example of the latter is the folk song *Bayan Khangain Khüder* (*Joyful Khangai Steppe*) sung in harmonies by an SATB chorus during a scene of a travelling show visiting a *ger* camp in the 1956 musical film *Our Melody*, the music of which was arranged by composer Sambyn Gonchigsumlaa (1915–91), the first Mongolian composer to receive formal musical training in the Soviet Union.

As well as harmonising and orchestrating melodies based on the pentatonic scale, another device composers used to blend genres was careful instrumentation. Many Mongolian composers scored pieces and cues for orchestral instruments with similar timbres to traditional Mongolian instruments. When discussing composing music for wide appeal, Jantsannorov (INT) told me:

> When I compose for a symphony orchestra, I always want to appeal to people who are not familiar with symphonic music, to people who are used to simple music. Using national or traditional music makes the music more powerful, so when I compose, I always emphasise the traditional elements. For example, the trumpet as an instrument expresses the European style more, but the clarinet, the flute, the strings, I can make these instruments sound like traditional Mongolian instruments. I therefore avoid using the trumpet and concentrate on the other instruments I mentioned, so the music will sound more like traditional Mongolian music. This makes the music more powerful.

Although composers had the training, the opportunity and even the obligation to compose for the symphony orchestra, the desire to make symphonic music sound more like Mongolian music was clearly present. In Jantsannorov's case, he believed not only that this method would fulfil the government's motive to make music appeal to the masses, but also that features of traditional music could make symphonic music 'more powerful'. Mördorj, the most prolific film composer of the Socialist era, used this technique in many of his early film scores. He used the oboe, which sounds like the *bishgüür*, in numerous cues in *Messenger of the People*, particularly during scenes of characters travelling alone or in pairs through the countryside to escape the White Russian Army. In Mördorj's score to the 1956 film *The Obstacles We Confront* (*Bidend Yuu Saad Bolj Baina*), which is largely set in Ulaanbaatar, he composed a solo flute melody, sounding like the *limbe*, to accompany a shot of the sunrise. The use of familiar sounds would help film viewers, particularly from rural areas, to associate with the images more readily, thereby enhancing their film-viewing experience.

Certain other cultural factors played their role in facilitating syncretism. From 1959, students at the State College of Music and Dance learned both classical music and traditional Mongolian music, albeit the new modified versions. Government policies of training, standardising and disseminating music were equally applicable to both genres. Furthermore, multiple music genres being present in the same context was the norm in Mongolia. Members of the Mongolian Composers' Union composed everything from ballets to songs. Later in the Socialist era, many film composers were also performers in the State Big Band, so they were used to composing classical and classical-influenced music and performing jazz and swing. The Mongolian Philharmony, the umbrella organisation for five music ensembles including a symphony orchestra and the state rock band, is managed by one director. Throughout the Socialist era, combining different musical genres would therefore not have been considered unusual.

Whether the new orchestral music heard in film soundtracks and concert platforms was a modified form of European classical music, a specifically new Mongolian branch of classical music, a recasting of folk music, or a new genre altogether – that is, professional music (*mergejliin khögjim*) – is a question worthy of debate. Given the overlap between these classifications, the music can rightfully be considered all of the above, although there are some differences of opinion amongst academics and Mongolian music professionals. Marsh (2009, p. 60) suggests that the new orchestral compositions were fundamentally European and that composers consciously, and possibly with difficulty, added a Mongolian element to them: 'Like their colleagues in other Soviet republics, Mongolian composers struggled to define a distinctly Mongolian sound within the late-Romantic European classical style of composition popular among Soviet musical institutions.' In contrast, when I asked the Executive Director of the Mongol Kino studio (the current name of the Film Factory studio), Jambyn Solongo (INT), about the European symphonic influence on Mongolian film music, he responded, 'I don't think the music is quite European in style. Mongolians have had orchestral music since the 1930s. Mongolian orchestras play Mongolian music despite using European orchestral instruments.' Whereas Marsh's quote suggests the music is fundamentally European with added Mongolian characteristics, Solongo believes it to be a distinctly Mongolian branch of classical music with European roots.

The term professional music has been applied to this syncretic music by Mongolian musicologists including Enkhtsetseg, who categorises it separately from classical music (*songodog khögjim*). She uses the term 'professional music' to a cover the broad spectrum of orchestral repertoire that combines characteristics of Russian symphonic music from Tchaikovsky to Shostakovich with elements of traditional Mongolian music, and cites the music of Jantsannorov as 'the pinnacle' of the genre (Enkhtsetseg, INT). Mördorj was one of the first Mongolians to compose professional music for films, early examples of which can be heard in his scores of the 1940s and 1950s. In addition to the professional music in *Tsogt Taij*, 10 out of the 14 cues in *The Obstacles We Confront* are professional music, with a primary melody built on the pentatonic scale, played by the woodwind, solo strings or French horns, and harmonised by the full string section.[15]

---

[15] See Chapter 4 for further discussion on the music of *The Obstacles We Confront*.

The issue of classification relates to the question of when orchestral music in Mongolia, including professional music, came to be considered a Mongolian tradition in its own right. The introduction of symphonic music to Mongolia from the Soviet Union was by no means an isolated example of Western music being instituted in a non-Western country, and it was during the twentieth century that this process was intensified worldwide. It was the relatively large extent of symphonic music in Mongolia, not to mention state endorsement, that led to its becoming a new Mongolian tradition. When exactly symphonic music was adopted as a tradition is difficult to determine and open to interpretation; however, the roots of professional music as a Mongolian tradition began in the early 1940s with works such as Damdinsüren's national opera *Three Dramatic Characters*. It is likely that symphonic music had not been heard in Mongolia at all before the Socialist era, yet by the 1940s it was present within every film soundtrack.

Workers of the State: The Public Status of Film Composers

During the Socialist era, composers were considered workers of the state, no different from herders or construction workers, and equally encouraged and obliged to dedicate their working lives towards building and furthering socialism. Since the government regarded composers as dedicated workers of the state, they were held in high esteem throughout the Socialist era, particularly in comparison to those considered a threat to socialism such as Buddhist lamas and noblemen. The MPRP introduced a number of measures to ensure that composers maintained their respected position within society and continued to compose music that met with governmental approval.

In the Soviet Union, composers were also held in high regard, and contemporary sources indicate that during the 1940s they often received state awards and even houses (Slonimsky, 1944, p. 15). On the other hand, compositions and composers were sometimes criticised publicly in the party newspaper *Pravda* for promoting counter-revolutionary ideas (Slonimsky, 1944, p. 7) so although many composers were rewarded for their compositions, they also had to exercise an element of caution in order to avoid criticism. The status of film and concert composers in the Soviet Union was very important to the new Mongolian composers, since they had no access to other role models. Following the practice in the Soviet Union, numerous Mongolian composers were awarded state medals during the Socialist era, and these awards had a twofold consequence. First, they served to encourage Mongolian composers to compose pieces that celebrated patriotism and socialism and that made use of the new standardised tuning system. Second, the awards demonstrated to the public that the MPRP and the official bodies that governed music approved of the compositions being produced. State medals were also awarded to other industrious workers of the state, such as construction workers and herders who met certain targets in building and breeding livestock respectively. The fact that composers were rewarded officially for using standardised tuning and composing pieces infused with patriotism and socialism would have shaped their decisions when scoring films.

Mongolians who studied composition in the Soviet Union, and at the State College of Music and Dance later in the Socialist era, learned the art of both concert and film composition. From the perspective of the MPRP, if the same composers' names appeared in film credits and concert programmes, concert-goers may have been more inclined to take note of the film soundtracks and film viewers more encouraged to attend classical concerts, thus maximising both film and concert attendance. Furthermore, it was more efficient and cost-effective for the MPRP to send composers to be trained in Moscow in both film and concert music rather than separating the two disciplines. Many early Mongolian composers also worked as composition teachers at the State College of Music and Dance and worked with new composers at the Film Factory, serving as mentors. Sharav states that his compositions are very influenced by his composition teacher Gonchigsumlaa and by Mördorj, with whom he worked at the Film Factory (Sharav, INT). In the early years of the Socialist era, all new Mongolian composers were trained by Soviet experts, but later in the era some of this work was taken on by Soviet-trained Mongolian composers.

Similarly, in the Soviet Union, certain celebrated concert composers also composed film scores, including Sergei Prokofiev and Dmitri Shostakovich to give two notable examples. Both of these composers made significant contributions to film composition in the early Soviet era which, given their achievements in art music, helped elevate film scoring to the same status as concert music in the Soviet Union. Notable early film scores include Shostakovich's music for the 1929 film *The New Babylon* and Prokofiev's score for Sergei Eisenstein's 1938 production of *Alexander Nevsky*. The fact that notable concert composers were commissioned to compose music for these early films demonstrates the positive and respectful attitude of Soviet filmmakers towards the new art of film music, and this opinion was consequently adopted in Mongolia.

The Mongolian composers played a crucial role in supporting the MPRP's socialist beliefs publicly, and the titles of many of their early concert pieces fall into two broad and overlapping categories: patriotic and socialist. Composing film cues founded on patriotism and socialism therefore became commonplace not only because of the subject matter of the films but also because composers had experience in composing patriotic and socialist-inspired music for the concert platform. Titles of concert pieces that suggest allegiance to socialist ideology include Gonchigsumlaa's opera *Truth* (*Ünen*) and Damdinsüren's aria *All the People Are Ours* (*Khamag Ard Bidniig*) from his opera *The Road to Happiness* (*Jargalyn Zam*). One of the most well-known concert pieces with patriotic undertones is Damdinsüren's *High in the Khentii Mountains* (*Khentiin Öndör Uuland*), a short piece for solo violin with orchestral accompaniment. Damdinsüren advanced the practice of harmonising folk tunes in this piece by composing the melodies he harmonised rather than using existing folk tunes. Another key piece is *My Motherland* (*Minii Ekh Oron*) by Mördorj, for which he won a state medal in 1945

New Beginnings: Patriotism, Propaganda and Professional Music   49

for his use of the European tuning system. Despite having composed numerous concert pieces and film scores, Damdinsüren and Mördorj are perhaps more well known for their composition of the new Mongolian national anthem, for which they were awarded a state medal in 1951. Many composers practised their craft and made a good name through composing concert pieces before they became known as film composers.

From 1957, all working composers in Mongolia had to be members of the Mongolian Composers' Union, and this institution was responsible for ensuring all compositions met government-stipulated criteria. Members composed both concert pieces and film scores, and these were heard only in state theatres, on state radio or within films produced by the Film Factory. Many composers also held positions of authority within the Mongolian Composers' Union and the other official bodies responsible for overseeing musical activity such as the Academy of Sciences or the Ministry of Culture. These measures ensured that later generations of film composers continued to work in the same politically acceptable manner as those of the early decades of Mongolian filmmaking.

Whereas Mongolia had had a rich musical heritage before Mongolian composers and musicians were trained in Soviet conservatoires, it had not had a film industry at all. The majority of Mongolian film composers received at least a partial traditional Mongolian musical upbringing before their formal training in the Soviet Union began to influence their music making; however, it was impossible for early Mongolian film professionals to draw upon a background of traditional Mongolian filmmaking, although many had experience of working in the theatre. Mongolian musicians and composers throughout the Socialist era worked with Mongolian musical instruments, albeit retuned and remodelled, whereas the film technology available to camera operators, editors and technicians came to Mongolia directly from the Soviet Union. Unlike Mongolian filmmakers, whose skills were acquired from Russian praxis, Mongolian film composers had only one foot in Soviet conventions and the other planted firmly in their own musical traditions. It was the film composers, therefore, who were in a better position to conserve elements of Mongolian traditions within their fledgling film industry.

The Dawn of the Golden Age (*Altan Üye*)

Although composers were considered workers of the state during the Socialist era, from 1990 they have been viewed from a different perspective and almost without exception the Mongolian film and music professionals I interviewed used the term *Altan Üye* (golden age) to refer to the film scores from the late 1950s.[16] The term 'golden age' has been applied to most areas of art and culture and refers to a period

---

[16]   This is in part due to the perception of film professionals and fans alike that the quality of film music declined rapidly after 1990, which adds to the sense of nostalgia surrounding film scores of the Socialist era. See Chapter 7 for further discussion of post-1990 film music.

50   *Mongolian Film Music*

of time considered the highlight of the art form in question. Defining a period as a golden age is always done retrospectively and invariably with a touch of nostalgia, and its time frame is often widely debated. The golden age of Mongolian film music continued well into the 1980s, although it is the film compositions of the 1950s that contained many of the musical characteristics that came to typify the golden age and laid the foundations for the film music that followed.

One important component of a golden age is a wealth of innovative artists in the field. Of the 29 composers employed by the Film Factory, 19 composed more than one film score during the Socialist era. Of the remaining 10, 8 composed only one film score ever whilst the other 2 continued to compose film music after 1990. The same few names therefore appeared recurrently in film credits as well as concert programmes, and it was these composers whose work is associated most closely with the golden age of Mongolian film scoring. Table 3.1 lists the most prolific film composers between 1940 and 1990, all of whom also composed concert pieces.

Table 3.1   The most prolific Mongolian film composers of the Socialist era

Composer	Number of films scored
Luvsanjambyn Mördorj	18
Zunduin Khangal	17
Gonchigiin Birvaa	15
Dagvyn Luvsansharav	12
Tsegmediin Namsraijav	12
Dambiinyamyn Janchiv	12
Bilegiin Damdinsüren	11
Natsagiin Jantsannorov	10
Jamyangiin Chuluun	8

In addition to these nine, other noted composers included Eregzengiin Choidog, Gonchigsumlaa, Tsogzolyn Natsagdorj and Sharav. The works of these composers are still performed regularly in theatres in Ulaanbaatar, which helps keep their music in the national consciousness.

From the late 1950s the professionalisation of traditional music was fully in progress, not only in Mongolia but also throughout the Soviet Union and Eastern Bloc. Other examples include state-sponsored concerts and music competitions in the Soviet Union and concerts of 'arranged folklore' in Bulgaria (Rice, 1994, p. 32). Creating music that was rehearsed, polished, technically proficient and tonally pleasing to the Soviet ear had replaced the improvisatory and domestic nature of the music Mongolians had previously practised. Within this musical context, certain musical symbols came to represent a typical Film Factory score,

New Beginnings: Patriotism, Propaganda and Professional Music   51

such as diegetic public songs with a one-instrument accompaniment during pastoral scenes, fast rhythmic string ostinati to echo the sound of galloping horses, and tremolo diminished chords to represent suspense, all of which came to be associated with this golden age.

Another determining factor as to what constitutes a golden age of film music is a wealth of excellent-quality film scores, particularly works that come to be considered classics and that have an impact on subsequent films and film music. It was during the golden age in Mongolia that some fruitful collaborations between directors and composers took place, resulting in the production of films and scores that are still held in high esteem within Mongolia. Table 3.2 shows the most prolific film directors of the pre-1990 era, the number of films they directed, and the number of films on which they collaborated with certain composers. Many of these directors received state medals, directed films that came to be considered Mongolian classics, and created some of the filmic characteristics and symbols typical within Film Factory filmmaking. Such collaborations gave key composers repeated opportunities to work closely with highly regarded and experienced directors and to score good-quality films, which in turn had an impact on their compositions.

Table 3.2   The most prolific film directors and their collaborations with composers

Director	Number of films	Number of collaborations with composers
Dejidiin Jigjid	24	Mördorj (4); Luvsansharav (4); Birvaa (4)
Ravjaagiin Dorjpalam	20	Mördorj (5); Chuluun (4)
Badrakhyn Sumkhüü	14	Luvsansharav (6)
Gombojavyn Jigjidsüren	12	Mördorj (4); Khangal (5)
Khaltaryn Damdin	11	Janchiv (6)

From the late 1950s, many composers and filmmakers who had finished their studies in the Soviet Union returned to Mongolia and put what they had learned into practice. By this time, the Mongolian film industry had had two decades of filmmaking experience, so professionals were practised in the skills necessary to produce films efficiently and to high standards. Likewise, due to training and experience, composers were able to create film scores that elevated the numerous on-screen images of hardworking ordinary Mongolians from scenes of hardship to scenes of the glorious struggle towards communism. Many films produced between the late 1950s and 1980s were large-scale, lavish productions, with sumptuous orchestral scores often featuring choirs and other instruments, which can compare favourably to the small-scale low-budget productions typical of the post-1990 era, when the term *Altan Üye* came into being.

From whose perspective a certain period is regarded a golden age is open to question and, due to the retrospective nature of the appellation, it is unlikely that artists would believe themselves to be in a golden age. Whether film audiences consider the late 1950s to mid-1980s the golden age of Mongolian film music is difficult to determine; many may be of this opinion due to an automatic agreement with the professionals and because of the importance given to films of these decades during national holidays. Mongolian films of the Socialist era are screened regularly on television during Mongolian New Year (*Tsagaan Sar*) and Independence Day. Since the labelling of any period as a golden age is based on judgements of quality, it is therefore more conceptual than historical labels that are based on events, for example the Mongol Empire. The boundaries of a golden age can therefore be shifted or the term applied later to a different period altogether.[17] Through the foundations laid in the early decades of Mongolian filmmaking, the status of Mongolian film composers of the Socialist era became elevated from 'workers of the state' to 'golden age' shortly after the era in question drew to a close.

Symphonic Music, Cinema and Propaganda

One of the principal tasks for the MPRP as soon as they came into power was to disseminate socialist ideology throughout Mongolia and to convince a nomadic society that industry and progress were the direction the country should take. To help achieve this aim, the government founded a film industry. Films and their accompanying music scores were disseminated to the entire population in addition to theatre, literature, art, public meetings and speeches, all of which were, essentially, propaganda. Yet the Mongolian people's inherent connection to their nomadic past could not be eradicated; the vast and sparsely populated geographical landscape made complete party control difficult to administer. In the 1930s, the state film studio gained initial experience in filmmaking, and, by the 1940s, films with socialist and patriotic themes were being produced, and two of these were scored by Mongolian composers. Symbols of pre-1921 life that did not support socialist ideals, such as Chinggis Khaan, were ignored in these films and the presentation of alternative ways of life from other nations – for example capitalism – were altogether avoided. Socialist society was promoted and Sükhbaatar became the new national hero, the 1942 film *Sükhbaatar* being the first of many such films. All of this helped to steer the population away from its pre-1921 past and in the direction of socialism.

Symphonic music had been used to score the majority of Soviet films, which encouraged the new Mongolian film professionals to adopt symphonic music as the

---

[17] One only need look at the various debates on when the golden age of British popular music is, for example, to see that once the term is applied, it can always be reapplied to a later period.

most appropriate genre for their fledgling film industry. New film composers were needed to score the films, so musically talented people from rural Mongolia were trained formally in composition by Soviet experts. On their return to Mongolia, the newly trained composers formed a close-knit community which, regulated by the Mongolian Composers' Union, played its part in promoting socialism collectively. Ample music budgets allowed film composers to utilise the symphony orchestra as a resource in virtually every film. MPRP initiatives to blur social, cultural and ethnic boundaries resulted in the modification of traditional music, making it compatible with the symphonic music that had been concurrently introduced. Mongolian composers embraced the variety of symphonic music introduced to the country by Soviet experts whilst maintaining a distinctly Mongolian stamp by combining the two musical disciplines, leading to the development of professional music. By the 1950s, Mongolia had gained initial experience in filmmaking and film scoring, and trained a cohort of new Mongolian composers who became respected as workers for the state and, ultimately, the first composers of the golden age of Mongolian film scoring.

Chapter 4

Socialist Cinema from Conception to Dissemination

A film goes through a number of stages from the devising of the initial idea through to its being viewed by the audience. In the case of Mongolian filmmaking of the Socialist era, the initial idea was devised by the MPRP, who wished to present to its people a strong image of socialist progress in which the proletariat and post-1921 heroes were exalted. Following the devising of the initial idea, the preproduction stage followed typical filmmaking procedure, which included writing the screenplay, designing sets and costumes, casting, and assembling the crew.

It was during the production stage that the imagined world of the plot, location, characters, themes, issues and ideology were brought to on-screen life. Mongolian films of the Socialist era portrayed the 1921 Revolution as a glorious victory that resulted ultimately in prosperity, equality and happiness, and it was the task of the film composers to create scores that helped filmmakers portray life under the socialist regime favourably. This chapter provides an overview of the main trends and themes presented on screen during the 1950s–1970s and a short discussion on one film, *The Obstacles We Confront* (*Bidend Yuu Saad Bolj Baina*, 1956), the only film of this period to be openly critical of the socialist regime.

The postproduction stage included editing, scoring, dubbing and censorship. This was followed by dissemination, which in the case of Mongolia involved a huge state operation to ensure the films were viewed by every citizen. Throughout each stage, Mongolian films were designed to champion the poor, repudiate feudal and religious authority, celebrate social and economic progress, and glorify the socialist policies that had stemmed from Marxist–Leninist doctrine. State-honoured film and concert composer Dagvyn Luvsansharav (1926–2014) had a prolific and varied career in music and film composition throughout the Socialist era, and his life and principal works are presented here as a case study.

Training, Preproduction and Production: A Brief Overview in the Mongolian Context

As was the case with musicians and composers, film experts from the Soviet Union came to Mongolia to provide training, whilst Mongolian film personnel who showed potential were sent to the Soviet Union, often to the VGIK film institute of the Moscow State University of Culture and Arts, to receive formal training as directors, producers, designers, cinematographers, camera operators, technicians and film researchers. This process ensured the best Russian and Eastern Bloc film techniques were being used to create Mongolian films of a comparable standard to those of its elder brother. Amongst the numerous film and music professionals and laypersons I spoke to during my time in Mongolia, opinion was divided as to whether training in the Soviet Union was wholly beneficial or tantamount to brainwashing. Prolific Film Factory film designer Püreviin Tsogzol (b. 1934), however, believes the best films were made by a crew comprising an equal split of those who were trained in the Soviet Union and those who had remained in Mongolia (Tsogzol, INT). The situation Tsogzol describes would have resulted in films being produced with the technical expertise of the Soviet Union combined with a markedly Mongolian stamp.

The series of five-year plans, starting with the first five-year plan of 1947–52, were the first step in the filmmaking process. Each five-year plan dictated how many films the Film Factory should produce in a given year, what themes and issues the films should address, and what budget they would be allotted. When discussing the filmmaking process, Tsogzol (INT) told me, 'Everything was organised by the socialist government, everything was part of the five-year plan, including film. Films had to show developments in socialism ... films had to promote socialist ideology.' The MPRP ordered the production of films that celebrated certain anniversaries, for example the 1921 Revolution or the establishment of herding collectives, thus numerous films on the same subject would be made within a given time period. To give examples, Sükhbaatar was a popular topic for films during the 1960s and there was a profusion of films about herding collectives in the 1970s. The prescriptive nature of filmmaking did not stop at the central subject of the story: certain actors became associated with particular types of roles. The actor Tseveliin Dashnamjil (1943–2002), for example, was only ever cast as Sükhbaatar, whom he played in *Morning* (*Öglöö*, 1968), *The Clear River Tamir* (*Tungalag Tamir*, 1970–73), *The Battle* (*Temtsel*, 1971) and *Five Colours of the Rainbow* (*Solongyn Tavan* Öngö, 1978). Films were also made to promote a particular ideological constituent or to appeal to a certain demographic, such as children. Propaganda was intensified in the run-up to important political events and professional propagandists were employed to operate and monitor this process. The socialist influence on filmmakers and composers, therefore, was not subliminal; their obligations were strategically and explicitly laid out in the form of well thought out, detailed governmental plans.

Once each five-year plan was issued, screenwriters could begin work on scripts, and the Mongolian Writers' Union provided them with strict guidelines regarding film plots and themes, thereby giving the writers limited scope on the topics and issues they could portray. Many of the films of the 1950s featured somewhat one-dimensional characters and stereotypes, so from the 1960s literary and film critics determined that screenplay writers should further develop characterisations. A screenplay department was set up within the Mongolian Writers' Union in the late 1960s to ensure that well-rounded characters coupled with verisimilar plots and clearly defined themes furthered the cause of socialism.

The influences exerted upon Mongolian filmmakers also came from the somewhat limited range of films to which they had access. Throughout the Socialist era, Mongolians had infrequent access to foreign films other than those from the Soviet Union and a few from other socialist countries. Soviet films dubbed in Mongolian were distributed widely in Mongolia in cinemas, mobile cinemas and on television, and Ulaanbaatar hosted Soviet film and documentary festivals and Soviet film poster exhibitions. The alleged popularity of Soviet films was publicised widely in Mongolian newspapers and other party publications. In addition to these Soviet films, the only other films Mongolian filmmakers and composers could watch and therefore be influenced by were films previously produced by the Film Factory.

Another important person during preproduction was the film's designer. Tsogzol, who worked as the designer on 29 films between 1961 and 1989, explained to me during an extended interview at the University of Film Arts in Ulaanbaatar the manifold duties of this job. Film designers at the Film Factory fulfilled a variety of roles including set design, costume design, creating the storyboard and even painting portraits of actors and characters. The skills needed to execute this role included artistic skills, historical research skills, knowledge of set construction, awareness of budget, and excellent communication with the director, screenplay writer, cinematographer, set builders and seamstresses. His professional training included filmmaking, so he could understand the technical considerations connected to his designs; history, so his designs would be authentic; and budgeting, since there would be little point in designing sets and costumes that were too expensive to make. The designers' storyboards, sets and costumes contributed to the common goal of reproducing authentic-looking film visuals.

One of the key roles throughout the filmmaking process was the director. During the Socialist era, as soon as film professionals started to gain experience and earn good reputations, the MPRP began to request certain directors for specific films. Dejidiin Jigjid (1919–89), for example, was well known for directing overtly ideological films and those about the 1921 Revolution. Once a director had proved adept at incorporating socialist ideology into a certain film genre, the MPRP could then rely on him to continue doing so in subsequent films.[1]

Directors, writers, designers and cinematographers, as well as composers, were highly trained, respected and often honoured with state awards and medals. Gifted actors also received state awards but they did not experience the adulation and fame of their Western counterparts. The concept of the film star or celebrity did not exist before 1990, and actors of the Socialist era were considered artists who held equal status to workers in any other field.

---

[1]   I use the masculine pronoun throughout this book to refer to film directors, composers and cinema projectionists of the Socialist era because, to my knowledge, they were all male.

58 *Mongolian Film Music*

The filmmaking process in Mongolia was similar to that of the Soviet Central Asian Republics, whose film studios were guided by the Politburo. The content of Mongolian films was dictated by the MPRP and it was the responsibility of the filmmakers to weave socialist ideology into the on-screen world of location, plot and characters, although this certainly does not mean that the films lacked aesthetic or artistic quality. Nonetheless, many of the resultant films portrayed an ideal existence that could be achieved through adherence to socialist policy.

Plot and Propaganda in the Middle Decades of the Socialist Era: 1950s–1970s

The obligation to depict socialist ideology in Mongolian cinema was profound. In addition to governmental directives and guidelines from the various unions, there were numerous articles in the party newspaper *Ünen* reinforcing the message that film and other art forms should portray the benefits of socialism. This excerpt from an editorial in the December issue of *Ünen* in 1968 is one such example: 'Our artists have no greater or more honorable duty than depicting realistically our today's life and proving the glorious triumph of communism' (Anon, 1968). It was the duty of Mongolian filmmakers to interpret the goals of the MPRP rather than cultivate their own ideas, although that is not to say that filmmakers were devoid of creative flair or socialist leanings. Their role in promoting socialism in a manner that would appeal to the masses was directed by the government and publicised in the media.[2]

The Film Factory produced eight films in the 1950s and most of these were uncompromisingly propagandist. The 1957 film *Awakening (Serelt)*, for example, highlights the benefits of Western medicine, brought to Mongolia by Russian doctors, in comparison to the traditional shamanic healing that had been widespread in Mongolia for some centuries. The most controversial film of the 1950s, however, was the 1956 release *The Obstacles We Confront (Bidend Yuu Saad Bolj Baina)*, directed by Ravjaagiin Dorjpalam (1930–90), which openly criticises bureaucracy and was the only film to make a firm stand against socialism until the late 1980s. This film, made in 1953 but not released for another three years, follows the story of Dalantai, who is dispatched to Ulaanbaatar to fetch tools for his herding collective. On arrival, he is sent from office to office to get a paper stamped and signed by various officials before he can collect the tools. The ironic message of the film, which is emphasised by Mördorj's orchestral score, is that this bureaucratic process was so time-consuming it detracted from the time he could have spent using the tools back at the collective.

The story of *The Obstacles We Confront* is told by means of an unseen narrator, who makes observations and comments on the on-screen action, and there is relatively little dialogue. Narrators were used in other Mongolian films of the Socialist era, for example *Tsogt Taij*, although usage in other films tended to be

---

[2]   This is comparable to socialist realism in the Soviet Union.

Socialist Cinema from Conception to Dissemination   59

limited to introducing the film and announcing major changes of time or location rather than providing a running commentary. The extensive use of voiceover and the realistic rather than idealistic subject matter makes the film a semidocumentary, which was a very unusual style for Film Factory feature films, although the studio produced numerous documentaries.[3]

The film opens with an up-beat diatonic cue in a major key played by full orchestra, whilst the narrator states, 'Mongolia is moving into socialism'. Such an opening is reminiscent of numerous Film Factory films and creates the impression that a typical propaganda film will ensue. Likewise, the plot appears at first to be standard fare, when Dalantai is given the task of collecting the tools and embarking on his journey. This is followed by a close-up shot of the traditional alcoholic beverage *airag* (fermented mare's milk) being poured into drinking bowls, accompanied by a cue of professional music, thereby creating a link between traditional music and the tradition of drinking *airag*. The narrator states at this point that Dalantai has not done his job properly since he does not yet have the tools, suggesting that his drinking may be the cause of the delay. When Dalantai arrives in Ulaanbaatar, the music is a triumphant anthem-like theme in a major key whilst the narrator says, 'Ulaanbaatar has developed well'. So far, the narration and accompanying scenes and music could be part of any Film Factory propaganda film; however, towards the end of the film the music is used to draw attention to the narrator's more controversial comments. During a cue featuring a pentatonic folk-like melody in the French horns with string accompaniment, the narrator's final statement is: 'It took Dalantai a long time to get the tools because of bureaucracy and this is one of the problems we now have in Mongolia.' It is the only cue of professional music in the film to employ the distinctly non-Mongolian sound of the French horns, which helps make this particular comment stand out.

In addition to emphasising the narration, music is also used during the film's numerous montages of Dalantai travelling from office to office to get the tools, which he does by car, on a bicycle and on foot. Each montage is accompanied by professional music. Professional music was used to enhance scenes of socialist progress in numerous propaganda films, and the familiar characteristics of traditional Mongolian music within this genre helped make it – and therefore the scenes – relatable, at least potentially, to the entire population. Conversely, in *The Obstacles We Confront*, Mördorj used professional music ironically to highlight one of the negative aspects of the new regime: increased bureaucracy. In one notable cue, Mördorj fused traditional and symphonic characteristics in a manner that became a musical symbol within Film Factory soundtracks: mid- and low-register strings playing a rhythmic ostinato reminiscent of the sound of a horse's hooves. This technique was used widely within horse-head fiddle and folk song repertoire in the abundance of songs about horses, although Mördorj used it ironically to accompany a car chase. The film ends with Dalantai back at

---

[3]   A semidocumentary is a fictional story with realistic subject matter presented as if it were a documentary. Examples of post-1990 semidocumentaries are discussed in Chapter 7.

60 *Mongolian Film Music*

the collective with the tools, telling his comrades that they would not believe how burdensome the bureaucracy is unless they experienced it personally. The function of the score is similar to that of numerous films of the Socialist era, and indeed of many films worldwide, in that it highlights key points in the story and the main messages of the film. The key points in question are the narrator's comments and the montages, the main message is one of irony rather than the direct promotion of socialism, and the music that enhances these moments is Mongolia's unique combination of traditional and Western symphonic music.

In addition to the blatant criticism of bureaucracy, *The Obstacles We Confront* briefly tackles other problems relating to the socialist regime. One technique common in Mongolian propaganda films was to depict dialogue between minor characters, unconnected to the main plot, expressing their admiration for Lenin or Sükhbaatar, or for progress and prosperity. Dorjpalam uses this technique ironically near the beginning of the film when some minor characters are discussing their boss. Instead of praising him, they report that he has been using collective money for his own gains. Whilst criticising people who embezzle communal funds was encouraged by the state, this scene highlights the fact that some socialist authority figures were in fact corrupt, in contrast to the lauding of socialist bosses in other contemporary films. In another scene, a party official flirts inappropriately with a woman, and two monkeys are shown to parallel and ridicule the official's behaviour. Animal fables were common in pre-1921 Mongolian folklore, so Dorjpalam employed a method common amongst pre-revolutionary storytellers, that of using animal imagery allegorically to criticise powerful members of society because it was not wise to do so openly.

Like all Film Factory films, *The Obstacles We Confront* went through numerous stages of control before it was screened publicly. The late release date and comparatively short running time of 36 minutes suggests that much of the original footage was cut.[4] Demchigsürengiin Myagmarsüren (b. 1944), one of five Mongolians trained in the Soviet Union as a film researcher, discussed this film with me at length. Myagmarsüren (INT) told me that audiences at the time were shocked the film got past the censors and he believes the Film Factory would not have got away with trying to make such a subversive film a second time. Yet if a Mongolian director dared to defy the state, the mid-1950s was the prime opportunity, given the easing of hard-line politics following the deaths of Choibalsan in 1952 and Stalin in 1953, and the consequent Khrushchev Thaw in the Soviet Union from 1956. *The Obstacles We Confront* was released in the same year as the Film Factory's only musical, *Our Melody* (*Manai Ayalguu*), which was also an unusual film because it featured songs and dances of many of Mongolia's ethnic groups, including the Tsaatan, Buryat and Torgut: 1956 was therefore a relatively experimental year within Mongolian cinema.

---

[4] The copy of *The Obstacles We Confront* I viewed at the University of Film Arts in Ulaanbaatar has a running time of 36 minutes, although it is possible that alternative cuts of this film are available elsewhere.

Socialist Cinema from Conception to Dissemination   61

In 1962, Mongolia joined COMECON, which strengthened Moscow's direct influence on Mongolian politics. In the 1960s, the Film Factory produced 32 feature films, including a batch of films about the 1921 Revolution, and without exception they depicted Sükhbaatar as the new national hero of Mongolia. Many of these films, such as *One of the Ten Thousand* (*Tümnii Neg*, 1962), *The Lost Finds His Way* (*Töörsöör Töröldöö*, 1966), *The Flood* (*Üyer*, 1966), and *Morning* are still considered amongst Mongolia's greatest films by film professionals and viewers alike. They were included in a limited edition celebratory DVD box set release of 10 classic Mongol Kino films in 2008, available only in Mongolia.[5] The other six films are *Tsogt Taij* (1945), *Awakening* (*Serelt*, 1957), *Messenger of the People* (*Ardyn Elch*, 1959), *Footprints* (*Khünii Mör*, 1965), *The End* (*Tögsgöl*, 1967) and *The Battle* (*Temtsel*, 1971). These 10 films are the only films of the Socialist era to be released on DVD, and *Tsogt Taij* is the only one with subtitles, in English. These 10 films are also screened regularly on Mongolian television during national holidays.

Comedy was a popular film genre in the 1960s, and these were no less propagandist than their historical drama counterparts. Social criticisms were made more subtly in the comedies, notable examples of which include *Oh, Those Ladies!* (*Ene Khüükhnüüd Üü?*, 1963), which criticises gender inequality in the veterinary profession, and *City Slicker* (*Niislel Khüü*, 1968), about a man born in Ulaanbaatar overcoming his struggle to adapt to countryside life. Comedies also formed part of the trend that began in the 1960s of celebrating anniversaries of socialist progress. The 1963 comedy *The Harmonica* (*Aman Khuur*), which celebrates the construction industry, is one such example. The humorous mood is maintained throughout with the aid of Luvsansharav's score of orchestral and piano cues and diegetic harmonica music.[6]

Certain events and character types appeared frequently and uniformly from the 1960s and thus became symbols representing a typical Mongolian film of this era. These included grandiose battle scenes, chases on horseback, brave Russian Red Army soldiers juxtaposed with incompetent Russian White Army soldiers, minor characters discussing Sükhbaatar's virtues, degenerate Buddhist lamas, and the sky euphemistically symbolising the death of a character. The link between a shot of the sky and death may relate to the Mongolian tradition of sky burial: when a person dies, the body is placed on a mountain to be taken by birds of prey, thus the body is 'buried' in the sky. The 1960s also saw the introduction of colour film to Mongolia, firstly with a co-production with the East German film studio DEFA Film, *Golden Palace* (*Altan Örgöö*, 1961), then with the Film Factory's first sole-produced colour feature, the short film *Two Friends* (*Khoyor Naiz*) in 1963.

It was not only films of the 1960s that depicted the 1921 Revolution but also plays, poems and novels, and many of these works were criticised at the Fourth

---

[5] The DVD box set release is under the Mongol Kino label, even though the original cinematic release of each was through the Film Factory studio (*Kino Üildver*).

[6] This score is discussed below.

62 *Mongolian Film Music*

Congress of the Mongolian Writers' Union in 1967. The result of such criticism was that films produced in the 1970s replaced the one-dimensional characters typical of the 1960s, who had been portrayed largely through either entirely heroic or cowardly actions, with characters who wavered in their convictions, changed allegiance and were fundamentally deeper and more fallible. In the early 1970s, films such as *The Clear River Tamir* and *The Battle* were produced to celebrate the fiftieth anniversary of the 1921 Revolution, and criticisms by the Mongolian Writers' Union were clearly taken on board. Nonetheless, despite the more realistic and rounded portrayal of characters, it was always the ardent socialist who ended up victorious, indicating that propaganda was still a strong force.

Like the majority of films of the 1950s and 1960s, films of the 1970s were principally set in the countryside, although scenes set in Ulaanbaatar were not uncommon. The Film Factory produced 47 films in the 1970s, of which 17 were in colour, the 1973 film *New Acquaintances* (*Shine Taniluud*) being the studio's first full-length sole-produced colour feature film. Many films of the 1970s were celebrations of anniversaries of industry or farming collectives. The MPRP's early attempts to collectivise Mongolia in the early 1930s were not successful, but new initiatives put into place in the late 1950s proved more fruitful and by the 1960s collectivisation was fully in progress. Cinema played a critical role in promoting collectivisation, demonstrating the advantages of joining a collective and the drawbacks of abstaining. Films about collectives include *The First Step* (*Ankhny Alkham*, 1970), *The Scent of the Land* (*Gazryn Üner*, 1978) and *Aurora of Venus* (*Üüriin Tsolmon*, 1979). Children's films were also popular in the 1970s in accordance with the MPRP's aim to disseminate films to every citizen and, by the end of the decade, precursors of the urban films popular during the 1980s started to appear.

Although the Film Factory produced films for Mongolian rather than global audiences, films of the 1970s would have been unlikely to fare well internationally. In addition to the country-specific subject matter and political bias, which could have alienated people outside Mongolia who may not have understood the cultural references, film technology was relatively old-fashioned. The technical equipment that had been new to the Film Factory in previous decades had not been upgraded. Whereas colour film was widespread worldwide, 30 out of 47 films of this decade were shot in black and white.

Postproduction, Dissemination and Archiving

Once a film had been planned, scripted and shot, it was subject to postproduction, censorship and dissemination, and it was during the postproduction phase, when a rough cut of the film was available, that the film composers were called upon. As is the case worldwide and not just within socialist cinema, it was the responsibility of the composers to complement and enhance the concept of the films. The fundamental concept in the case of Mongolian cinema of the

Socialist era was always socialist ideology, and film composers had an obligation to take this on board.

Whilst the MPRP sometimes suggested a certain director for a specific film, the director in turn often chose a film composer who had become associated with that particular film genre. Luvsansharav, for example, became renowned for scoring revolutionary films. When a film composer heard a film on a certain theme was being made, he sometimes guessed in advance that he would be commissioned to compose the score. Music budgets were usually generous enough to allow film composers to score films for full symphony orchestra and additional ensembles, instruments or singers if they so wished. The scores were handwritten in Western notation: a skill the composers had learned during their formal musical training in the Soviet Union. The music was recorded at the Film Factory studios and the recordings stored in the Mongolian Film Archive. To what extent the composers had artistic freedom is a question to which each composer has his own answer. Luvsansharav (INT) claims he had almost complete freedom when composing film scores whilst film designer Tsogzol (INT) says many other composers were given strict guidelines regarding the music they were required to compose.

Once the soundtrack had been synchronised to the picture, each film was put through a lengthy series of controls to ensure good artistic and technical quality, and that the film achieved the ideological goals set out by the MPRP. Literary and artistic criticism published by the Mongolian Writers' Union also played an important role in ensuring films were ideologically appropriate and that insurrectionary content was absent. Inevitably, many films were heavily censored before release. Tsogzol (INT) told me that the censorship process often improved the artistic quality of the film and helped ensure high standards, but at other times some artistic merit was lost to the cutting-room floor. In both cases, he says, 'By the time the film was controlled through the various stages, it may have ended up as a very different film compared to the filmmaker's original intentions.' The music editing in many films of the Socialist era can provide clues as to where films had been cut. There are numerous incidences of cues being cut short in the middle of a phrase or bar, followed swiftly by a totally different and often musically incongruous cue. It is unlikely that highly trained and experienced composers would have composed the music in this way.

As soon as a film had been produced and monitored, the final cut was ready to be released to the proletariat, and massive state operations were put into place to ensure every citizen had access to the propaganda. New permanent and mobile cinemas were constructed throughout the Socialist era to accommodate population growth and to ensure every citizen had access to the films. The number of permanent cinemas countrywide increased from 7 in 1950 to 27 in 1985 (State Statistical Office of the MPRP, 1991, pp. 114–15). In the 1960s, cinemas and permanent projectors were set up in mines and factories (UNESCO, 1982, p. 29). A cultural reform in the 1960s decreed that films should be disseminated to people in the countryside and not just people in more densely populated areas such as Ulaanbaatar. Furthermore, the MPRP introduced measures to criticise, improve and disseminate symphonic music. These measures included taking symphony orchestra tours to the countryside to bring symphonic music to the rural population and escorting parties of workers and school pupils to see operas and ballets in Ulaanbaatar.

Collectivisation made it easier for officials to gather the rural population, and trained projectionists travelled from province to province with mobile cinemas to screen films in cultural clubs and red corners (*ulaan bulan*). The number of red corners increased from 334 in 1950 to 1,535 in 1975 (Central Statistical Bureau of the Council of Ministers of the MPRP, 1977, p. 303). When it was noted that herders in very remote areas of Mongolia still had no access to films, mobile cinemas were taken to individual *ger* encampments. The number of mobile cinemas increased from 44 in 1950 to 502 in 1985. The Central Statistical Bureau of the MPRP in Ulaanbaatar monitored not only how many cinemas and mobile cinemas were in operation, but also the average number of films viewed by each citizen in a given year: 1 film in 1950, rising steadily to 10 films in 1985 (Central Statistical Bureau of the Council of Ministers of the MPRP, 1981, p. 222). Film festivals were also held on public holidays, and this tradition endured long after the fall of the socialist regime. Films of the Socialist era are still screened throughout the day on Independence Day every 26 November and during Mongolian New Year (*Tsagaan Sar*) in February. During the Socialist era, large colourful film posters were displayed in public places, film music was broadcast on the radio, and the State Symphony Orchestra and singers of the Mongolian Philharmony toured film song concerts at cultural clubs in provincial centres throughout the country.

After arriving in a village or *ger* encampment and setting up the screen, mobile cinema projectionists were expected to give talks about political activity before playing the film. Film screenings often coincided with public meetings, special occasions and holidays, so gathering film audiences was not problematic since a crowd of people was already present when the mobile cinema arrived. In addition to the political message of the films, audiences were simultaneously exposed to speeches and campaigns. The growing numbers of libraries and travelling musical performance troupes from the 1960s further reinforced the political messages present in the films and accompanying speeches.

Tsagaan Nokhoi, a film technician I interviewed in Ulaanbaatar, worked as a mobile cinema projectionist during the 1970s and 1980s. He used to screen films in *ger* encampments throughout Mongolia, and he remembers this job fondly as a wholly enjoyable experience. Tsagaan Nokhoi (INT) explained that due to lack of motorised transportation he travelled by camel caravan with a screen measuring 4 metres by 3, which he would mount on two poles. The projector was powered with a Russian engine called an AV, which served as a generator, to screen both Mongolian and Russian films dubbed in Mongolian. The state supplied him with a selection of films that audiences should watch in a particular month, though ultimately he could choose which films he screened. Before he arrived in a particular village or encampment, local people were already familiar with the music and songs in the films, since they were broadcast on state radio, to which almost every citizen had access. When Tsagaan Nokhoi arrived at encampments, villagers would greet him eagerly, unload the camels for him and help set up the screen. Tsagaan Nokhoi's description of herders embracing the new films with enthusiasm may well be tinged with nostalgia. Nonetheless, it does indicate that people were happy to accept the new media at least as a form of entertainment if not consciously for the political messages they contained.

Danzanvaanchigiin Ukhnaa was trained as an opera singer in Bulgaria then as a concert producer in Moscow, and has worked as the General Director of the Mongolian Philharmony since the 1980s. I interviewed him at the Central Palace of Culture in Ulaanbaatar in 2008, when he discussed the State Symphony Orchestra film song tours to the countryside before 1990. Ukhnaa (INT) described a similarly enthusiastic response by herders to the arrival of the orchestra in rural areas to that of Tsagaan Nokhoi's account of mobile cinemas. Ukhnaa recounted how herders became aware of the arrival of the orchestra in advance through word of mouth and would wait eagerly, bestowing gifts of livestock and food upon the musicians. Apart from the tours of the State Symphony Orchestra, the only access most of the rural population had to symphonic music was through radio and film soundtracks, making cinema one of the greatest contributors to the dissemination of orchestral music in Mongolia.

Articles in party newspaper *Ünen* and reports by the various unions describe the process of cultural reform and propaganda dissemination as being thoroughly organised, well executed and both successful and popular amongst the population. Such reports, however, were as much propaganda as the films, music and art works themselves. Some anecdotal evidence suggests that the reality was not as idyllic as the MPRP liked to portray. Urtnasan, an English teacher and self-professed Socialist-era film buff, whom I interviewed in 2008, was born in Ulaanbaatar in the early 1970s. In an interview she explained that she and her classmates were regularly accompanied *en masse* to the cinema by their teachers, as well as to the opera and ballet, during the 1970s and 1980s. Pupils who played truant during these cultural excursions were given poor grades in examinations and end-of-term reports. Groups of workers were similarly escorted to the cinema by their bosses for regular film viewings and accompanying speeches. This idea of compulsory film viewing is in stark contrast to Tsagaan Nokhoi's descriptions of herders waiting eagerly for the mobile cinema to arrive in their locality.

The decline of the mobile cinema started in the mid-1980s when television sets became more widespread in the countryside. Films for television started to be produced and earlier films were broadcast on television, ensuring herders still had access to films without the need for mobile cinemas. The steady growth in film production and dissemination since the Cultural Leap Forward in 1959 meant that the MPRP was successful in its efforts to distribute propaganda to every citizen. One problem the Film Factory had to solve as a result of these efforts, however, was deciding what to do with the film reels and scores they had already produced.

On 5 September 1960 construction began on a building to store the increasing number of film reels, sound recordings and still photographs. This building was named the Mongolian Film, Photograph and Sound State Archive in 1967 and is today commonly known as the Mongolian Film Archive. The archive retains close links with the renamed Mongol Kino film studio and University of Film Arts, although it is now considered a separate institution. All three buildings are within a few minutes' walk of each other in the same area of Ulaanbaatar. The archive stores every feature and documentary film ever produced by the studio, although some of the earlier reels are in too deteriorated a state to be viewed. The archive holds 212 Mongolian feature films, 1,013 documentary films, 1,011 official documentaries (that is, footage of current affairs and historical events), 128,565 photographs, numerous foreign films dubbed in Mongolian, and 1,376 sound recordings in a variety of formats (Baigalmaa, INT). The purges of the 1930s involved the destruction of monasteries and many musical instruments in an attempt to eradicate material symbols of pre-1921 Mongolia. In contrast, the archiving of socialist films, photographs and sound recordings helped to preserve Mongolian socialism in material form.

The Mongolian Film Archive has taken great care since the 1960s to preserve films and their associated sound recordings, yet this was not the case for handwritten film scores, film sets and costumes. The archive holds only 27 film scores, the University of Film Arts has 3 and the score to *Tsogt Taij* is kept in Moscow. These are the only film scores of the Socialist era to survive. When composers had finished handwriting their scores, they had to submit them to the Film Factory finance department in order to get paid. Intermittently, the finance department burned or otherwise destroyed the scores in order to create space. Likewise, the costume and set departments at the Film Factory cleared out the wardrobe and set stores on occasions. The studio carefully conserved finished films yet took little care to conserve the constituent parts of the film – those being the costumes, sets and scores – suggesting that studio officials were confident that the funding ploughed into their industry would continue well beyond the five and a half decades of Socialist-era filmmaking.

From Monastery to Moscow to Maestro: A Case Study of Dagvyn Luvsansharav

Luvsansharav is a prolific and three-time state-honoured film and concert composer whom I interviewed in Ulaanbaatar in 2008. His twelve film scores of the Socialist era include orchestral cues in a late-Romantic symphonic style, professional music, Buddhist temple music, traditional music, music with a clear jazz influence, and cues with atypical instrumentation within the context of the era such as the vibraphone and electric organ. Certain of his film scores are emblematic Film Factory soundtracks whilst others embrace an element of experimentation and can rightfully be described as his own style.

Luvsansharav (INT) told me the story of his musical background and how this influenced his subsequent film compositions. He was born to a family of herders

Socialist Cinema from Conception to Dissemination 67

in Khentii province in 1926. As the youngest child in the family, he was sent to a Buddhist monastery to become a monk at the age of five, as was customary in those days. In the monastery, he learned to read Tibetan and Mongolian, to dance the ritual masked dance, the *Tsam*, and to play the *bishgüür* and *ikh büree*. During visits to his family in Khentii, he would participate in family feasts and celebrations, during which elder members of his family would sing long-song (*urtyn duu*) and short-song (*bogino duu*). It was musical activity both at home and in the monastery that sparked the young Luvsansharav's interest in becoming a composer.

The repression of Buddhism in the 1930s prompted Luvsansharav to leave the monastery, so in 1937 he returned to Khentii to help his parents herd their livestock. In 1943 he started work at a cultural club in Khentii as a musician, singer and dancer, and whilst working there he learned to play the accordion and to read music. In 1945, he was auditioned and chosen to move to Ulaanbaatar to work as a singer and dancer with the newly formed Mongolian People's Song and Dance Ensemble.[7] In 1947 he started to compose long-song and short-song and one year later started to compose public songs (*ardyn duu*) in what he describes as his 'own style' (Luvsansharav, INT). He was appointed chorus master of the Mongolian People's Song and Dance Ensemble in 1949, where he remained for three years until the MPRP sent him on a two-year ethnographic project in Khovd province, western Mongolia, which involved the collection and analysis of the music of the ten or so ethnic groups who lived there.

Luvsansharav had learned Buddhist temple music at the monastery, domestic music (*geriin khögjim*) with his family in Khentii, Russian accordion music at the cultural club, and new professional folk music (*yazguur khögjim*) in Ulaanbaatar. He had gained experience in composing traditional Mongolian forms such as long-song and short-song, and with the structures and styles of the new public songs. Between 1954 and 1959 he received formal training as a composer and chorus master at the Tchaikovsky Conservatoire in Moscow. These diverse musical influences laid the foundations for his personal style of composition that would later emerge through his film scores.

Luvsansharav's first film score was for the 1962 film *Bayasgalan*, a fictional story about a horseman of the same name. Regarding his musical influences for this score, Luvsansharav (INT) says:

> When I was composing [*Bayasgalan*] there were two main influences, and one of them was my upbringing in the countryside. I was knowledgeable about agriculture and countryside life, and this was hugely beneficial to me since I was composing music to a film about a horseman. The other big influence was my education in Russia. These two things influenced my composition greatly.

---

[7] This was later renamed the Mongolian National Song and Dance Academic Ensemble, which is what it is called today.

In addition to Luvsansharav's training in the Soviet Union, it was not only domestic music that influenced his film scores but also his personal experience of herding and the context in which domestic music was created and performed. Film designer Tsogzol (INT), with whom Luvsansharav worked on the 1966 film *The Lost Finds His Way*, told me, 'I think that many of these great old composers knew a lot about people's lives. They had a great deal of experience in working with people. They had extensive knowledge of music that they acquired in famous institutions. This all helped towards making good films and great film soundtracks.'

The culture and environment in the case of Socialist-era composers was that of a one-party state. When I asked Luvsansharav (INT) whether the filmmakers of *Bayasgalan* had exerted any political influence on him, he answered, 'I had freedom. No one controlled me. I watched the film and then composed the music corresponding to the action.' When talking about the development of his music during subsequent film scores, however, he said, 'I was influenced by socialist ideology a little bit. There was one party at the time and we had to represent the ideology in our films ... but I was not influenced that much. I always composed music as dictated by the action of the films.' Although Luvsansharav claims not to have been influenced heavily by socialist ideology, the fact that his music followed the action of the films, which in most cases were imbued with an overt political agenda, meant his music was in fact influenced by socialist ideology, albeit indirectly.

Luvsansharav's second film score was for the 1963 comedy *The Harmonica*, a propaganda comedy in praise of the construction industry. The film tells the story of Dari, an elderly lady whose *ger* compound is being destroyed to make way for new buildings, and the comedy element revolves around her busybody nature. Tömör, the harmonica-playing construction worker responsible for the demolition, is in love with Dari's daughter, Badam, and concocts a plan to ensure he becomes their neighbour in their new apartment block. The harmonica – a foreign musical instrument new to Mongolia – is a symbol of progress in the film, representing the construction programmes and urbanisation also recently introduced to the country. At first Dari is reluctant to accept either the harmonica or the progress in the construction industry, yet she eventually embraces both. Despite the light-hearted nature of the story and score, the message that lives are improved considerably by the construction of new buildings is heavily present throughout.

The most significant music in the film is the harmonica piece that serves as the introduction to the opening titles and that reappears regularly throughout, played by Tömör. The piece is a pentatonic melody with a waltz accompaniment, which would need to be played on two harmonicas despite being presented diegetically as a solo. The pentatonic melody is influenced by traditional Mongolian music and the waltz by the European classical music Luvsansharav studied in Moscow, and the harmonica was a relatively unfamiliar sound in Mongolia at the time. This unique blend of traditional music, Western classical music and a new instrumental sound echoes the theme of the film – Mongolians accepting a new way of life – and demonstrates Luvsansharav's experimental side.

Figure 4.1   Dari's happy expression on hearing the harmonica at the end of the film. Myatavyn Badamgarav as Dari, *The Harmonica* (*Aman Khuur*), Film Factory (Mongol Kino), 1963

Following the opening titles, the first time Tömör plays the piece we see a close-up of Dari's bewildered face, as she tries to figure out what the sound is and where it is coming from. On subsequent instances of this cue, Dari's facial expressions demonstrate that she is becoming increasingly annoyed with Tömör's harmonica playing, mirroring her attitude towards the construction of the new buildings. By the end of the film, however, she has come to love the harmonica, Tömör and the buildings, and on the final occurrence of the harmonica piece, the camera closes in on her smiling face as she says Tömör's name with a sense of happiness and pride (Figure 4.1). The fact that the harmonica music does not change yet Dari's attitude towards it is completely different each time it is heard adds to the comedy value, particularly during this final cue. It is also during this cue that the ideological message of the film reaches its culmination: Dari's initial scepticism about new construction has given way to acceptance and happiness. The delivery of this message through the medium of comedy ensured it appealed to a broader spectrum of audience members than the dramas of the previous decade and at a more subliminal level.

Other key cues in *The Harmonica* include a revolutionary song (*khuvsgalyn duu*) sung by SATB chorus, which accompanies a construction montage, and a Romantic-era style violin solo accompanied by piano underscoring a scene in which Tömör takes Badam to the top of a hill to show her how 'beautiful' Ulaanbaatar now looks with all the new buildings. In another cue, fast military-style music is played when Dari's husband cycles home on new tarmac roads to bring her good news about their new apartment. In this score, Luvsansharav demonstrated his ability to compose the genres typical of the Socialist era, thus paving the way for subsequent scores in which he blended his musical influences. Luvsansharav composed one more film score in 1963, *Sin and Virtue* (*Nügel Buyan*), and with these early films he became established as one of Mongolia's most respected new composers.

For the remainder of the Socialist era, Luvsansharav collaborated with only two directors: Jigjid and Badrakhyn Sumkhüü (1929–2003). Three-time state-honoured director Jigjid began his career as a cinematographer on films such as *Tsogt Taij* and *Awakening*. He made his directorial debut in 1959 with the propagandist and highly regarded *Messenger of the People* (*Ardyn Elch*). Propagandist revolutionary films became Jigjid's trademark, and it was in his films that certain filmic symbols came about, such as scenes of minor characters discussing Sükhbaatar's merits. Sumkhüü, who received two state medals, also directed propaganda films and those about the 1921 Revolution, although he is perhaps better known for his introspective films of the 1970s, which paved the way for the urban dramas that became popular during the 1980s.

Luvsansharav scored four films between 1966 and 1972, all of which were set in and around 1921 and featured the revolution. The first of these was Sumkhüü's *The Lost Finds His Way*, which tells the story of Balt, who hides in a remote cave after escaping an unjust prison sentence ordered by corrupt noblemen. After witnessing a battle the between the Russian White and Red armies, Balt takes an injured soldier from each side into his cave to help them recover. At first Balt does not understand the hostility between the two Russians, as he thinks of them as 'the same people'. As time passes, the Red Army soldier tells Balt of Sükhbaatar's heroism whilst the White Army soldier's aggressive and deceptive ways are revealed. After much soul searching, Balt 'finds his way'. Finally, Balt is shot by a nobleman, and his dying wish is to support the Red Army and the Mongolian People's Party. As was customary in Mongolian films of the 1960s, the characters are divided clearly into 'good' Red Army soldiers and 'bad' White Army soldiers and noblemen. Balt, an honest and just man, eventually chooses the right path, which, in the case of films about the 1921 Revolution, was always that of Sükhbaatar and the Russian Red Army.

The thirteen cues in *The Lost Finds His Way* appear in significant points in the plot and share traits with many Mongolian film scores of the 1960s, such as string ostinati echoing the sound of a horse's hooves and professional music to accompany pastoral images. One of the first cues of the film, during a scene of Balt camping by a river, features a violoncello solo similar in sound to traditional horse-head fiddle music in terms of register, use of pentatonic scale, free rhythms and ornamentation. The symphonic influence is apparent in the accompaniment of *pizzicato* strings and the echoing of fragments of the melody by the orchestra. Similar cues follow, including a pentatonic oboe solo with string accompaniment as Balt watches the countryside from his prison, a melody in unison strings during a shot of the river and an orchestral *tutti* melody as he watches a bird fly above his cave. Other cues include diminished chords played in tremolo strings, which was a common technique in Mongolian, Russian and Hollywood films to denote

Socialist Cinema from Conception to Dissemination

suspense. This technique has become something of a cliché in Western cinema, although it would have been relatively novel within Mongolia in the 1960s. The film ends with a triumphant brass fanfare in a major key when Balt declares his loyalty to the Red Army and the Mongolian People's Party, which provides contrast to the minor keys and diminished chords of previous cues.

Luvsansharav's next two scores were for Jigjid's *Morning* and its sequel *The Battle*, both of which starred Dashnamjil, an actor renowned for playing Sükhbaatar. Luvsansharav (INT) says he believes these to be his best film scores, saying of them, 'The music expresses the action of these films better than any of my other film scores'. He told me that these films were given a larger music budget than other films he had worked on, thereby giving him the financial freedom to compose exactly the music he wanted. As was typical of Jigjid's films, socialist ideology was heavily present in both *Morning* and *The Battle*, sometimes subtly, at other times blatantly. In both films, Red Army soldiers are portrayed favourably whilst members of the White Army are not. Sükhbaatar gives numerous rousing speeches and he is portrayed as a kind and caring family man as well as a strong leader, and there are several scenes in which minor characters extol Sükhbaatar's manifold qualities. The music, like the action, is grand, dramatic and on a large scale regarding the size of the orchestra and the rich textures of the cues. The title music for *Morning* is representative of Film Factory film cues that were strongly influenced by late-Romantic to early twentieth-century European symphonic music. Scenes of processions, festivals and award ceremonies are enhanced with orchestral cues based on revolutionary songs with added military band instruments such as the snare drum, and military-inspired musical figures such as the fanfare. By the time *Morning* was released in 1968, the Mongolian Military Song and Dance Academic Ensemble had been in existence for 36 years, so viewers of these two films would have been very familiar with the sounds and instruments of a military band and would have associated them with patriotism and victory.

Traditional Mongolian instruments and vocal styles are presented only diegetically and these cues are given somewhat negative associations: a drunken man sings a short-song, a *shanz* is played to entertain drunken soldiers in a Chinese restaurant, and an unruly shaman plays the drums. Since traditional music would have been associated with the era before 1921, representing traditional music negatively was a method of tainting the image of pre-1921 culture. Since traditional music had been given new performance contexts in the form of cultural clubs and theatres, such scenes reinforced the message that any other performance spaces for traditional music were not desirable.

Buddhist temple music makes an appearance in *The Battle* during a scene in the Bogd Khan's palace. The non-metric rhythms of the drums and drones of the *bishgüür* and *ikh büree* give way to timpani, brass fanfares and rousing diatonic symphonic music followed by an instrumental rendition of a revolutionary song when Sükhbaatar arrives. Although Buddhists are not portrayed in an obviously negative manner in this scene, the music – temple music being subdued by military-style music – signifies the ultimate victory of Sükhbaatar and the Mongolian

72 Mongolian Film Music

People's Party over religion and pre-1921 customs. The shaman from *Morning* also reappears in *The Battle*, and is portrayed in a similar manner.

Mongolian cinema in the 1970s saw a broadening of film genres and deeper characterisations, and Luvsansharav's scores likewise comprised a wider variety of musical influences. There is a clear jazz influence in some of his scores of this decade, reflected largely through the instrumentation, which included the saxophone, guitar and vibraphone. His next score was for *In the Nest* (*Icheend Ni*, 1972), directed by Sumkhüü, which completed his contribution to celebrating the 1921 Revolution through his music. Although he claims not to have been controlled or strictly influenced by the government regarding his film compositions, an ideological film about the 1921 Revolution calls for revolutionary songs and music that enhances the ideological content. Luvsansharav's choice of musical genres was therefore the result of artistic decisions and filmic compositional technique, that of following the action of the film, rather than a conscious and direct consequence of political obligations. His next three films of the 1970s were also directed by Sumkhüü: *The Sound of the Engine* (*Motoryn Duu*, 1973), *The Beloved* (*Khani*, 1975) and *Tales of First Love* (*Ankhny Khairyn Duuli*, 1975).

The Beloved is the story of Naran, a woman with a heart condition that would make it unsafe for her to give birth. She keeps this secret from her husband and father-in-law, until she overhears the two men arguing about her not having borne children. She decides to conceive and discovers she is pregnant whilst her husband is in Turkey at an international wrestling competition, yet she almost loses the unborn child. This is a relatively forward-looking film in terms of its subject matter, introspective nature, and music. Its central theme of individuals coping with hardship is more typical of films of the 1980s rather than the themes common in the 1970s, namely collectivisation and socialist progress, and the score is similarly progressive within the context of Mongolian film scoring. Luvsansharav maintains the tradition of scoring scenes set in the countryside with traditional instruments, thereby underpinning connections between nomadic instruments and nomadic life. The music accompanying the central plot, which is located in Ulaanbaatar and deals with fresh ideas and themes within the context of Mongolian films, utilises the vibraphone, electric organ, saxophone, guitar, drum kit, and a wordless female chorus in addition to the orchestra. This is one of the few film scores that used voices when the script did not call for a text to be set to music and is amongst the first to use instruments more associated with jazz music, thereby highlighting the fact the film depicts themes and issues at the cutting edge of Mongolian cinema.[8]

---

[8] The first Mongolian film score to feature jazz music was for the 1969 crime thriller *The Secret of the Cave* (*Agüin Nuuts*) by composers Pürevjavyn Khayankhyarvaa and Natsagiin Mendbayar. This was the sole film score for both composers. Instruments associated with jazz music, including the saxophone and guitar, were used within orchestral cues in the 1968 film *City Slicker* (*Niislel Khüü*), although the music is not in a jazz style.

Socialist Cinema from Conception to Dissemination 73

The melodies of certain cues, especially during scenes when Naran overhears her husband and father-in-law arguing, are based on jazz modal scales rather than pentatonic or diatonic scales, which, in addition to the instrumentation, gives the music a definite jazz quality. The final scene alternates between Naran successfully giving birth and her husband winning the wrestling competition, accompanied by a cue of swing music played by a jazz big band. Although jazz had not formed part of Luvsansharav's musical background, the State Big Band at the Mongolian Philharmony had been fully established by this time and was likely to have influenced his score, indicating that Luvsansharav remained receptive to new musical influences and was willing to experiment by combining them with the styles and techniques in which he had been trained.

Tales of First Love is a film in two parts, framed in the context of two friends, Gansükh and Dembii, looking back at their first loves. Gansükh's story, filmed in colour, is a romantic comedy and Dembii's, shot in black and white, a mournful drama. The score, co-composed by Batsükh, is very different in the two parts of the film, suggesting that Luvsansharav was responsible for one part, namely Gansükh's story, and Batsükh the other. Luvsansharav's cues include those played on traditional instruments including the *bishgüür* and *yatga* to portray Gansükh's teenage life as a herder, but traditional music is used in combination with other genres as the story progresses in less nomadic settings. A voice from a loudspeaker announces that a concert will soon begin in the nearby cultural club, and the music used to accompany this scene is military-style marching music in 4/4 played by a traditional-instrument orchestra with a *shanz* solo. Such use of military-type music played on instruments not associated with military bands was uncommon within Mongolian film soundtracks. This shows Luvsansharav's experimental side in that he blended traditional Mongolian music and music introduced by the Soviet Union – in this case military bands – in a novel way.

There are a number of cues in *Tales of First Love* that demonstrate an interesting development in professional music and are what Luvsansharav (INT) calls his 'own style'. These idiosyncratic cues are professional music with added percussion and non-orchestral instruments such as the electric organ, adding a contemporary element to this already syncretic music. In one scene, when Gansükh is trying to ascertain whether the object of his affections, Büjen, likes another man named Oidov, the music is an up-tempo cue of professional music with added woodblock, castanets and electric organ. In another scene, when the jealous Gansükh gallops past Büjen and Oidov, the music is an orchestral ostinato reminiscent of the sound of a horse's hooves but with added electric organ and a jazz guitar solo. Luvsansharav's modern take on professional music in these cues complements the more modern subject matter of the film, namely personal relationships and feelings.

Luvsansharav's compositional output of the Socialist era concluded with two more collaborations with Jigjid: *Wings of the Land* (*Gazryn Jigüür*, 1978) and *Happiness Taken for Granted* (*Jargal Daakhgüin Zovlon*, 1982). These films were more clearly propagandist than Sumkhüü's films of the 1970s, and Luvsansharav's scores developed from the music he had created for the earlier 1921 Revolution films to his own distinctive style of professional music with added percussion and non-symphonic instruments. *Wings of the Land* is a celebration of the railway industry, loosely disguised as a romantic drama based on a love triangle. The film includes typical Jigjid traits such as minor characters appearing only to talk about the virtues of socialism. The score similarly contains what had developed throughout the 1970s as the distinctive Luvsansharav sound of professional music with added percussion, in this case the vibraphone and snare drum.

Luvsansharav's musical background was diverse and he was continuously receptive to new musical influences, which he combined in ways that were original in Mongolia at the time. When I asked him how he believes his music contributed to the films he scored, he said, 'Music is all imagination; it's not like real life. Life in films [of the Socialist era] was nicer than real life: the music made the life seem nicer.' Luvsansharav composed numerous concert pieces in the nine years before he scored his next film in 1993, after which he continued to compose both concert pieces and film scores.

The Filmmaking Process and a Composer's Perspective

From the early days of the Socialist era, the MPRP recognised the importance of propaganda and realised that cinema was an extremely effective tool for propagating ideology countrywide. Every aspect of the filmmaking process from conception to production through to composing the music and dissemination was controlled as part of a strategic and comprehensive governmental plan. Films about the most pressing political issues of each decade were consequently produced, from the patriotic films of the 1940s and 1950s to celebrations of anniversaries of the 1921 Revolution, industry and collectives in the 1960s and 1970s, and music was used to highlight key points. As directed by the five-year plan, cinema was used to convince a nomadic society that industry and progress were the direction Mongolia should take. Film music enhanced this ideological image by highlighting scenes that portrayed the professed prosperity of post-1921 life, which, in Luvsansharav's words, 'made the life seem nicer'. The entire population was catered for through the dramas, comedies and children's stories produced each decade, and all films throughout this time were about Mongolian matters, whether historical, current or ideal.

Within this context some composers worked within film music very briefly, in some cases for only one film, whilst others such as Luvsansharav flourished and composed numerous scores throughout the Socialist era. Each composer has a different perspective regarding their personal political leanings, and Luvsansharav is an example of one who, on the whole, did not feel influenced directly by socialist ideology when composing film scores. Nonetheless, his eagerness to learn different musical styles and genres in addition to his feelings of artistic freedom helped him create a unique style of music and make an important contribution to combining musical styles and influences within film soundtracks.

Chapter 5

A Standard of Socialist Cinema: *The Clear River Tamir* (*Tungalag Tamir*, 1970–1973)

In the early 1970s, the hundredth anniversary of Lenin's birth in 1870 and the fiftieth anniversary of the 1921 Revolution were celebrated in Mongolia. This was a countrywide endeavour and a prime opportunity for the government to bolster the dissemination of socialist ideology. Meanwhile, by the early 1970s, an increasing proportion of the public had gained experience in film viewing in comparison to previous decades, so filmmakers began to use more sophisticated methods to get their message across. New films and their scores had to move away from one-dimensional characterisations and explicit propaganda to arouse fresh interest amongst audiences. The MPRP commissioned numerous novels, plays and documentary films in honour of the double celebration in addition to a three-part epic feature film *The Clear River Tamir* (*Tungalag Tamir*, 1970–73). The film was, in many ways, exemplary of the Film Factory's output of the 1970s in terms of cinematic style, ideological content and soundtrack. It combined successfully the propagandist imagery of the 1960s whilst simultaneously acknowledging Mongolian folklore and looking ahead to the introspective stories that started to become popular from the mid-1970s. Similarly, the score comprised a variety of styles and genres that appealed across the broad spectrum of citizens of socialist Mongolia.

Part 1 of *The Clear River Tamir* is set shortly before 1921, and juxtaposes corrupt members of the ruling classes against the courageous Mongolians who allied with the Russian Red Army. The principal characters of Part 1 are the herder Erdene and the nobleman Itgelt. It explores the volatile relationship between these two men and introduces the insurgent activities of local hero Tömör, who steals from the rich to give to the poor. Sükhbaatar and the battles of 1921 are the focus of Part 2. Throughout this part, Erdene's loyalties alternate between the White and Red Russian armies as he undergoes his personal struggle to decide which of the two sides he should follow. Part 3 represents the betterment of society due to socialism set against the roguery of Buddhist lamas. The principal character of this part is Itgelt's son, Khongor, a young boy from Part 1 who is now an adult. Like Erdene, Khongor strives to decide which side he should join, yet whereas Erdene's decision is ultimately based on choosing the 'right way', Khongor's loyalties fluctuate depending on which side will provide him with the greatest material advantages at any given time. Images of the river Tamir run throughout all three parts and serve as a symbol of Mongolia's constant natural beauty.

76 *Mongolian Film Music*

An Exemplary Socialist Mongolian Film

Chadraabalyn Lodoidamba (1917–69) wrote the novel *Tungalag Tamir* in 1962 when he was working as the Mongolian Minister of Culture, and it was lauded at the Fourth Congress of the Mongolia Writers' Union in 1967 (Dashdondog, 1964). The MPRP deemed the novel, which had also been translated into Russian and released in the Soviet Union, a suitable story to celebrate the double anniversary of Lenin's birthday and the 1921 Revolution and was accordingly adapted into a film screenplay of the same title. It was the Film Factory's most ambitious project to date in terms of length, scale and scope, and with two simultaneous anniversaries at stake, the filmmakers and composer were under pressure to create something truly magnificent.

In some earlier Mongolian films, the music editing can provide clues as to the amount of censorship to which the film was subject. In several films, many cues are cut short mid-melody, indicating that the censors removed portions of the films after the postproduction stage before they were disseminated to the public. *The Clear River Tamir*, however, has a total running time of 267 minutes and the music cues flow smoothly throughout the film, suggesting that less cutting due to censorship took place in comparison to many earlier films. The MPRP chose the topics of films that were to be produced under the five-year plan, yet in the case of *The Clear River Tamir* they chose the actual story: Lodoidamba's novel. Given that the government chose the story and left it relatively uncensored, *The Clear River Tamir* is an excellent example of a tale depicting the socialist society the MPRP was eager to promote.

Within the 47 feature films produced by the Film Factory in the 1970s, three themes appear frequently: the 1921 Revolution, collectivisation and, later in the decade, family problems exacerbated by society. In the early 1970s, films celebrating the 1921 Revolution were still as prevalent as they had been in the 1960s, largely on account of the double anniversary. In addition to *The Clear River Tamir*, Jigjid's *The Battle* (*Temtsel*, 1971), the sequel to *Morning* (*Öglöö*, 1968), is perhaps the most well known. After a wealth of experience in producing such films, the Film Factory was in a position to tackle the 1921 Revolution with further profundity, greater technical and artistic skill, and a more subliminal level of propaganda.

There was a small number of films about collectivisation in the 1960s, including the comedies *Khökhöö Almost Gets Married* (*Khökhöö Gerlekh Dökhlöö*, 1962) and *City Slicker* (*Niislel Khüü*, 1968). This theme became well established by the 1970s with films such as *The Bridegroom* (*Khürgen Khüü*, 1970), *An Unforgettable Autumn* (*Martagdashgüi Namar*, 1975) and *The Scent of the Land* (*Gazryn* Üner, 1978) and, as was the case in the 1960s, the propaganda element often took precedence over feasibility of plot or rounded characterisations. *The Clear River Tamir* deals directly with the 1921 Revolution, yet scenes showing the decay of feudal structures, which paved the way for more centralised control of rural and agricultural areas, namely collectivisation, also place the film within this second theme, making it directly relevant to collectivised 1970s audiences.

The third theme, family and relationship problems, appeared in urban drama films such as *The Beloved* (*Khani*, 1975) and *Wings of the Land* (*Gazryn Jigüür*, 1978), and these films foreshadowed the main issues filmmakers covered during the following decade. Family and relationship problems are explored as comprehensively in *The Clear River Tamir* as they are in the later urban drama films, although the former is set in an earlier era and a more rural environment. *The Clear River Tamir* is a rare example of a film that addresses all three themes common in Mongolian films of the 1970s.

In addition to the themes of *The Clear River Tamir*, two further components make it the epitome of 1970s Mongolian filmmaking: the imagery and the score. Common images throughout the film include socialist progress, heroes (folk and political), battles, rivers, countryside traditions and festivities, minor characters praising Sükhbaatar, corrupt lamas and princes, untimely killings, and shots of the sky symbolising death. All of these images made regular appearances in the films of the 1960s and 1970s and became classic symbols of the Film Factory film style, and all of them appear in *The Clear River Tamir* in abundance.

The film utilised the best available sets, costumes and technical equipment, and was the first Mongolian film to be produced in widescreen, although it was shot in black and white, as were the majority of films of this decade. The lavish score comprises every type of music ensemble heard in a Film Factory soundtrack to date: a symphony orchestra, numerous traditional instruments, Buddhist temple music, a military band, an accordion, a chorus and solo singers. Since the film was produced in honour of the double anniversary, the MPRP would have undoubtedly provided the Film Factory with a relatively generous budget, and this is reflected in the resources used. *The Clear River Tamir* is still broadcast regularly on Mongolian television during public holidays, and is widely regarded within Mongolia as one of the country's greatest achievements in filmmaking.

Key Personnel

The director, film designer and composer for *The Clear River Tamir* were all born in the countryside, trained in Moscow, and had worked on several films before being chosen to bring Lodoidamba's novel to life on the big screen. State-honoured film director Dorjpalam was born in Selenge province and studied at the VGIK Film Institute in Moscow between 1949 and 1955. Dorjpalam's first film was the controversial *The Obstacles We Confront* (*Bidend Yuu Saad Bolj Baina*, 1956) and he directed a further nineteen films before the end of the Socialist era on a variety of subjects so wide that he could rightfully be considered one of the Film Factory's most daring and experimental film directors. He gained extensive experience by directing nine films before *The Clear River Tamir*, including the 1961 co-production with DEFA Film (Deutsche Film-Aktiengesellschaft) *Golden Palace* (*Altan Örgöö*). This film for children is famous for its special effects, for which Dorjpalam had the advanced technical equipment of this East German film studio at his disposal. Throughout the late 1950s and 1960s, many of Dorjpalam's films dealt with modern issues in small communities, such as the 1963 comedy *Oh, Those Ladies!* (*Ene Khüükhnüüd* Üü?), a criticism of gender inequality in modern society in which a female veterinarian disguises herself as a man in order to get a job in a village. Despite Dorjpalam's substantial experience, he was perhaps a risky choice as director for the epic production of *The Clear River Tamir* in comparison to Jigjid, who could be seen as the more obvious man for the job. Jigjid had directed many films about the 1921 Revolution, including *Messenger of the People* (*Ardyn Elch*, 1959), *One of the Ten Thousand* (*Tümnii Neg*, 1962), *Footprints* (*Khünii Mör*, 1965), *The Flood* (*Üyer*, 1967) and *Morning*. Jigjid, however, was otherwise engaged during the production of *The Clear River Tamir*, when he directed three other films, *The Bridegroom*, *The Battle* and a film about agricultural developments called *The Community of Bayan Bulag* (*Bayanbulgiinkhan*, 1973). In addition to directing *The Clear River Tamir*, Dorjpalam co-wrote the screenplay with Chimidiin Dolgorsüren (1920–2002) based on Lodoidamba's novel.

Another key member of the crew was the state-honoured and prolific designer Tsogzol. In addition to the 29 films on which he worked as film designer during the Socialist era, he directed a film for children, *The Story of Büshkhüü* (*Büshkhüügiin Ülger*) in 1979. He was born in Dornod province, studied at the Mongolian National Art College in Ulaanbaatar, then at the VGIK Film Institute in Moscow between 1956 and 1961. The 10 films he worked on during the 1960s before *The Clear River Tamir* covered a wide range of genres, giving him experience of designing sets, costumes and storyboards for historical battles, comedies, rural dramas and thrillers.

Tsegmediin Namsraijav (1927–87), composer and recipient of two state medals, was born in Arkhangai province, performed at the Bömbögör Nogoon Theatre at the age of 8 and composed his first instrumental ensemble piece aged 18. Between 1952 and 1957 he studied at the Tchaikovsky Conservatoire in Moscow along with Luvsansharav, who was there between 1954 and 1959. Namsraijav's first film score was for Dorjpalam's 1958 film *Three Friends* (*Gurvan Naiz*), then 12 years passed before the pair collaborated again on *The Clear River Tamir*. During this time Namsraijav scored four films, all designed by Tsogzol, including two films directed by Jigjid about the 1921 Revolution and its aftermath: *One of the Ten Thousand* and its sequel *Footprints*.[1] With these two film scores and his association with Jigjid, Namsraijav had made a name for himself as a composer for historical battle films, making him a fitting composer for *The Clear River Tamir*. Namsraijav's scores for Jigjid's films mostly comprised dramatic orchestral cues, military bands and revolutionary songs. One particular cue in *Footprints* demonstrates not only that Namsraijav was influenced by what he had learned in Moscow but that traditional Mongolian music was still an integral part of his compositional output. The cue in question accompanies a scene of two Mongolian soldiers in a trench writing a letter home. The patriotic content of the letter refers to defeating the enemy and

---

[1] Namsraijav's other two film scores before his second collaboration with Dorjpalam were *Before Dawn* (*Üüreer*, 1961) and *The Misfortune of Khovd* (*Khovdgiin Gai*, 1964).

A Standard of Socialist Cinema   79

protecting Mongolia. The music, however, is not new folk music (*yazguur khögjim*), public song (*ardyn duu*), a military or orchestral piece, or any of the new genres introduced to Mongolia since the onset of socialism. It is a traditional horse-head fiddle solo, creating the impression that, despite military campaigns and the desire to defend Mongolia from non-socialist enemies, it is traditional Mongolian music that lay within the hearts of homesick soldiers. Namsraijav's training in Moscow and his exposure to new genres of music heavily influenced his score for *The Clear River Tamir* yet he managed to retain elements of traditional Mongolian music other than the new genres developed during the Socialist era.

The Clear River Tamir was the first film on which Dorjpalam, Tsogzol and Namsraijav worked together, although the composer had previously worked with both the director and the designer. Dorjpalam and Tsogzol worked together on a further six films after *The Clear River Tamir* and Namsraijav and Tsogzol worked together on a further two. Dorjpalam had previously displayed something of a rebellious streak in his filmmaking, Namsraijav had composed music with a heavy Russian influence whilst maintaining traditional Mongolian music, and Tsogzol had worked on virtually every genre covered by the Film Factory and with almost every key member of the crew. The combination of these diverse talents and influences made for a fresh take on the 1921 Revolution and a more in-depth exploration of Mongolia under the Socialist regime.

Characters and Plot

Key Characters

Erdene	a herder, works for Itgelt, joins White Army then Red Army (Parts 1, 2 and 3)
Itgelt	a wily, opportunist local nobleman (Parts 1, 2 and 3)
Tömör	the local hero, steals from the wealthy to give to the poor (Parts 1, 2 and 3)
Khongor	Itgelt's son (a boy in Part 1, a teenager in Part 2, an adult in Part 3)
Tügjil	a policeman who tries to capture Tömör (Parts 1 and 3)
Dolgoor	Erdene's wife (Part 1, also in Parts 2 and 3 in Erdene's memory, via flashbacks)
Dulmaa	Erdene's sister and later Tömör's wife (Parts 1 and 2)
Petr	a Russian Bolshevik (Parts 1 and 2)
Gerel	a wealthy Mongolian noblewoman who befriends Erdene (Parts 1 and 2)
Bat	Khongor's friend, Erdene and Dolgoor's son (a teenager in Part 2, an adult in Part 3)
Sükhbaatar	military leader of the 1921 Revolution (Part 2)
The Bogd Khan (Part 2)	

80 *Mongolian Film Music*

Synopsis

Part 1, 98 minutes It is 1911 in Central Mongolia. In this year, Mongolia declared independence from China following the demise of the Qing Dynasty (1644–1911) and the Bogd Khan was proclaimed Mongolian head of state. Local hero Tömör, renowned for stealing from the rich to give to the poor, has escaped prison and falls into the river Tamir. Local boy Khongor recognises him and helps him. Local herder Erdene's horses have been stolen and policeman Tügjil tells him Tömör is the rustler, which makes Erdene happy since he knows the horses will be used well. Meanwhile, nobleman Itgelt rewards his workers with a game of hide and seek at the end of the working day; however, this is a ploy so he can seduce Erdene's wife, Dolgoor. Later, Tügjil finds Tömör and, after an unsuccessful attempt at capturing him, begs to join him. Itgelt sends Erdene on a bogus errand then goes to his *ger* and blackmails Dolgoor into sleeping with him.

Tömör and Tügjil are on the steppe stealing horses to give to the poor, but Tügjil is secretly plotting Tömör's demise. Itgelt celebrates Mongolia's freedom from Manchu (Qing) rule with a group of wealthy Russians at a *Naadam* festival. Back on the steppe, Tügjil stabs Tömör and steals the horses. Erdene meets Petr, a Russian Bolshevik who tells him to beware of the White Army.

Some days later, Tömör is riding across the steppe when he meets Erdene's sister, Dulmaa, and they fall in love. She wants to elope, partly due to her new love for Tömör and partly to escape from her lazy, alcoholic husband. Tömör, however, says he has important work to do first. Itgelt and Erdene attend a party near a Buddhist temple, where Erdene meets Gerel, a wealthy married lady. A few days later, Erdene is riding across the steppe when he meets his sister Dulmaa, who tells him Dolgoor has cuckolded him (with Itgelt). He confronts Dolgoor, who confesses. Erdene throws Dolgoor out then beats up Itgelt.

Some years later, Tömör is now married to Dulmaa and he sings happily near their *ger*. He is falsely imprisoned a few months later. Meanwhile, Erdene has become an officer in the White Army but is considering changing allegiance. Part 1 ends with a chance encounter between Khongor and Dolgoor, who is wandering alone in the snow against the backdrop of the frozen river Tamir.

Part 2, 80 minutes Tömör escapes from prison and returns to his *ger*, where Dulmaa wants him to lead a normal life, but he refuses. Erdene and his son, Bat, watch mounted troops of the Mongolian People's Party and Erdene considers defecting to the Red Army. It is 1921, and Sükhbaatar's army defeats a Chinese battalion. Sükhbaatar orders his men to pool their looted resources but Erdene, who has now joined Sükhbaatar's forces, is reluctant to give up a silk *deel* (traditional robe) he was intending to give to Dolgoor, should they be reunited.

The Mongolian People's Party and the Red Army defeat the White Army in battle. Two minor characters discuss Sükhbaatar's victory. Tömör and Dulmaa are reunited. Sükhbaatar summons Erdene to his office and orders him to retrieve an important document from Gerel's house, which he does. Bat and Khongor,

A Standard of Socialist Cinema 81

now teenagers, play near a Buddhist temple. The Mongolian People's Party successfully takes over the capital (then named Niislel Khüree) and Sükhbaatar rewards Erdene with a new *ger*. Sükhbaatar visits relatives in the countryside, Erdene misses Dolgoor, and the Mongolian People's Party plans further military action. Part 2 ends with Sükhbaatar promoting Erdene and giving a rousing speech about defeating enemies of Mongolia.

Part 3, 89 minutes It is the early 1930s, by which time the Bogd Khan is dead, Mongolia has been declared a republic, the capital city has been renamed Ulaanbaatar after Sükhbaatar, the MPRP has become the ruling party of Mongolia, and the Great Leap Forward has begun. Khongor, now a young man, is at a *Naadam* festival with Itgelt and Tügjil. Erdene still misses Dolgoor. Some days later Itgelt visits Erdene and asks for friendship. Itgelt's workers gossip that whoever marries Khongor is a lucky woman, since he is wealthy. Khongor chooses a bride and gets married. Khongor has participated in a bout of stealing, so Tömör advises him to change his ways. Meanwhile, Buddhist lamas conspire to overthrow the MPRP and order local people to bring their belongings to them. The MPRP gives Dulmaa's ex-husband a new *ger*. Bat and Khongor meet up by chance whilst riding through the steppe. Tügjil and the lamas send out scouts in preparation for their counter-revolutionary battle.

Back at the temple, the remaining lamas are trying to recruit more men. Tömör speaks out against the lamas and a monk shoots him dead. Khongor has now joined the lamas in return for help in further unlawful activity. During a battle between the MPRP and the rebel forces, Tügjil is killed and Bat, who fights for the MPRP, is captured. Khongor offers to kill Bat, but releases him as soon as his colleagues' backs are turned. Bat immediately re-joins his fellow soldiers whilst Khongor gallops away from the problem. Back at the battle, Bat spots a member of the rebel forces galloping by and shoots. Only when the victim dies does Bat realise that the person he has shot is Khongor. Victorious MPRP soldiers ride by as Bat holds his dead friend. The film ends with Erdene riding alongside the river Tamir.

Key Characters: A Brief Analysis

Although certain supporting characters are portrayed in the one-dimensional manner of previous propaganda films, such as the honourable and virtuous Sükhbaatar and the cunning and deceitful Buddhist lamas, the principal characters of *The Clear River Tamir* – Itgelt, Tömör, Erdene and Khongor – are given considerably more depth. Both Lodoidamba's novel and Dorjpalam's experience in directing personal stories about contemporary society and culture provided the basis for these more believable characterisations. Furthermore, each of the principal characters is associated with a relatively one-dimensional supporting character, which by contrast makes the former appear more realistic. These lifelike depictions of the main characters made it possible for the filmmakers and actors to

82   *Mongolian Film Music*

express the socialist ideology of the story with greater subtlety than in the explicit propaganda films made in previous decades.

Itgelt the nobleman represents the capitalist principles the Mongolian People's Party opposed. He is a cunning sycophant who changes allegiance depending on which side provides him with the greatest benefits at any given time. His devious ways are introduced at the start of the film when his workers discuss what a good boss he is, followed swiftly by his blackmailing and seducing Dolgoor. She spends the rest of the film lonely and miserable as a result of Itgelt's actions. Tügjil the policeman is a one-dimensional evil character, whose actions, unlike Itgelt's, are not driven by clear motives. This consequently makes Itgelt appear more realistic.

The outlaw Tömör is a similar character to the Mongolian folk hero Toroi Bandi, who is popularly referred to as the Mongolian Robin Hood.[2] By stealing from the rich to give to the poor, Tömör displays morals that would have appealed to older members of 1970s audiences' sense of nostalgia and tradition as well as chiming with socialist ideology. He speaks out against the lamas' counter-revolutionary plans, demonstrating that traditional values are compatible with socialism in that they oppose the views of religious leaders. His love story with Dulmaa serves to make him more human than super-human, thereby making him more relatable to audiences. Tömör's death is also significant: although he is of a virtuous disposition, he decides to remain independent rather than joining ranks with either side. As a result, he is murdered, and his unexpected and dishonourable killing by a Buddhist monk enhances the anti-religious propaganda.

Whereas propaganda films of the 1950s and 1960s explicitly portrayed socialism as the 'right way', and indeed the only way, Erdene demonstrates that it is acceptable to have doubts about socialism provided you adhere to it ultimately. Audience members who may have started to question socialist dogma by the early 1970s could therefore relate to Erdene whilst being reassured that socialism was the right way after all. On a personal level, Erdene is torn between his friendship with the cunning nobleman Itgelt and the Bolshevik Petr, yet it was Itgelt who slept with Erdene's wife and Petr who is portrayed throughout as generous and courageous. It is Erdene's questioning that makes him more human and his overcoming of his misgivings that makes him a suitable protagonist for socialist propaganda cinema in the 1970s.

Like Erdene, Khongor is similarly confused about whom to side with but, unlike Erdene, he fails to make the right choice. As a child at the start of the film, Khongor shows kindness by rescuing Tömör from drowning in the Tamir, yet by the time he reaches adulthood he has inherited his father Itgelt's materialistic ways and ultimately chooses the wrong path. This is highlighted further by his friendship with Bat, who embraces socialism from the onset and leads a successful life. Significantly, it is Bat who finally kills Khongor, albeit inadvertently, symbolising the victory of socialism over doubt. The film ends with Khongor's

---

[2] See Mend-Ooyo (2007), for the story of Toroi Bandi, who stole gold and silver from the rich to give to the poor.

funeral followed by a shot of Erdene riding happily alongside the river, which leaves the audience with the lasting view that the character who rejected socialism died and the one who followed it found peace of mind.

Some comic minor characters provide light relief from the intense battle scenes, fraught personal relationships and weighty propaganda. Dulmaa's maudlin ex-husband is amusingly overjoyed when he is presented with a new *ger* and there is a memorable scene in which an elderly man shouts about Sükhbaatar's virtues to his partially deaf neighbour, who mishears everything to great comic effect. In the latter example, Dorjpalam satirised the Mongolian filmic cliché of minor characters praising Sükhbaatar – a common feature of Jigjid's films – whilst still conveying the message that Sükhbaatar is worthy of commendation.

It is significant that Itgelt's story does not reach as dramatic a conclusion as the other principal characters; he fades out of the story approximately half way through Part 3. Propaganda cinema was concerned not only with promoting new initiatives, for instance collectivisation, and defaming old institutions such as religion, but also with deliberately omitting certain actions that would tarnish the image of the socialist regime, for example the purges. In the 1930s, hundreds of noblemen were assassinated and this was a macabre side of socialism that Lodoidamba and the Film Factory would have been reluctant to divulge. By phasing Itgelt out of the story, the studio could avoid presenting the inglorious fate of Mongolia's noblemen. It is also significant that Part 3 focuses on a negative portrayal of Buddhist lamas rather than the similar fate that the lamas met in the 1930s.

The Score

As was the case with the majority of Film Factory films, the symphony orchestra featured most prominently in the soundscape of *The Clear River Tamir* and 33 of the 80 cues are in the style of late-Romantic symphonic music. There are 20 cues of traditional Mongolian music, making it the second most prevalent genre in the film, and many of these cues are diegetic rather than underscoring. There are seven cues of military-inspired music, including three revolutionary songs, two brass band cues and two cues of military-style music played by the orchestra. There are six cues of professional music (*mergejliin khögjim*) and a further seven 'mixed' cues, in which the cue begins with either traditional or symphonic music then develops or cuts into the other of these two styles, with the traditional and symphonic elements being clearly separated. The mixed cues accompany longer scenes, and the shift in musical style underpins a change of action, time or place. The remaining cues comprise five played on Buddhist temple instruments, two accordion pieces and a composed song (*zokhiolyn duu*) that concludes the film and serves as the film song. In many Russian and Hollywood films, melodic fragments

84 *Mongolian Film Music*

of the film song are used as the basis of a number of cues.[3] This is not the case with the film song in *The Clear River Tamir*, and this convention is generally not prevalent in Mongolian films.

There are no noticeable cases in *The Clear River Tamir* of cues being cut short mid-melody, which suggests the censors did not cut out much footage in scenes that had music. The sound mixing is also consistent in that each instrument in any given cue can be heard clearly, and there are no instances of music drowning out the dialogue or sound effects eclipsing the music. This demonstrates technical expertise in creating a soundtrack on the part of the sound crew in comparison with some earlier Film Factory films. The consistent quality of the music editing and mixing is complemented by the fact that many consecutive cues are in the same key, thus providing continuity to this film of great length, numerous characters and multiple plot lines.

There are certain functions that the cues of *The Clear River Tamir* fulfil and these contribute to the overall understanding of the nuances of the plot and enhance the drama of the story. The music also provides signposts for the audience as to the important elements of propaganda, such as glorious battles or the moral disposition of the characters. Certain cues are used to glue scenes together, by starting towards the end of one scene and continuing into the next and there are cues that segue into subsequent cues. For example, a horse-head fiddle solo played when Dolgoor is wandering alone flows into Tömör's song in a scene that takes place some years later when he is married to Dulmaa, suggesting that Dolgoor's loneliness has continued throughout these passing years.

One function of music in many Hollywood films and in Mongolian comedies of the Socialist era is the matching of hit-points, when the music matches exactly the on-screen action. Namsraijav composed two such cues in *The Clear River Tamir* but for dramatic scenes that highlight character traits rather than for the film's comedic moments. In Part 1, a diminished stinger chord in the strings is heard when Tömör subdues Tügjl in a fight after the latter tried to capture him. This very short cue foreshadows the next and most significant cue that matches hit-points, when the two men meet again later in Part 1. During this scene, Tömör tells Tügjil the history of the nearby mountains whilst the two relax on the steppe. The music is a *limbe* solo, which creates a peaceful atmosphere and suggests the two are now friends. The camera closes in on Tügjil and the music cuts to a low string tremolo, thereby hinting that something bad is about to happen. A cymbal crash is then heard as Tömör falls to the ground clutching his chest (Figure 5.1). It is only when Tügjil rides away to the sound of a string ostinato and a dotted rhythm on the woodblock that echoes a galloping horse that we realise that Tügjil has stabbed Tömör and run away with his horses. The music highlights Tügjil's actions and therefore emphasises his negative character traits as well as the sense of shock felt

---

[3] An example is the song *My Heart Will Go On* from the 1997 film *Titanic*, throughout which composer James Horner uses the film song melody as the basis of numerous symphonic cues.

A Standard of Socialist Cinema

Figure 5.1 Tömör is stabbed by Tügjil, accompanied by a cymbal crash. Togtokhyn Sanduijav as Tömör, *The Clear River Tamir* (*Tungalag Tamir*), Film Factory (Mongol Kino), 1970–1973

by both Tömör and the audience regarding the stabbing. Not only does the use of music help the audience understand what has just happened, particularly since it happened so quickly, but it also serves to guide the audience's sympathies towards Tömör. Namsraijav used music to match Tügjil's wicked actions in the same way that music had been used in numerous Film Factory comedies to highlight amusing moments. Although Namsraijav may not be credited with composing the most innovative music for this film, he certainly brought about developments in the use of music to highlight character traits and psychology.

An important piece of music in any film is the opening cue, as this sets the mood or provides a sense of time or place from the onset. Part 1 of *The Clear River Tamir* takes place in 1911, before socialism was introduced in Mongolia, when traditional nomadic lifestyle was the norm, and the opening cue is a four-minute traditional long-song (*urtyn duu*) accompanied by horse-head fiddle and *limbe*. The final cue of Part 1, a two-minute dramatic, diatonic symphonic cue, is played again at the start of Part 2, which deals with the 1921 Revolution and the birth of Soviet influence in Mongolia. Not only does this cue create the atmosphere for the battle scenes that follow, but it also glues Parts 1 and 2 together. Part 3 takes place in the early 1930s, when socialism was being established in Mongolia, and the opening cue is a piece of professional music, indicating the merging of Soviet and Mongolian cultures (see Example 5.1 below).

Another important element of film scoring is the spotting, or the decision as to which scenes should have music and which should not. One reason not to add music to a scene is to create a greater impact when music appears in subsequent scenes, therefore there are often periods with no music just before a dramatic cue. In *The Clear River Tamir*, there is no music during the scenes of preparation for battle, which provides contrast to the rich symphonic cues of the battle scenes. Likewise, when Khongor gallops away just before Bat shoots him, the only sound

86 *Mongolian Film Music*

is that of the horse's hooves. The sombre music that follows when Bat realises what he has done is all the more poignant for the sparse soundtrack that precedes it. Other notable moments without underscoring are the amusing scenes, making the comedy element of this revolutionary drama more subtle than if Namsraijav had used instrumental cues to highlight the humour. Music typically used in many Hollywood and Mongolian films to enhance the comedy, such as trombone slides, staccato bassoon melodies and xylophone glissandi, would be inconsistent with the style and mood of *The Clear River Tamir*; Namsraijav avoided these instrumental techniques altogether. Dulmaa's ex-husband sings drunkenly when he is awarded his *ger* but no instrumental cue is used, and there is no music at all when the elderly man discusses Sükhbaatar with his partially deaf neighbour.

Underscoring

The main functions of the underscoring cues are to enhance the crisis points of the story, to create a pastoral atmosphere, to differentiate good and evil supporting characters, to foretell a misfortune and to parallel a character's state of mind, especially when there are doubts and fluctuations. Thrilling and suspenseful scenes in *The Clear River Tamir* are enhanced by powerful symphonic sounds, and film music of this nature is in keeping with the Russian convention of using symphonic music for dramatic and historical films. The musical characteristics of such cues include rich textures, *tutti* sections, crescendos, dynamic contrast, tremolo, diminished chords and fast scalic passages. Many Mongolian film composers, as well as many of their Soviet counterparts, gained much of their experience in dramatic orchestral writing from their concert pieces. Scenes requiring and thus using dramatic orchestral music include Tügjil attempting to capture Tömör, Erdene learning of Dolgoor's infidelity, the battle scenes and Tömör's death.

When the music differentiates good and evil characters, it is lavish *tutti* orchestral cues that are associated with the former and specific orchestral effects such as tremolo or drones with the latter. When clear-cut wicked characters such as Tügjil and the Buddhist lamas are introduced, appropriate underscoring is used to indicate their villainy. When Itgelt is introduced in the ninth minute of the film, however, there is no music in any of his scenes until the 27th minute, when he blackmails Dolgoor. Since Dorjpalam presented Itgelt as one of the multidimensional principal characters, music was not used immediately to indicate his wickedness, as this would render him a one-dimensional roguish character from the start.

Since diatonic harmonies and retuned folk music had been promoted countrywide from early in the Socialist era, by the early 1970s all citizens were familiar with the diatonic sound and its connotations of perceived modernity and progress. By contrast, non-equal-tempered pre-revolutionary folk and Buddhist temple music at this time seemed passé. Scenes in which Sükhbaatar makes rousing speeches and presents awards are scored with triumphant anthem-like orchestral cues in major keys. These scenes appear more real because of the casting of the actor Dashnamjil as Sükhbaatar, since this is the only film role he ever played, and audiences would have been familiar with his portrayal of the revolutionary hero from the widely screened 1968 film *Morning*. In contrast, orchestral effects such as the low drones and tremolo used for Tügjils's scenes create a sinister atmosphere, and the discordant Buddhist temple music used for the lamas would have sounded outmoded in comparison to the progressive anthem-like music based on the equal-tempered scale associated with the revolutionaries.

Using music to foreshadow misfortune was (and still is) a scoring technique commonly used in both Russian and Hollywood films, since it heightens the sense of anticipation felt by the audience as they wait for something unfortunate to occur. A diminished chord warns the audience something sinister will happen to Dolgoor when Itgelt arrives in her *ger*, and ominous music at the temple foretells not only the lamas' misdeeds but also that something bad will happen inside the temple itself: Tömör's death. Another notable cue of this nature is the low-pitched minor-key melody, bassoon pedal point and tremolo strings heard when Khongor and Bat meet by chance towards the end of Part 3, which foretells the ill-fated conclusion of the two friends.

The characters of most previous Mongolian historical dramas can be divided into two camps: supporters of the Mongolian People's Party and the Red Army on one side and their enemies on the other, namely the ruling classes, lamas, the White Army and the Chinese. Erdene and to a lesser extent Khongor alternate between the two camps, and their emotional turmoil as they decide which side to favour displays a depth of character previously unexplored by the Film Factory. Consequently, this calls for a depth of understanding previously not demanded of the audience. Music was therefore used to help audiences become acquainted with this new concept, so many of the orchestral cues parallel Erdene and Khongor's fluctuating states of mind. This music is an essential part of the film since it facilitates an understanding of what these two characters do not say; it reads between the lines, as it were, of the screenplay. Given that the psychological function of *The Clear River Tamir* was to disseminate propaganda, such music enables a more profound reception of the ideological elements of the film on the part of the audience.

The use of music to correspond to Erdene's state of mind is employed from his very first scene, when his horses are stolen, which is accompanied by a slow minor-key string melody. A major-key variation on this cue is heard when he first talks to Petr, who tells him to beware the counter-revolutionaries and convinces him that Bolshevism is the way forward. These two cues represent Erdene's dissatisfaction with his present life and his hopes for what it may become if he follows Bolshevist ideology. The emotion of the scene in which Erdene beats up Itgelt is enhanced by an orchestral *tutti* crescendo, yet the slow music played when Petr talks about Bolshevism reappears when Erdene rides away from the fight. The immediate return to this slow cue suggests that Erdene, after witnessing Itgelt's wickedness, is now seriously considering Petr's encouraging views on Bolshevism. When Erdene becomes an officer in the Russian White Army, a horse-head fiddle solo with a light orchestral accompaniment is heard as he rides across the steppe. When he comes across his old friend Tömör's discarded shackles, rousing orchestral music of bold brass statements and flourishing woodwind fragments enters, representing Erdene's memories and uneasiness regarding his position in the White Army. He consequently throws down his gun and talks to a passer-by about Sükhbaatar, at which point the music becomes soothing with a steady beat and in a major key. Further horse-head fiddle cues represent Erdene's sorrowful and nostalgic state of mind as he reminisces about Dolgoor.

Khongor's changing state of mind is a little more transparent than Erdene's and is scored more bluntly in two main cues. When he meets the woman he wants to marry, the ornamented melodies and harp glissandi suddenly play at double tempo, representing his increased heart rate and excitement. Khongor's other major turning point is when Tömör advises him to forgo his criminal ways. The music in this scene is a modern, experimental orchestral cue of note clusters and discords with added reverb, which blends into a diatonic flute melody as Khongor daydreams about a crime-free life. This cue is the only one of its kind in the film and signifies Khongor's chaotic state of mind, which would explain why he ultimately ignored Tömör's words and continued living his misguided lifestyle.

Although the majority of scenes that depict the river Tamir are underscored with traditional Mongolian instruments, namely the shots of happy characters at the flowing Tamir, the two scenes of unhappy characters alongside the frozen Tamir are accompanied by symphonic music. By scoring joyful shots of the river with traditional music and the mournful ones with orchestral music, Namsraijav has subtly created positive associations for the audience between the river, happiness and traditional Mongolian instruments and vocal styles. When traditional music is performed or heard on screen by the characters, however, not all of the cues come with clearly favourable connotations.

Diegetic Cues

There are 21 cues of diegetic or semidiegetic music in *The Clear River Tamir* comprising 13 pieces for traditional instruments or vocal styles, four instances of Buddhist temple music, two accordion pieces and two revolutionary songs. That musicians are shown on screen or their presence implied in just over a quarter of the film's 80 cues demonstrates that Dorjpalam and Namsraijav wished to present live music making as habitual before and during the Socialist era. The 13 diegetic or semidiegetic traditional music cues make up the majority of the film's 21 cues in this category, suggesting that traditional music in films was deemed most appropriate when the action called for it directly.

The Khalkha folk songs sung by characters on screen in *The Clear River Tamir* are well known throughout Mongolia, thereby appealing to the audience as a whole. The songs in question are *Erdene Zasgiin Unaga* (*The Foal from Erdene*),

Figure 5.2   Erdene and Itgelt at a party in a wealthy family's house. Norovyn Baatar as Erdene (left) and Ayuurzanyn Ochirbat as Itgelt, *The Clear River Tamir* (*Tungalag Tamir*), Film Factory (Mongol Kino), 1970–1973

which Tömör sings when he is happily married to Dulmaa in their new *ger*, and *Eruu Tsagaan Bolimor* (*White-Breasted Sparrow*), which Dulmaa's ex-husband sings drunkenly to express his happiness at receiving a new *ger* of his own. These songs would have provided audience members with feelings of both familiarity and solidarity, and it was not uncommon for audiences to sing along to well-known songs whilst watching films.[4]

There are many scenes in films of the Socialist era that depict the opulent lifestyles of higher-ranking members of pre-1921 feudal society, and these are typically scored with traditional music, often diegetically. One such scene in *The Clear River Tamir* is the party in Part 1 that Erdene and Itgelt attend in the lavishly decorated home of a wealthy family. Along with the other party guests, both Itgelt and Erdene wear expensive clothes, eat and drink heartily and relax on the luxurious furniture (Figure 5.2). Throughout the scene we hear a *shanz* solo and men singing drinking songs, and although neither a *shanz* player nor singers are seen, their presence at the party is implied. Namsraijav and Dorjpalam would have chosen (semi)diegetic traditional music here since this is what the action calls for, yet this scene gives these cues unfavourable associations, albeit subtly. The party is attended by Itgelt, the main villain of the film, and Erdene before he chooses the 'right way', rather than any of the characters who support socialism from the onset, such as Bat, Petr or Sükhbaatar. The opulence of the scene is in stark

---

[4] Many of my informants, most notably Ukhnaa of the Mongolian Philharmony, described film viewings in which audience members sang along to songs.

contrast to the simple game of hide and seek that Itgelt organised as a celebration for his workers at the start of the film. Furthermore, Erdene is seen flirting with the married lady, Gerel, just moments before he throws out Dolgoor on account of her dalliance with Itgelt. This association of traditional diegetic music with pre-1921 feudal values, which the MPRP considered negative in comparison with new socialist values, was commonplace in films before the late 1980s.[5]

Ironically, although the rhythms and structures of these semidiegetic *shanz* and vocal cues sound improvisatory, thereby corresponding with what is known about historical performance practice, they are based on equal-tempered scales. Even if Namsraijav and Dorjpalam had wanted historical accuracy in the form of pre-revolutionary tunings for this scene, this would have been very difficult since both men were born after 1921 and would not have known exactly what pre-1921 traditional music sounded like. Furthermore, Namsraijav wrote the score by hand using the Western staff notation he had studied in Moscow, making it difficult for him to compose music based on anything other than equal-tempered scales. The traditional music used in this historical film was therefore not the music that would have been heard before 1921 but that which had been modified and promoted by the MPRP.

Similarly, the *Naadam* festival scene in Part 3, set in the 1930s, is attended only by characters who have decided not to follow socialism, namely Itgelt, Tügjil and Khongor. The music of this scene is *uukhai* and so negative associations are made subtly by linking this genre with people who have not embraced socialism. Erdene, meanwhile, is sitting on the bank of the Tamir reminiscing about Dolgoor when he is disturbed by two passing children singing a revolutionary song. This genre, new to Mongolia since it became a socialist country, is therefore associated with Erdene, who by this point in the film has chosen socialist progress, whilst traditional music is associated with the characters who shunned socialism and ultimately fade out of the story or die.

The choice of whether musicians and singers in the story are visible (diegetic cues) or their presence is implied (semidiegetic) may have come down to practical reasons. It is easy to incorporate one accordion player into the celebratory scenes whereas showing the *uukhai* singers in the *Naadam* festival scenes would detract from the dialogue, and showing the array of sizeable Buddhist temple instruments could be problematic for the cinematographer regarding the composition of the shots. Moreover, there was a shortage of temple instruments in the 1970s to use in film scenes since many were destroyed along with the temples during the purges of the 1930s. The use of semidiegetic cues similarly helped create atmosphere but with a greater awareness of its source than the underscoring cues. Nonetheless, representing a variety of musical genres as live performances on screen was clearly an important element of Dorjpalam and Namsraijav's musical agenda.

---

[5] Traditional music was portrayed in a far more positive light from 1988 following the release of *Mandukhai the Wise Queen* (*Mandukhai Tsetsen Khatan*). See Chapter 6 for a discussion of this film.

Professional Music Cues

The six instances of professional music in *The Clear River Tamir* perform the contradictory functions of providing contrast with the two dominant musical genres of the film – symphonic art music and traditional music – whilst giving a sense of continuity to the whole soundtrack by sharing musical elements with both. The characteristics of symphonic art music in these six cues include the instrumentation, notation, some structural devices and diatonic harmonies. The structural elements of symphonic art music Namsraijav used include canonic imitation, theme and variation form, playing a melody over a drone or pedal and the division of phrases into bars of equal length. The traditional Mongolian features of these cues include the use of the pentatonic scale, the music being melodically rather than harmonically or rhythmically driven, and the extensive use of melodic ornamentation and *rubato* to create an improvisatory feel. Namsraijav's usage and combination of these musical characteristics is typical of professional music throughout Film Factory soundtracks, although the ratio of professional music cues to other genres differs greatly from film to film.

The six cues in *The Clear River Tamir* are played on orchestral instruments, which sometimes emulate the sounds of traditional Mongolian instruments, such as the low register of the violin imitating the horse-head fiddle, the oboe corresponding to the *bishgüür*, and the *limbe* sounding like the flute. The cues combine the melodic components of traditional Khalkha music and the structural and harmonic components of European symphonic music and are mostly performed with instrumental sounds common to both genres.

The sparing use of professional music in *The Clear River Tamir* helps to highlight significant moments in the plot. The first of these cues occurs when Tömör steals horses from the rich to give to the poor, and the orchestral strings echo the sound of galloping horses' hooves. Given Tömör's portrayal as a traditional hero in the manner of Toroi Bandi, professional music is more suitable for this scene than the dramatic, diatonic symphonic music that accompanies Sükhbaatar's heroic actions. There are two moments in the story when principal characters fall in love: Tömör in Part 1 and Khongor in Part 3, and both scenes utilise professional music. In both cases, the orchestra is used to imitate the sounds of traditional Mongolian instruments, such as the harp and flute for the *yatga* and *limbe* respectively. Characteristics of Khalkha musical traditions are also employed such as ornamentation and the use of the pentatonic scale. These romantic subplots provide relief from the intense political agenda and action scenes, and the use of professional music helps maintain a light atmosphere, where Romantic-era orchestral music could be too melodramatic and traditional music too incongruous with the romantic mood within the context of Mongolian film-scoring conventions.

Two of the professional music cues are solos: an oboe imitating the *bishgüür* when Erdene returns to his village and is berated by an acquaintance, and a solo violin in its lower register sounding like a horse-head fiddle during Tömör's death scene.

The latter scene includes the characteristic shot of the sky to symbolise death. The use of solos during these moments is effective since they represent Erdene and Tömör being alone, which contrasts with the orchestral *tutti* and military band sounds during scenes of collective activity. In contrast with traditional music cues such as the *limbe* solo and *shanz* solos, Namsraijav has chosen to score these two cues for Western orchestral instruments rather than traditional Mongolian instruments. This brought about an interesting development in combining traditional Mongolian music and symphonic music: these two cues are not harmonised, thereby creating a simplified version of professional music within the repertoire of Mongolian film scores.

The most substantial and perhaps most significant instance of professional music is the opening cue of Part 3, which is set in the 1930s. At this time, ordinary Mongolians had to create a balance between the traditional lifestyle they had led before the 1921 Revolution and the emergent socialist society. It is fitting for the music at this point in the film to be a combination of traditional Mongolian music and the symphonic music that had around this time been introduced to Mongolia from the Soviet Union. This cue is based on the pentatonic scale of G, B flat, C, D and F and is melodically driven with light accompaniment and only the slightest suggestion of harmony. The cue opens with an ostinato pedal in the lower strings that is reminiscent of the horse's hooves figures common in horse-head fiddle pieces. The pentatonic scale is then introduced by a descending figure in the brass. At bar 6, whilst the ostinato continues, the first statement of the melody is played by the violins in their low to mid-register, corresponding with the alto-register sonority of the horse-head fiddle. The very first note of the melody is set against a B natural, making the tonality of the cue ambiguous, given the B flat of the pentatonic scale. Ornamentation and *rubato* are employed and the flexibility of the rhythm creates an improvisatory feel (Example 5.1). The flute then takes over the melody from bar 13 and it is ornamented further with trills on the longer note values, which is typical of *limbe* performance practice.[6] The symphonic element is brought into the cue by the use of canonic imitation of the flute melody by the horns. The end of the cue blends immediately into the traditional wrestlers' song (*uukhai*) of the *Naadam* festival scene.

Although there are few cues of professional music in *The Clear River Tamir*, they play an important role in highlighting pre-1921 traditional society juxtaposed with the new socialist culture. Symphonic music in the style that Namsraijav studied in Moscow is used for battle scenes of the 1921 Revolution, and traditional music is mostly presented on screen. Significantly, professional music is used for scenes that combine the new socialist Mongolia with pre-revolutionary traditional values. Tömör steals horses from the rich to give to the poor in the manner of folk hero Toroi Bandi, yet his magnanimity and sense of equal fiscal entitlement are congruous with the socialist ideology promoted in the film. Tömör's death

---

[6] Bars 6 and 13 according to my transcription, not necessarily according to Namsraijav's score.

Example 5.1 The first statement of the melody of the opening cue to Part 3, *The Clear River Tamir*

scene plays the dual role of condemning the lamas whilst making Tömör a martyr to his beliefs and good morals. Although Namsraijav may not be credited with bringing about the most innovative musical developments in professional music, he succeeded in using this genre to highlight traditional values combined with socialist ideology whilst supporting the deeper psychological elements of the film.

Film Music and a Deeper Psychological Impact

Mongolian films of the 1950s and 1960s were imbued with socialist ideology and the characters divided clearly into good and bad. The music often supported these dichotomous portrayals, with major-key anthem-like pieces being associated with the former and low-pitched diminished chords or sinister minor-key melodies with the latter. By the 1970s, however, audiences had become familiar with propaganda films and would not have been so easily influenced by one-dimensional characterisations enhanced by bold cues. Furthermore, there was a disparity between the hardships many people experienced in real life and the idyllic life portrayed on screen. The solution was to show that socialism sometimes caused hardship but – most importantly – that this hardship could be overcome. Namsraijav's use of music to help the audience understand what the characters do not say, for example Erdene's fluctuating state of mind but ultimate embracing of socialism, was a major development in Mongolian socialist propaganda. Namsraijav's score for *The Clear River Tamir* is a showcase for the music genres prevalent in the films that preceded it, and was important regarding developments in the function of Mongolian film music in that it played an essential role in highlighting the psychological elements of the film.

Dorjpalam had previously directed the provocative 1956 film *The Obstacles We Confront* and had made numerous films dealing with personal emotions. Given that psychology and subliminal propaganda were more significant in *The Clear River Tamir* than other films about the 1921 Revolution, Dorjpalam is an appropriate choice for director, rather than the risky choice he may at first appear. Namsraijav's experience in scoring revolutionary films made him a suitable composer for this large-scale anniversary celebration. Yet his sensitivity to Mongolian musical traditions, as evidenced by his notable horse-head fiddle cue in *Footprints* ensured he was able to match the subtleties of the deeper psychological character portrayals necessary in *The Clear River Tamir* to appeal to 1970s audiences. This deeper understanding of 1970s Mongolian society and the complexities of human psychology on the part of Dorjpalam and Namsraijav paved the way for some of the subversive Mongolian films and music of the following decade.

Chapter 6
Perestroika, a Wise Queen and a Delinquent Rock Star

The Mongolian national revolution started in 1985 with Gorbachev and perestroika, not in 1990 with the Mongolian Democratic Revolution. He broke down the socialist system, and this made me change my style of composition.

Jantsannorov, INT

From the mid-1970s in the Soviet Union, the problems of over fifty years of socialism and corrupt administration manifested in the form of economic hardship and social unrest. In the mid-1980s, Gorbachev publicly acknowledged the disparity between reality and the way life was portrayed through socialist propaganda. He consequently promised political transparency and drastic change in the Soviet Union through his policies of glasnost (openness) and perestroika (restructuring). The reaction to these policies in the Soviet Union was unprecedented and led inadvertently to its dissolution, the downfall of socialism throughout the Eastern Bloc and the end of the Cold War.

Gorbachev and perestroika had a momentous impact on a number of Mongolian film composers, filmmakers, and students who were studying in the Soviet Union during the 1980s. I conducted extended interviews with composer and civil servant Jantsannorov and film director Choimbolyn Jumdaan (b. 1948), both of whom cite perestroika and Gorbachev as the principal influences on their compositions and films respectively during the latter half of the 1980s, particularly on the ground-breaking score for *Mandukhai the Wise Queen* (*Mandukhai Tsesten Khatan*, 1988) and the controversial *Whirlpool* (*Ergüüleg*, 1989).

The Road to Perestroika: Mongolian Cinema in the 1970s and 1980s

In *The Clear River Tamir* (*Tungalag Tamir*, 1970–73), the protagonist Erdene's fluctuating state of mind emphasised by the music was one of the first instances of Mongolian filmmakers showing it was acceptable to question socialism, although they added the proviso that socialist ideology should be followed ultimately. Many of the films that followed took a similar introspective approach by depicting emotions and relationships in a variety of contexts. Filmic celebrations of socialist progress were replaced with reflections on societal and interpersonal problems. Examples include *Tales of First Love* (*Ankhny Khairyn Duuli*, 1975), *The Beloved*

(*Khani*, 1975), and *Naidan the Shepherd* (*Khonichin Naidan*, 1979), which is about a young boy who escapes from a monastery due to ill treatment. Despite deeper characterisations and the coverage of personal and societal problems, propaganda was still a prominent force, the negative portrayal of Buddhist lamas in *Naidan the Shepherd* being a good example. These films paved the way for cinema of the 1980s, which dealt with issues in Mongolia that paralleled the problems in the Soviet Union that Gorbachev intended to tackle through his new policies.

The 1980s was the Film Factory's most prolific decade, during which 64 feature films were produced, and in many of them the action was moved from the countryside, as had been the case throughout the previous five decades, to Ulaanbaatar. This shift in milieu reflected the urbanisation in Mongolia at the time. The urban drama films focused on city life and the plight of the individual, and often drew a fine line between supporting socialism and criticising it. Many Mongolian films of the 1980s featured one family rather than military companies and collectives, time periods of a few weeks rather than several years, and local Ulaanbaatar neighbourhoods as opposed to vast expanses of disputed territory. Fewer characters were presented, so scriptwriters could afford to make them deeper, more rounded and introspective. The MPRP still dictated the themes of films but they were less patriotic and celebratory, and more governed by displaying social behaviours that were desirable (or otherwise) to the state.

Governmental campaigns appeared throughout the 1980s to rehabilitate offenders, warn against the dangers of alcohol abuse, and to remind citizens of their moral obligations regarding fidelity and childcare, and these issues became common themes within films. Notable examples include *Not Yet Married* (*Gerlej Amjaagüi Yavna*, 1981) about a man who has not had time to find a wife due to his dedication to the mining industry, *Five Fingers* (*Garyn Tavan Khuruu*, 1983) about five children left to fend for themselves when their mother dies after her husband leaves her for another woman, and *The Forgotten Tale* (*Martagdsan Duuli*, 1989), which deals with single parenthood and the reforming of criminals. The emphasis on societal problems caused people to question socialism and wonder what the alternatives might be. Gorbachev's suggested solutions to these problems were glasnost and perestroika, and these policies had a profound influence on the new wave of Mongolian film directors and composers.

In 1986, the name of the sole Mongolian film studio was changed from Film Factory (*Kino Üildver*) to the State Film Head Office (*Ulsyn Kinony Yerönkhii Gazar*), and this name remained until 1991 when it was renamed the Mongol Kino Company (*Mongol Kino Negtel*). Scores by the prolific composers of the first two decades of the golden age (*Altan Üye*) such as Damdinsüren, Mördorj and Luvsansharav became less frequent and a new generation of film composers began to establish reputations. Amongst these were Jantsannorov, the composer for *Mandukhai the Wise Queen* and Gaadangiin Altankhuyag (b. 1948), the composer for *Whirlpool*, both of whom have also held prominent positions in the governmental and organisational bodies that regulated professional music making, such as the Mongolian Composers' Union and the Ministry of Culture.

The Catalyst for New Mongolian Films and Music

In April 1985 at the Plenary Meeting of the Central Committee of the CPSU, perestroika was inaugurated. Perestroika was a collection of proposed reforms and strategies created to avoid economic collapse in the Soviet Union and to promote further development. Gorbachev attributed the urgent need for economic reform to a number of factors including vast expenses procured through acquiring material resources, the cost of developments in construction, corrupt officials taking unearned bonuses, and the erosion of moral values amongst the Soviet populace (Gorbachev, 1987, pp. 20–21). Further explanations for the Soviet Union's economic problems include expenditure due to the arms race, the Cold War, and policies of finding employment for every citizen leading to the creation of unnecessary jobs.

Through perestroika, Gorbachev advocated a move towards his vision of democratisation, whereby regional leaders were to be elected rather than appointed by the state. This would allow for greater local management and reduce the CPSU's direct involvement in local affairs. Furthermore, technological advancement was to be encouraged, laws were to be more strictly observed, the role of trade unions was to be evaluated, and women were to spearhead a drive towards strengthened family values. Other major objectives of perestroika included improved relations with the world's superpowers and worldwide nuclear disarmament, although it could be argued that the move towards nuclear disarmament was a means to alleviate the economic strain caused by military expenditure during the arms race.

Gorbachev also blamed the Soviet Union's problems on destructive traits such as corruption and alcoholism, and the tendency to conceal faults through propaganda. Similar cover-ups had occurred in Mongolia, such as the Film Factory's deliberate omission within films of the true fate of noblemen and lamas. Gorbachev commanded the exposing of faults through the policy of glasnost, the counterpart of perestroika, which urged greater freedom of speech in the media and culture. At the meeting in April 1985, Gorbachev declared that glasnost and perestroika should be implemented throughout the Soviet Union with immediate effect.

Glasnost and perestroika called for what was to all intents and purposes a second revolution, albeit one that did not involve overthrowing the current system of government. Gorbachev envisaged a scenario in which all socialist citizens should come together in the struggle to revive Lenin's ideals in the spirit of the October Revolution in 1917 (1987, p. 25). Gorbachev's desire for democratisation, power to be less centralised, more openness and freedom of speech eventually came to be, but as a result of the fall of socialism and the dissolution of the Soviet Union rather than his vision of reviving Marxist–Leninist ideology.

Mongolia, meanwhile, was suffering similar economic and societal problems, and news of elder brother Soviet Union's new policies of glasnost and perestroika spread quickly and came to be viewed as a solution. Perhaps more important than the actual reasons for Gorbachev's call for perestroika was the fact that change

98 *Mongolian Film Music*

was deemed necessary. If the MPRP had also acknowledged publicly that reform was imperative, it would have been tantamount to admitting that socialism as it had been for the last sixty years was not working. The MPRP made no such proclamations, however, so it was left to others with a public voice, such as filmmakers and composers, to do so.

Looking to the Past: Jantsannorov and a Wise Queen

> When I am dead, I don't want people talking about me as a good composer. I want people to remember me as someone who successfully introduced Mongolian music to the world. That is my only wish.
>
> Jantsannorov, INT

I interviewed Jantsannorov in Ulaanbaatar in April 2008, and we discussed at length his musical background and training and his compositional process for the score to *Mandukhai the Wise Queen*. He also told me about his contribution to Mongolian cultural policy through his various posts in the Ministry of Culture and other official governing bodies for music and the arts.

Jantsannorov was born to a herding family approximately 40 kilometres from Kharkhorin, which had been the capital of Mongolia briefly during the Mongol Empire.[1] He learned to sing long-song (*urtyn duu*) from his elder brother and mother, and to play the accordion from his school teacher, Ochirbat. He moved to Ulaanbaatar in 1967 to study at the Teachers' [training] College (*Bagshiin Deed Surguuli*), where he learned piano and started to compose short piano pieces. After graduating as a music teacher in 1971, he remained at the college as a lecturer for a further two years before attending the Kiev Conservatoire between 1973 and 1979 to study composition.

Jantsannorov told me that whilst he was studying in Kiev, he noticed that, unlike conservatoires in Moscow and Leningrad where music was divided into 'Russian/Soviet' or 'rest of the world', people in Kiev recognised Ukrainian national music as a distinct and separate style. When he returned to Mongolia after six years in Kiev, he compared the traditional music of his childhood to what was being presented as traditional music in 1979 and noted that, 'the costumes were traditional Mongolian costumes but the music was not traditional Mongolian music' (Jantsannorov, INT). He felt dismayed that traditional Mongolian music had been changed so drastically by external forces, namely Soviet-inspired cultural policy, so he made the decision to become involved in cultural policy in order to influence Mongolian music making. Between 1979 and 1990, Jantsannorov held various positions at the Ministry of Culture, the Mongolian Arts Committee and

---

[1] Kharkhorin, also known as Karakorum, was a supply base during Chinggis Khaan's time, and it became the capital during his son Ögedei's reign. The capital was then moved to Khanbalik (now Beijing) in 1272 during Chinggis' grandson Khubilai Khan's time.

the Mongolian Association of Musicians. In these posts, he was responsible for policy making regarding music concerts, celebrations, reforms and promotions throughout Mongolia. During this period he also composed symphonic music, chamber music and pieces for traditional instruments during his free time.

Jantsannorov's first film score was for the 1983 drama *Five Fingers*, for which he composed cues for solo jaw harp (*aman khuur*) as well as symphonic cues. Also in 1983, he composed the score for *The Wrestler* (*Garid Magnai*), an historical drama set in pre-revolutionary times, an era rarely covered by the Film Factory. *The Wrestler* was the first in a trilogy about Mongolia's three manly sports, the traditional sports of the *Naadam* festival. The other two films, also scored by Jantsannorov, are *Champion Horse* (*Tod Magnai*, 1990) and *The Archer* (*Tsets Magnai*, 1995), although there may have been no intention to make a film trilogy during production of *The Wrestler* in 1983. Despite the traditional Mongolian subject matter of *The Wrestler*, the score mostly comprises symphonic cues typical of Film Factory productions of the 1970s and early 1980s. Jantsannorov scored a further four films between 1984 and 1986, *The Sound of Victory* (*Yalaltyn Duun*, 1984), *Hot Autumn Day* (*Namryn Khaluun Ödrüüd*, 1985), *I Love You* (*Bi Chamd Khairtai*, 1985) and *Dew* (*Süüder*, 1986), before he composed the pioneering music to *Mandukhai the Wise Queen* in 1988. This score earned him a reputation as one of Mongolia's most accomplished and innovative film composers.

A True Mongolian Historical Epic

Mandukhai the Wise Queen is an historical epic based on the true story of the fifteenth-century queen, Mandukhai. Like *The Clear River Tamir*, the film is in three parts but is to all intents and purposes one long film rather than a trilogy of separate films. It was directed by Begziin Baljinnyam (b. 1943), who had previously worked as the cinematographer on 15 films and had directed 5 films, including 3 collaborations with Jantsannorov: *Five Fingers*, *I Love You* and *Dew*. The epic production of *Mandukhai the Wise Queen*, which has a total running time of 305 minutes, involved a large cast, opulent sets and costumes, and two teams of stuntmen to perform the grand battle scenes, one of which was led by film director Jumdaan. Film researcher Myagmarsüren (INT) told me the production utilised the best film technology Mongolia had to offer at the time and there was stiff competition amongst actors to play the lead characters. He explained that Namsrain Suvd (b. 1948), who played Mandukhai, received threatening and insulting anonymous letters believed to be written by envious actresses who failed to land the role (see Figure 6.1 below). Many of the cast and crew received state awards for their contribution to this production and it is widely considered within Mongolia one of the country's greatest films. It was screened throughout Mongolia when it was released in 1988, and school children and workers were escorted to the cinema by their teachers and bosses to watch all five hours of the film in one sitting.

100　　　　　　　　　　*Mongolian Film Music*

It is still broadcast regularly on Mongolian television, particularly during the *Tsagaan Sar* (Mongolian New Year) holiday period.

The plot is as follows. It is the fifteenth century. Manduul Khan (king) marries the young Mandukhai, who he hopes will bear him a son, since his first wife has failed to do so. Mandukhai falls pregnant, Manduul Khan, who is an alcoholic, dies, and Mandukhai gives birth to a baby girl. Following Manduul Khan's death, the throne is hotly contested since there is no male heir. Ismel, one of Manduul Khan's men, and Önöbold, Mandukhai's former lover, are involved in the contest. Manduul Khan's advisor suggests Mandukhai should choose who becomes the next khan. Mandukhai chooses Manduul Khan's seven-year-old nephew, Batmönkh, purely for his name, since he is too young to rule.[2] She marries him, thereby making him khan and uniting feuding factions. Neither Ismel nor Önöbold is happy with the decision and they plot their revenge. When Batmönkh Khan turns 18, Mandukhai bears him twin sons and wishes to leave him in charge of Mongolia so she can retire in peace. Ismel, however, is causing trouble, and Önöbold returns and declares battle. Further fighting ensues, this time against the Chinese, and Mandukhai leads her troops to victory on horseback. Mandukhai returns to the palace to find Ismel sitting on the khan's throne. The two fight and she is shot by one of Ismel's archers. Ismel administers the fatal stab with his sword. Önöbold arrives and captures Ismel, who is consequently buried alive for killing Mandukhai. Batmönkh Khan promises to rule the newly unified Mongolia well to honour her memory.

The caption at the start of the film states, 'This film is dedicated to Mandukhai, a wise queen from the fifteenth century, who helped unify the Mongols.' Lengthy tales of heroes and battles, such as the story of Mandukhai, had been popular in Mongolia for centuries as part of the country's rich tradition of bardic storytelling. In the late 1980s, people became interested in Mongolian history other than the rise of socialism and, due to public demand, the MPRP set up a commission to investigate blank spots in history, such as the purges of the 1930s. Furthermore, it was extremely rare during the Socialist era for Mongolian films to display patriotism overtly unless it was linked directly with socialism, *Tsogt Taij* being the other principal example. Although *The Wrestler* covered traditional Mongolian subject matter, it did not evoke the same scale of patriotic feeling as *Tsogt Taij* and *Mandukhai the Wise Queen*. This is partly due to its conventional score and partly because the latter two films were based on well-known true stories of heroic combat and Mongolian victories. The only possible link with the socialist cause in *Mandukhai the Wise Queen*, given the contemporary drive to combat alcoholism, was the portrayal of Manduul Khan's alcoholism contributing to his early demise, although this link is tenuous.

Whereas the key members of the crew of *Tsogt Taij* were Russian, the entire cast and crew of *Mandukhai the Wise Queen* were Mongolian, leading many film

---

[2]　Mandukhai's young husband, Batmönkh, remained in power from 1470 to 1504, making him one of the longest-ruling khans in the history of Mongolia (Baabar, 1999, p. 57).

fans and professionals to consider it the first truly Mongolian historical epic film. It is also the first Mongolian film in which Chinggis Khaan is openly revered: in addition to numerous references to his descendants and heirs, there are scenes depicting Manduul Khan praying to a Chinggis Khaan shrine and Sartai, the palace advisor, telling stories of Chinggis Khaan to the young Batmönkh. There are further touches of nostalgia in the film such as captions in classical Mongol script despite the fact that the majority of film audiences would have been able to read only Cyrillic. In the context of perestroika and the MPRP's aim to revitalise socialism, and in the context of state film studio's series of urban dramas in the 1980s, *Mandukhai the Wise Queen* was a rare piece of filmmaking, and it was Jantsannorov's responsibility to compose a fitting score.

Reimagining History through the Score

When Jantsannorov composed his first film scores, he was influenced by traditional methods of Mongolian film scoring, which accounts for the Soviet-inspired orchestral music of *The Wrestler* despite the timeless traditional Mongolian subject matter. After the inauguration of perestroika in the Soviet Union, Jantsannorov began to question socialism and to think about the Mongolian traditions that had been lost and the rich history that had been ignored during the Socialist era. His re-evaluation of where his national loyalties lay – either with pre-revolutionary Mongolia or post-1921 Soviet-influenced Mongolia – led to a change in his compositional style. In his dual role as member of the Ministry of Culture and film composer he felt able to provide the Mongolian public with the new sense of patriotism he felt they desired in the form of his music.

Jantsannorov told me he always works very closely with film directors when scoring films to ensure the music he composes expresses the director's intentions. He had worked with the director Baljinnyam on three films before *Mandukhai the Wise Queen*, so the two men could reach a mutual understanding quickly since they were familiar with each other's working methods and they shared the same sentiments regarding perestroika and patriotism. Nonetheless, Jantsannorov faced an interesting challenge in having to compose a score for a story set five centuries earlier, and his ideas on how he approached the scoring process are, in his own words:

> Films are dedicated to the public. My music [for *Mandukhai the Wise Queen*] is dedicated to people living in the twentieth century. My music is therefore all about the twentieth century, even if the film is set in the fifteenth century; it doesn't matter. My music must be relevant to twentieth-century people. Second, Mongolian films are aimed at Mongolian audiences, so the music I compose is only for Mongolians.

102   *Mongolian Film Music*

Given Jantsannorov's dedication to composing music relevant to twentieth-century audiences and his patriotic feelings aroused by perestroika, he employed a process of composition he had never before used. Jantsannorov took three recordings of the celebrated long-song singer Namjilyn Norovbanzad (1931–2002) singing the same song, *Uyakhan Zambutiviin Naran* (*Sun of the Placid Universe*). The first recording was made in the 1960s, the second in the 1970s and the third in the 1980s. Jantsannorov noted how Norovbanzad's style of singing had changed over the three decades and he analysed the differences in the vocal techniques she employed. Using this analysis as a basis, he then imagined how the song would have sounded in the 1950s, then the 1940s, then the 1840s and so on. By imagining changes in music, working chronologically backwards, he eventually reached the fifteenth century and had an idea of what this music may have sounded like. He then combined his imagination of historical music with modern scoring techniques in order to compose an historically influenced score that was relevant to twentieth-century audiences. The public's reaction to Jantsannorov's score was unequivocally positive. Film researcher Myagmarsüren (INT) acknowledges that 'This score made huge changes and reforms to Mongolian film music. He combined modern music with some of the more interesting Mongolian musical traditions. This is quite unusual music.' Referring to musical traditions lost during the Socialist era, film viewer Urtnasan (INT) asserts that, 'Thanks to the historical topic of this film, Jantsannorov could express our traditional music identity.' Jantsannorov's score for *Mandukhai the Wise Queen* is one of the few pre-1990 film soundtracks to be released commercially on CD in Mongolia, and excerpts from the score are broadcast regularly on national radio.[3] Jantsannorov acknowledges the widespread appeal of his score and its unique place in twentieth-century Mongolian film scoring. He told me:

> After I composed this music people were proud of me because they thought it represented the fifteenth century very well. People believed the music could have originated in the fifteenth century. But my music was not genuine fifteenth-century music. It was music of the end of the twentieth century.

The instrumentation of *Mandukhai the Wise Queen* comprises a symphony orchestra with a large percussion section including timpani, gongs, cymbals, claves and xylophone; horse-head fiddles, *khuuchir, limbe, yatga* and *yoochin*; shaman's drums; and overtone singing (*khöömii*), long-song, whistling (*isgeree*), and a male and female chorus. Prior to 1988, Jantsannorov had used traditional Mongolian instruments only for diegetic cues and not for underscoring. His use of traditional instruments in *Mandukhai the Wise Queen* helped change viewers' perception of these instruments by portraying them in a considerably more positive context than that of earlier films.

---

[3]   N. Jantsannorov, *Manduhai the Wise*, ADMON Co., recorded February 1988 at the Mongol Kino studios (no release date given).

Figure 6.1 Mandukhai becomes queen on her wedding day. Namsrain Suvd as Mandukhai, *Mandukhai the Wise Queen* (*Mandukhai Tsetsen Khatan*), State Film Head Office (Mongol Kino), 1988

The film opens with a cue of traditional vocals including long-song and *khöömii* accompanied by *yoochin* and symphonic strings, which is followed by a shaman's ritual involving vocals and drums. One of the most significant cues of traditional music occurs 10 minutes into the film during Mandukhai and Manduul Khan's wedding. The scene depicts the lavishly dressed newly-weds seated on ornate thrones, surrounded by dignitaries enjoying a sumptuous feast, entertained by a troupe of traditional dancers and a large traditional-instrument orchestra. The music is an extended piece of Jantsannorov's reimagination of palace music (*ordony khögjim*), a genre associated with the pre-1921 ruling classes and therefore rarely heard during the Socialist era. In the midst of the celebrations, the camera closes in on Mandukhai's grave countenance as she accepts her position as queen, the starting point of her unification of Mongol peoples (Figure 6.1). The music, the action and the imagery at this point all portray a society that was the antithesis of socialist ideals, yet they are presented in this scene in a respectful and nostalgic manner. This is in stark contrast to the portrayal of pre-1921 special occasions in earlier films of the Socialist era, such as the party in *The Clear River Tamir* where Erdene and Itgelt meet Gerel, a scene imbued with negative connotations. The sounds of the traditional-instrument orchestra introduced during Mandukhai and Manduul Khan's wedding scene appear throughout the remaining five hours of the film, as part of Jantsannorov's intention to 'restore lost traditions rather than promote nationalism' (Jantsannorov, INT).

Before 1988, professional music (*mergejliin khögjim*) cues were predominantly based on pentatonic scales, harmonised, and played on symphonic instruments. In *Mandukhai the Wise Queen*, Jantsannorov developed the idea of combining Western and Mongolian musical elements by composing cues based on eight-note scales and diatonic harmonies to be played on the traditional instruments heard in the wedding scene, sometimes with light orchestral accompaniment and even some modern discords. The result was a music that was unique and easily identifiable as Jantsannorov's idiosyncratic musical voice, and what musicologist Enkhtsetseg (INT) calls 'the pinnacle of professional music'. Jantsannorov's music was both traditional and progressive. His direct inversion of previous compositional practices in professional music was symbolic of the attitudes of many Mongolians in the late 1980s who had wearied of the socialist struggle and wanted a new future based on traditional values and customs.

One example of Jantsannorov's new sound is a leitmotif used throughout the film to signify Mandukhai's relationship with Önöbold (Example 6.1). The key of the cue is F minor, yet each time it reappears the instrumentation and accompaniment are different. Structurally, the melody does not fit into a regular time signature or into a pattern of two- or four-bar phrases,[4] making it sound more improvisatory in the manner of traditional Mongolian music and concurrently more like modern twentieth-century music. The use of traditional instruments in the various appearances of this cue helps associate the music with the historical period of the story. The use of the F minor scale is clearly influenced by the diatonic music Jantsannorov studied in Kiev, yet he juxtaposes the scale with a drone on the note G, making the F minor tonality less obvious. The use of traditional instrumentation with diatonic scales and subtle discords is a novel combination of tradition and modernity, making Jantsannorov one of the foremost innovators in the development of professional music.

Another theme that appears at various times throughout the score is a brass fanfare figure used in scenes of battles and *Naadam* ceremonies (Example 6.2). Fanfares on brass instruments made regular appearances in military music and revolutionary songs, yet it is the context and musical interval of these cues in *Mandukhai the Wise Queen* that differentiates them from fanfares in other film scores and gives them an historical and nostalgic feel. These fanfares appear in the film to herald the start of a traditional festivity or battle, thereby creating new associations with this familiar musical device by linking it with history and tradition rather than twentieth-century battles. The interval of this fanfare is a perfect fourth, the same as that of the standardised open tuning of the horse-head fiddle, therefore a familiar sound to twentieth-century Mongolian audiences and one readily associated with this iconic traditional Mongolian instrument.

Jantsannorov also combined traditional and symphonic music through mixed cues, cues that begin in one musical genre then cross-fade into another, as Namsraijav had done in his score for *The Clear River Tamir*. There is a bittersweet scene in which Mandukhai brings her new seven-year-old husband Batmönkh into the palace and he is too scared to sleep so she tells him a bedtime story. The cue begins with a *yatga* solo as she takes the child in her arms, strokes his

---

[4]   In my transcription, the melody fits into 10 bars, 2 of which are in a different time signature from the other 8, although this may not be strictly as Jantsannorov composed these cues.

Example 6.1   The melody of Mandukhai and Önöbold's theme, *Mandukhai the Wise Queen*

Example 6.2   Fanfare figure, *Mandukhai the Wise Queen*

hair tenderly and begins the story. As the boy falls asleep, the camera closes in on Mandukhai's troubled countenance and the music cross-fades into a densely textured orchestral theme that builds into an intense crescendo. The dramatic contrast between the peaceful *yatga* music and the orchestral crescendo highlights Mandukhai's loneliness and predicament that she is officially bound to a child, leaving her unable to pursue a fulfilling relationship with a man.

The use of percussion is notable in Jantsannorov's score, not only because of its scope and variety but also because of the nod to history provided by the timpani during the battle scenes. In the thirteenth-century chronicle *The Secret History of the Mongols* drums are mentioned five times, with reference to them being used in battle during the reign of Chinggis Khaan.[5] Jantsannorov also uses percussion with note clusters, stinger chords and drones in the strings to create striking sounds during the scenes when Ismel is plotting against Mandukhai and scenes of characters' deaths.

Throughout the Socialist era, the celebration of traditional customs from shamanism to *Naadam* was suppressed, and reverence for Chinggis Khaan was replaced with devotion to Lenin and Sükhbaatar. Through Jantsannorov's score, Mongolians regained access to sporting songs (*uukhai*), shaman's rituals and traditional vocal techniques in a respectful and celebratory context, rather than their being presented on screen as an outdated lifestyle waiting to be liberated by socialism. His score combined European and Mongolian, and ancient and modern musical elements in innovative ways, creating a nostalgic celebration of a lost history made relevant to twentieth-century film audiences, reminding Mongolians of traditions that had been overshadowed by socialism for over sixty years.

---

[5]   See Anon., 1982, pp. 40, 42, 169, 170 and 220.

106 *Mongolian Film Music*

Dancing Like Capitalists: Popular Music Comes to Mongolia

Whilst the Film Factory was producing introspective urban dramas and Jantsannorov was developing his idiosyncratic compositional style, the consumption of popular music increased gradually as the government reduced previous strictures on this genre. Popular music was discouraged and largely unavailable in Mongolia until the 1970s, although it had never been outlawed officially. The socialist regime made performing and listening to popular music almost impossible by promoting, broadcasting, funding, and providing training only for genres of music the government deemed acceptable: classical (*songodog khögjim*), military bands, professional music and new folk music (*ardyn khögjim* and *yazguur khögjim*). Large ensembles such as orchestras and professional folk troupes were compatible with the idea of collectivisation, whereas small pop or rock bands were associated with capitalism and decadence. It was difficult for Mongolians to establish pop and rock bands modelled on the likes of The Beatles or the Rolling Stones, since access to musical instruments such as guitars and drum kits was limited and only members of the Mongolian Composers' Union, who followed strict socialist guidelines, could get music performed or even rehearsed.

In the late 1960s, the Minister of Culture and author of the novel *The Clear River Tamir* Lodoidamba visited the United Kingdom, where he heard the music of The Beatles. On his return to Mongolia, he asked the government to provide support for popular music. In the 1960s and 1970s, several Mongolians studied at the University of Leeds on cultural exchanges funded by United Nations scholarships and the British Council. Although the Mongolians in question were carefully selected by the MPRP to be trusted to maintain socialist ideals, they too encountered The Beatles and other pop and rock bands and took cassettes back to Ulaanbaatar. At this time, it was rare for Mongolians to own music in the form of cassette recordings; the government still had control over what the public listened to and when, since music was available only via radio, television, cinema or concerts. Only after the cultural exchanges and acquisition of cassettes did it become possible for some Mongolians to listen to the popular music of the West, even though some composers such as Luvsansharav had desired it for some time. Speaking of the early 1960s, Luvsansharav (INT) said, 'Many film composers were curious about Western popular music. I was interested in listening to these modern styles too, just to listen, that's all. But we could not listen to popular music in public. All I wanted to do was listen but we were not allowed.'

As a result of these prominent personalities' interest in popular music, the MPRP finally allowed it in Mongolia, albeit strictly regulated. In 1971, the first state rock band, Soyol Erdene (lit. Cultural Treasure) was founded by the Ministry of Culture and managed by the Mongolian Philharmony, which was also home to the State Symphony Orchestra. Soyol Erdene was an early example of the manufactured pop group and everything from their lyrics to their image was carefully crafted and monitored. Manufactured pop groups were by no means a phenomenon of Mongolia, and similar bands existed worldwide at the time, notably The Monkees in the USA. Soyol Erdene and other pop and rock groups that followed would have appealed to Mongolia's predominantly young population.

An underground popular music scene in which individuals played home-made instruments in secret had begun in Ulaanbaatar in the mid-1960s, and from the early 1970s it started to gain momentum. I interviewed producer of popular music and journalist B. Dolgion in Ulaanbaatar in 2008, and he told me about his involvement in the underground popular music scene. Whilst Soyol Erdene was giving official performances, groups of amateur musicians such as Dolgion met unofficially in discreet locations to play popular music, including cover versions of Western pop songs to which they had access and some original compositions. Dolgion formed a band called Ineemseglel (Smile), whose line-up included himself on guitar, his sister B. Angirmaa on vocals and the drummer Lkhagvadorj Balkhjav, all of whom remained prominent figures in the Mongolian popular music industry. Dolgion has worked as a producer of popular music, founded Mongolia's first music television channel and was the presenter of the reality television singing competition *Universe Best Songs* in 2009. Angirmaa has worked as a singer, songwriter, film composer and manager for a number of Mongolian girl groups, and Balkhjav has worked as a film composer and songwriter in addition to being the General Director of Ulaanbaatar-based television channel UBS Television. Meanwhile, in the Soviet Union, pop and rock bands that had similarly played in secret began to perform in public, and the first rock festival in Soviet history, named Spring Rhythms, took place in Tbilisi in 1980.

Although instruments associated with popular music genres, such as saxophones and guitars, had featured within orchestral cues as early as the 1960s in films such as *City Slicker* (*Niislel Khüü*, 1968), it was the mid-1970s when popular music ensembles appeared in soundtracks. One of the first occurrences was in the 1975 film *An Unforgettable Autumn* (*Martagdashgüi Namar*) about teenagers on a compulsory work placement in the countryside. During the Socialist era, groups of teenage school children used to be sent to work at herding collectives for two months every autumn. The film features a scene in which some of the teenagers are dancing whilst listening to an instrumental piece on the radio, with the melody and chords based on jazz modes and featuring a saxophone solo, electric bass, guitar, keyboard and drum kit. As they dance, another group of children appears and one says, 'Why are you dancing like capitalists? Our teachers say this is rubbish.' Although the MPRP had finally allowed popular styles in film soundtracks, it did so with an element of caution by retaining the attitude that it was a bad influence on socialist society.

Throughout the 1980s, popular music was heard more regularly in film soundtracks, especially those scored by Dambiinyamyn Janchiv (b. 1940), Zunduin Khangal (1948–96) and Altankhuyag. The spectrum of popular genres in film soundtracks expanded to include disco, progressive rock and psychedelic rock, with bands such as Boney M and Pink Floyd being popular choices, and Mongolian film composers began to emulate these styles. Likewise, in the Soviet Union, the bands that had formed the pre-perestroika underground rock scene,

108 *Mongolian Film Music*

which was particularly prominent in Leningrad, made appearances in Soviet film soundtracks.

During the final years of the 1980s further pop and rock bands were established in Mongolia, including Chinggis Khaan, Kharanga (Gong) and Khonkh (Bell). Prior to the introduction of popular music in Mongolia, the main foreign musical influences were those from the Soviet Union. Through the appearance of popular music since the 1960s and 1970s, Mongolians gained access to musical and cultural influences from the West that had previously been denied. The burgeoning popular music scene was initially present only in Ulaanbaatar; since capital cities tend to have greater trade links with other countries, they generally have more access to the music of those countries too. Towards the end of the decade, Ulaanbaatar-based musicians who had formerly played popular music in secret were finally afforded more freedom to express themselves musically.

Whereas Jantsannorov's score to *Mandukhai the Wise Queen* was a reimagination of the past, another film was produced the following year that depicted an imagined future: *Whirlpool*, whose soundtrack contained a number of cues of popular music. The main character was neither a socialist hero like Sükhbaatar nor a struggling member of the proletariat, but a lead singer of a rock band, and the score by Altankhuyag was similarly seditious.

Looking to the Future: Jumdaan, Altankhuyag and a Delinquent Rock Star

> I felt like a crazy person making this film [*Whirlpool*], a crazy person against craziness!
>
> Jumdaan, INT

One year after directing *Mandukhai the Wise Queen*, Baljinnyam wrote the screenplay for a controversial and unashamedly anti-socialist film, *Whirlpool*. He worked on this film with the prolific cinematographer Delgeriin Battulga, who had provided the cinematography for *The Clear River Tamir*, and the director Jumdaan, who had worked on *Mandukhai the Wise Queen* as team leader for the stuntmen on horseback. Along with his predecessors Tsogzol and Dorjpalam, Jumdaan had trained at the VGIK Film Institute in Moscow, and the film's composer, Altankhuyag, had trained at the Sofia Conservatoire in Bulgaria.

Due to glasnost and the consequent relaxation of censorship in the Soviet Union, filmmakers there began to produce films in stark contrast to the celebratory socialist realist cinema of previous decades. These films of the 1980s became known as the Soviet Black Wave and depicted the darker side of society including crime, violence and alcoholism, and many of them were scored with rock music from the erstwhile underground rock music scene.[6] Likewise, *Whirlpool* was a dark and violent film that criticised socialism strongly and utilised pop and rock

---

[6] See Egorova, 1997, pp. 273–80.

music in the soundtrack. Whereas *Mandukhai the Wise Queen* offered a rare opportunity to celebrate lost customs, *Whirlpool* offered a glimpse of a possible alternative future.

I interviewed the film's director, Jumdaan, in Ulaanbaatar in November 2008. He spoke good English, which he learned after 1990 by working on films. Jumdaan studied double bass at the State College of Music and Dance in Ulaanbaatar but his musical career was cut short when he broke his fingers whilst practising kendo, a Japanese martial art, which he now teaches to the Mongolian police force for a living. He consequently switched to filmmaking, and studied film directing in Moscow between 1980 and 1986, throughout the perestroika era from its conception to its implementation and during the Soviet Black Wave. In 1987, a year after he had returned to Mongolia, he directed his first film, *The Stranger* (*Khünii Khün*). The music was composed by his fellow student in Moscow and good friend Tseden-Ishiin Chinzorig (1953–2002), who shared Jumdaan's anti-socialist sentiments aroused during the perestroika years. In some ways *The Stranger* is typical of films of the 1980s in that it deals with relationship problems, specifically those of an alcoholic man, Tseveen, whose wife leaves him on account of his alcoholic tendencies. The anti-socialist sentiment of the film is expressed mainly via Tseveen's rebellious friend Badarch, who complains to his university lecturers about socialist policies and claims his fellow students share his opinions but are too afraid to speak up. Chinzorig's score includes diegetic pop songs during party scenes, modern orchestral cues with discords and note clusters, vibraphone solos and an electronic version of the English tune *Greensleeves*. The young rebellious protagonist and the electronic version of a folk melody were two of the key ideas at the core of Jumdaan's next film, *Whirlpool*. In 1988, Jumdaan's experience as the team leader for mounted stuntmen in *Mandukhai the Wise Queen* provided him with further inspiration and experience in working on a film that did not directly promote socialist ideology.

The plot of *Whirlpool* is as follows. After a rock concert, the lead singer of the band, Batbold, sees a female fan being attacked by a gang of rapists outside the venue. He saves the girl, Khulan, and she consequently falls in love with him. In a dreamlike sequence, Batbold is woken the following morning by the voice of his computer telling him to get out of his home. The walls of his *ger* promptly disappear, leaving Batbold in an open space littered with debris. He then goes to a sauna with his band members and some groupies, where they take drugs. Although drugs are not mentioned explicitly during this part of the film, everyone present in the sauna takes a tablet and they consequently behave in a manner that suggests the tablets were hallucinogens.

Khulan is now infatuated, and is soon drawn in to the brutal and hedonistic world of Batbold and his recalcitrant band members. During a surreal sequence, Khulan watches quietly as the boys dance around a campfire on a mountain, performing deviant versions of traditional Mongolian rituals: they cut themselves and pour their blood into a silver cup, parodying a rite in which milk should be poured. Khulan then follows Batbold to a house party, during which he is beaten up until he passes out as part of an initiation ceremony into a gang. When Batbold comes round, he is welcomed into the gang and he departs the party happily, leaving Khulan, who is being harassed by gang members, to fend for herself. Batbold later confesses that he orchestrated the attempted rape at the rock concert in order to meet her. She responds by telling him he is like a robot with no soul.

Khulan introduces Batbold to her family but he wishes to keep their relationship a secret. Later that night, Khulan cuts Batbold's long hair whilst he sleeps. When he wakes up, he is horrified and seeks revenge by pouring a jug of boiling water over her face, scalding her badly. Batbold is put on trial for assaulting Khulan. In court, he makes an impassioned speech to the judges about how socialism has reduced people to an army of robots. The heavily bandaged Khulan is called to testify against him but she does not want him to be sentenced; she claims that she is his heart.

Jumdaan told me with a hint of both amusement and pride that *Whirlpool* had divided the critics when it was released in 1989. He was glad that people liked his film and somewhat pleased that it provoked such a reaction. He said of the many reviews and articles written about the film that approximately half appreciated its defiance of socialism whilst the remainder found the violence, iconoclasm, and candid attack on the political regime disconcerting. This divide in opinion may be indicative of the ratio of opponents to supporters of socialism in Mongolia in the late 1980s. The diminishing morals of Soviet citizens that Gorbachev wanted to challenge through perestroika – such as partying, drinking, drug taking and iconoclastic behaviour – were glorified in *Whirlpool*. The desire for a Mongolian equivalent to perestroika was felt amongst many Mongolians at this time, and numerous articles about restructuring appeared in the party newspaper *Ünen* throughout 1989 (Kaplonski, 2010, p. 1,045). Following decades of cinema portraying socialist heroes, Batbold, a delinquent rock star, was the ultimate anti-hero. He is portrayed as a victim of socialism, on which his cruel behaviour is blamed; however, through his participation in formerly suppressed activities such as singing rock music, he also represents freedom.

Whirlpool had already caused a stir during the shooting stage, when Jumdaan filmed a scene that presented Mongolian life as equivalent to that in Europe and more affluent Asian countries. Approximately 90 percent of cars in Mongolia in the 1980s were older Russian models, and it was only diplomats who owned newer Japanese, Korean or European cars. Jumdaan (INT) told me he wanted to film a scene that would make Ulaanbaatar look more cosmopolitan and 'less like a Russian colony'. He asked the police to stop the traffic at the main crossroads in Ulaanbaatar for a whole hour so he could usher the newer cars into the scene. The main crossroads is the intersection between what is now called Peace Avenue and Chinggis Avenue, near the Central Post Office, and has always been one of the busiest in Mongolia, so stopping the traffic for an hour would have caused major disruptions. He filmed the scene successfully but it made him temporarily unpopular with Ulaanbaatar's motorists. Jumdaan (INT) claims there is 'a strong Western influence in this film. People at the time wanted what Western countries had.'

Jumdaan's idea of presenting desirable material possessions is supported by Batbold owning a computer, an item very few Mongolians had at the time. The influence of capitalist countries, however, was not limited to shots of expensive cars and defiance of Soviet-inspired politics; it was also heavily present in the score.

Before *Whirlpool*, Altankhuyag had previously combined different musical styles in his score for the 1987 film *At the End of the Tale* (*Ülger Duussan Khoino*), in which a cue of professional music returns in a later scene with added drum kit. In *Whirlpool*, Altankhuyag further developed the use of popular music in films by combining it with traditional Mongolian music in certain cues. The *Whirlpool* soundtrack incorporates a wide variety of music genres, including pop and rock songs by bands such as Pink Floyd and The Beatles, pop ballads and rock songs composed by Altankhuyag, electronic keyboards, a traditional Mongolian folk song, and solos for traditional vocal styles and instruments accompanied by symphony orchestra. There are also two cues of electronic versions of famous European classical music pieces. What is also noteworthy about the music of *Whirlpool* is the absence of the genres that had become customary in Mongolian film scoring, such as military bands and new folk music. The strong presence of popular music and conspicuous lack of the conventional music genres of Mongolian cinema indicates the shifting trends of preferred music styles in 1989, which concurs with Jumdaan's words (INT), 'People at the time wanted what Western countries had.'

The opening cue of the film is a piece of rock music, performed diegetically by Batbold's band. Given that rock music in Mongolia had been taboo for the majority of the Socialist era, and was associated with youth, subculture and rebellious attitude, this cue sets the atmosphere appropriately for the rest of the film. Since rock music had been introduced when Mongolians visited Western countries and subsequently impelled the government to support it, it had become a symbol of citizens pressurising the government to forge stronger links with the rest of the world.

The popular songs by well-known bands used in the film are *Let It Be* (1970) by The Beatles, *The Happiest Days of Our Lives* from Pink Floyd's progressive rock concept album *The Wall* (1979) and Jan Hammer's instrumental *Crockett's Theme* from the American television series *Miami Vice*, which was released as a single and reached the Top 10 in numerous European countries in 1987. These songs are used during the party scene in which Batbold is initiated into the gang, thereby creating the impression that Western popular styles had become the preferred genres amongst young Mongolians during parties, whereas previously it was customary for people to sing traditional songs at social gatherings. A version of Mozart's *Rondo alla Turca* for electronic keyboard and drum kit is heard in the scene in which Batbold, his band members and the groupies take (hallucinogenic) tablets in the sauna, and a similar arrangement of Bizet's *Carmen* accompanies a scene of Batbold and the gang gambling. These distortions of well-known classical pieces highlight the theme of insubordination and add to the element of the grotesque within the film. These latter two cues are reminiscent of Wendy

Carlos's electronic versions of Beethoven's ninth symphony and Rossini's *William Tell Overture* in Stanley Kubrick's *A Clockwork Orange* (1971), which are used ironically to represent the delinquent protagonist's state of mind, although Jumdaan and Altankhuyag may not have been familiar with this film.

Of the few orchestral cues in *Whirlpool*, most appear in the scenes when Batbold and Khulan are alone. Since the mood of these scenes is generally unhappy, Altankhuyag has eschewed the filmic cliché of composing slow orchestral melodies with lush string accompaniments for love scenes. He uses equivalent lush string passages and leisurely paced melodies ironically to highlight their one-sided and troubled relationship. The scenes in question include Batbold's confession to orchestrating the attempted rape and Batbold's visit to Khulan's family in the countryside, when he rides a horse badly, demonstrating that he is a modern city boy at heart rather than a typical traditional Mongolian. Orchestral music is also used in conjunction with long-song when Batbold has the vision of the walls of his *ger* disappearing. The use of this traditional vocal technique during a scene in which the traditional Mongolian home is destroyed is in keeping with the iconoclastic imagery of the film and foreshadows the boys' deviant execution of traditional rituals later in the story.

Jumdaan told me he chose the folk song *Khar Torgon Khamjaar* (*Black Silk* Deel *Piping*)[7] for use within *Whirlpool* on account of its subject matter of unrequited love. The lyrics tell the story of a girl who makes a beautiful silk *deel* in order to attract a boy. The boy, however, is not interested and he eventually forms a relationship with another woman, leaving the girl with the *deel* heartbroken. There is a clear comparison between the girl in the song and Khulan's unrequited love for Batbold. Altankhuyag composed a number of variations on the *Khar Torgon Khamjaar* melody for *Whirlpool*, including a complete rendition for solo female voice with orchestral accompaniment, which was used as the film song.

The folk song is first heard the morning after the feigned attempted rape at the rock concert, emanating from Batbold's computer one note at a time in a robotic manner. This is the first of numerous references throughout the film to Batbold metaphorically turning into a robot. When Batbold confesses he set up the attempted rape, the folk song reappears on the horse-head fiddle with electronic keyboard accompaniment. One of the most striking cues in which the folk song is employed, however, occurs during the scene when Batbold wakes up to discover Khulan has cut his long hair. When Batbold looks at Khulan sleeping soundly, the folk-song melody is played on the horse-head fiddle. When he looks in the mirror at his short hair, discords played on an electronic keyboard are heard. He looks alternately between the sleeping Khulan and the mirror, and the music alternates between the folk song and the electronic chords. The cue stops abruptly when Batbold reaches for the jug and throws boiling water on Khulan's face. The subject matter of the lyrics of *Khar Torgon Khamjaar* associates the song clearly

---

[7] Piping refers to the decorative sewn border on a *deel*, the unisex traditional Mongolian robe.

with Khulan, whilst Altankhuyag's treatment of the melody – scoring it first for computer tones then finally alternating it with electronic keyboard discords – represents Batbold's attitude towards her.

The innovative ways Altankhuyag combined the folk song with electronic and computerised music further develops previous combinations of traditional music with symphonic music. Mongolian composers had been heavily influenced by and trained in the Soviet Union for decades and had combined Soviet music with their own musical traditions. In the late 1980s, Mongolian composers such as Altankhuyag started to combine Mongolian traditional music with that of their new place of inspiration: the West.

Both *Mandukhai the Wise Queen* and *Whirlpool* echoed and simultaneously aroused public attitudes at the end of the 1980s in Mongolia by representing two sides of the same anti-socialist coin. The Ministry of Internal Affairs is thanked in the final credits of *Mandukhai the Wise Queen*, suggesting the film had governmental backing, yet Baljinnyam and Jantsannorov managed to express anti-socialist feeling through the celebration of lost traditions and a history that had been ignored by the socialist regime. *Whirlpool*, on the other hand, was deliberately subversive, and negative attitudes towards the socialist regime were expressed explicitly in the screenplay. In *Mandukhai the Wise Queen*, the use of traditional musical instruments, the depiction of an historical figure uniting warring Mongolian factions and the portrayal of customs that had been suppressed during the Socialist era appealed to people's nostalgia for lost traditions. The use of popular and rock music in *Whirlpool* in conjunction with the portrayal of the rebellious anti-hero and cosmopolitan imagery became part of the subversive Zeitgeist in the twilight years of the Socialist era.

Foreshadowing the Fall of Socialism in Mongolia

Jantsannorov had worked in prominent official positions and had already composed film scores incorporating the symphonic compositional techniques he had learned in Kiev before perestroika led to the monumental change in his thinking and musical style. Jumdaan, on the other hand, had already been influenced by perestroika before he made his first film. Gorbachev's economic and cultural reforms, therefore, incited a desire for independence from Soviet influence in people who were already established workers of the Mongolian film industry and those who had yet to make their first film. After decades of films glorifying Sükhbaatar and socialist progress, it was a fifteenth-century queen and a delinquent rock star who provided challenging and subversive images of lost traditions and future possibilities, and it fell to Jantsannorov and Altankhuyag to score befitting music. The scores for *Mandukhai the Wise Queen* and *Whirlpool* were largely devoid of music associated with the genres that had been promoted by the socialist regime, and it was the past and the future respectively that provided inspiration.

Aided by Jantsannorov's reimagination of fifteenth-century Mongolian music, *Mandukhai the Wise Queen* appealed to a reimagined past, a past that socialism had attempted to erase or modify. The twentieth-century thinking behind Jantsannorov's historical score made his nostalgic reimagined past relevant to audiences in 1988 and beyond. *Whirlpool* appealed to an imagined future, in which Mongolians drive expensive cars, own computers, listen to rock music and participate freely in activities the socialist state had never approved of. The soundtrack, which includes computerised music, British pop and rock songs, and a Mongolian folk song mixed with electronic sounds, was relevant to those Mongolians who wanted to move forward and who wanted, as Jumdaan (INT) stated, 'what Western countries had'.

Although the two scores were musically dissimilar, both composers were making the same point: it was time for the end of the socialist regime and for the resurgence of traditional Mongolian music in a modern way. Not all Mongolians agreed with Jantsannorov's and Jumdaan's sentiments, however, and there were many who still supported socialism. Yet the film viewers who had tired of socialism by the late 1980s could relate to the portrayal of the past and the future in these two film scores, especially since the present they had tired of was conspicuously absent from both.

Chapter 7

New Directions: The Democratic Revolution and the Aftermath of the Socialist Era

Around the time Jantsannorov was composing his first film scores and Jumdaan was learning the art of filmmaking in Moscow, another Mongolian student, Sanjaasürengiin Zorig (1962–98), was studying philosophy and social science at Moscow State University and was equally influenced by perestroika. After returning to Mongolia, he spearheaded a series of (largely) peaceful demonstrations in Ulaanbaatar at the turn of the decade, which provided the catalyst for the Democratic Revolution in 1990 and the end of the Mongolian socialist regime. Mongolia's consequent independence from Soviet influence and move towards democracy had relatively little impact on the Soviet Union, which was in the process of being dismantled throughout the period of demonstrations in Ulaanbaatar. The end of the Socialist era in both Mongolia and the Soviet Union resulted in drastic changes within the Mongolian music and film industries and manifold new directions in film composition.

The Sound of a Bell and a Musical Revolution: Zorig and the Fall of Socialism

After graduating from Moscow State University in 1985, Zorig returned to Mongolia and in the following year became a lecturer at the National University of Mongolia. Inspired by what he had seen in Moscow, he discussed the need for political change in Mongolia with his students and colleagues. In 1988, the year *Mandukhai the Wise Queen* was released, Zorig and his associates placed anti-government posters around Ulaanbaatar. Meetings and secret yet peaceful activity against the socialist regime continued until December 1989, when the protest became public. On 10 December 1989, celebrations were due to take place in Sükhbaatar Square for International Human Rights Day but instead of the customary military marches, song and dance performances and political speeches, Zorig and approximately two hundred associates marched through the city centre with banners emblazoned with slogans calling for reform. The protestors wanted changes equivalent to those proposed by Gorbachev in the Soviet Union, namely *il tod* (glasnost) and *öörchlön baiguulalt* (perestroika). The rock band Khonkh accompanied the protest with their song *Khonkhny Duu* (*The Sound of a Bell*), which became the unofficial anthem of the pro-democratic demonstrations. The protest was peaceful and, due to Gorbachev's call for freedom of speech and

116   *Mongolian Film Music*

the international outrage at the handling of the Tiananmen Square protest in Beijing in June 1989, the Mongolian police and military were not called to disperse the crowd (Rossabi, 2005, pp. 1–24).

Another significant demonstration took place in Sükhbaatar Square on 21 January 1990, during which the actor and singer Dogmidyn Sosorbaram (b. 1958) led the crowd in renditions of folk songs in praise of Chinggis Khaan. This was one of the first public displays of admiration for Chinggis Khaan since 1921 other than *Mandukhai the Wise Queen*. From February 1990 groups of Mongolians started to form their own political parties and on 22 February protestors took down the statue of Stalin from outside the state library.[1] On 7 March, 10 men wearing traditional costume went on hunger strike in Sükhbaatar Square and were later joined by several university students and monks from Gandan monastery, the only working monastery in Mongolia at the time. This protest continued into the following day, during which violence broke out, one person died and several were injured. The Politburo resigned in March, and the series of demonstrations came to an end in May when the MPRP announced there would be a free election in Mongolia in July (Rossabi, 2005). Political activists consequently concentrated on the election campaign rather than protesting; however, the new political parties had no experience of campaigning and little money for publicity. Furthermore, the opposition parties did not unite, which would have greatly improved their chances of success in the election. The MPRP gained the overall majority during the July 1990 election and remained in power. Nonetheless, from the election onwards, Mongolia was no longer a Soviet satellite and no longer a socialist country, and the monopoly of the state film studio over Mongolian film and film scoring came to an unexpected end.

Mongolia and the Dissolution of the Soviet Union

The withdrawal of Soviet troops from Mongolia as a consequence of improved Sino-Soviet relations had started as early as 1986, and this heralded the waning Soviet interest in Mongolian affairs. Furthermore, epoch-making changes occurred throughout the Eastern Bloc from the late 1980s, which contributed to the Soviet Union turning its attention away from Mongolia. These included demonstrations against Soviet rule in the Baltic States as early as 1987 and the fall of the Berlin Wall in November 1989, one month before the first pro-democracy demonstration in Ulaanbaatar. In the spring of 1990, when the demonstrations in Mongolia were well under way, Lithuania became the first Soviet republic to declare independence

---

[1] The 7-metre statue of Stalin was subsequently placed inside Ismuss nightclub on Peace Avenue, the main street in Ulaanbaatar, but was removed in early 2009 to make more space on the dance floor.

New Directions

and protests took place in Belarus. In 1991, long after Mongolia had already had its democratic election, a series of demonstrations took place in Moscow.[2]

One of the most significant events in the Soviet Union was the failed coup of 18–21 August 1991, during which party members appointed by Gorbachev and representatives from the military and the KGB formed a State of Emergency Committee whilst Gorbachev was on holiday. The Committee demanded, amongst other things, a ban on strikes and demonstrations and a return to pre-perestroika governing. The coup failed in part because Gorbachev refused to comply, although he lost public credibility since it was he who had appointed the Committee members to their governmental positions. The person who reaped the greatest advantages was Russian president Boris Yeltsin, who publicly resisted the coup and came across as a strong leader (Strayer, 1998, pp. 187–96)

Within a fortnight of the failed coup, Latvia and Estonia's independence was recognised, and Ukraine, Belarus and Moldavia (now called Moldova) declared independence. Throughout the following four months, referendums were held and an overwhelming majority in all the remaining Soviet republics voted in favour of independence (Marples, 2004).[3] The newly independent republics became known collectively as the Commonwealth of Independent States on 10 December 1991, exactly two years to the day after Zorig and his associates demonstrated for the first time in Ulaanbaatar. Gorbachev resigned on 25 December, an agreement to dissolve the Soviet Union was made on 26 December and the following day, Yeltsin took over from Gorbachev. By the end of 1991, the Soviet Union no longer existed.

The exact reasons why the Soviet Union and its satellite states moved away from socialism have always been and are likely always to be hotly debated. Yet since the dissolution of the Soviet Union, the Mongolian film and music industries could no longer be influenced directly by the country's former elder brother, whether people wanted this to be the case or not. Although Mongolia officially loosened its ties with the Soviet Union after July 1990, there were no ties whatsoever by the end of 1991, since the Soviet Union had ceased to be.

Opportunities and Losses after July 1990

After July 1990, there was much economic, political and societal disarray in Mongolia whilst people became accustomed to the fall of the socialist regime, the transition to democracy and the influx of new opportunities this brought about. The change in the political system and the move towards a market economy from July 1990 meant that the State Film Head Office (*Ulsyn Kinony Yerönkhii Gazar*, formerly the Film Factory) was no longer the only film studio, and film composers were not obliged to be members of the Mongolian Composers' Union.

---

[2] For further information, see Marples, 2004.

[3] Ibid.

Although the state film studio and Mongolian Composers' Union continued to operate, new independent film studios and film composers unaffiliated to the Mongolian Composers' Union began to emerge. The loss of state control over the film industry and the depletion of state funding meant that filmmaking and film composition changed irrevocably, and a plethora of low-budget, low-quality films were produced hastily.

With very few exceptions, each film of the Socialist era was scored by only one composer, whereas after 1990 film soundtracks were often a collaborative effort. The government no longer stipulated the themes of films or the preferred genres of music for the soundtracks. The result was greater artistic freedom and increased opportunities for those who wished to be part of the film industry but had not been chosen as state workers at the Film Factory. Furthermore, Mongolia was now open to influences from the cinema and music industries of Western Europe and elsewhere in Asia as well as America. On the other hand, the dissolution of the Soviet Union and the change in the political system of Mongolia meant that the film industry was not supported by the generous funding, comprehensive training programmes or guaranteed job opportunities of the Socialist era. The result was the production of low-budget films made with inadequate technology by inexpert personnel who had not been trained in the art of filmmaking or composition. As a result, post-1990 Mongolian film scoring diverged significantly from that of the Socialist era.

Mongolia's transition from socialism to democracy required acclimatisation and came with inevitable teething problems. The post-1990 democratically elected MPRP introduced a series of reforms to facilitate the change to a market-led system and to deal with the financial deficit that followed the withdrawal of Soviet funding and trade. From 1991, the privatisation of state property and the dissolution of collectives began and, as a consequence, many people's incomes decreased, unemployment rose and inflation soared. The lack of public funds meant that standards in education and health provision declined and public buildings that were the pride of the Socialist era started to deteriorate. State support for the arts was reduced or, in some localities, stopped altogether, causing many rural artists, as well as people from former collectives, to move to cities to find work. As a result, urban populations expanded rapidly, particularly the *ger* districts on the outskirts of Ulaanbaatar. Moscow issued Mongolia with a 'bill' of several billion roubles for aid given between 1949 and 1990, and Mongolia responded in 1993 by billing Russia for 'damage' inflicted by Soviet policies (Sanders, 1996, p. 202). Nations other than the former Soviet Union became interested in Mongolia, and foreign charitable organisations and missionaries started to arrive in the country. It was in this context of poverty, social upheaval and increasing interest from foreign organisations that the state film studio, renamed Mongol Kino in 1991, ceased to have monopoly over Mongolian filmmaking, and new filmmakers and composers struggled to make a living in a precarious industry.

Developments in the Music Industry

After July 1990, musicians had the liberty to express themselves free from the confines of censorship and the control of the Mongolian Composers' Union and without the obligation to promote socialist ideology. Opportunities arose for anyone who wished to be a musician and those who had played outlawed genres such as popular music in secret under the socialist regime were now able to perform publicly. Genres previously absent in Mongolia emerged in the 1990s, such as heavy metal and hip-hop, and the popularity or prevalence of certain genres resulted more from the personal choice of citizens rather than governmental backing. Shops began to sell records and cassettes, giving people more choice over what they listened to and when, since they no longer had to rely on the government to provide concerts, radio broadcasts and film screenings as their sole means of listening to music.

On the other hand, the withdrawal of Soviet funding had an impact on musicians' salaries and job opportunities, and many left the music profession to pursue other careers.[4] The state support for musicians during the Socialist era had to all intents and purposes disappeared and formal musical training became the privilege of people born in Ulaanbaatar. There were insufficient funds to accommodate students from rural areas in student dormitories in Ulaanbaatar and there was no longer a programme of sending young rural Mongolians who showed musical potential to foreign conservatoires. As a result, there has recently been less of a nomadic influence on film scoring, since new composers have been mostly born and brought up in Ulaanbaatar.

During the Socialist era, music was recorded only at the state film, radio or television studios, in which state-approved genres such as new folk music (*ardyn khögjim* or *yazguur khögjim*) or symphonic music were recorded. After 1990, numerous independent recording studios were established, many of which recorded the plethora of Mongolian pop and rock bands that had recently emerged. The majority of these studios, however, were poorly equipped and managed, and music producers had little knowledge of music marketing, relying instead on word of mouth to distribute their recordings. Consequently, many independent studios ceased to operate after producing only a small number of records.

Whereas official performing artists of the Socialist era were considered workers of the state and others had to perform in secret, the post-Socialist era saw the advent of Mongolia's first stars and idols and the notion of celebrity, especially within the popular music scene. After 1990, popular music began to be performed regularly in bars, clubs, cafés and hotels, many of which host resident bands. Ulaanbaatar has become home to a flourishing live popular music scene, in which

---

[4] It should be noted that many Mongolians wanted to work in the film and music industries during the Socialist era but did not get the opportunity to do so. There are others who worked in these industries only briefly, as was the case with the eight composers who composed only one film score each.

120   *Mongolian Film Music*

live bands and solo artists can be seen each evening around the city and concerts are advertised in local newspapers, with posters and on the radio. Yet whilst some artists prospered, others faded into obscurity due to lack of funding, contacts and popular acclaim.

During the latter part of the Socialist era, some Mongolians had had exposure to Western popular music such as The Beatles, yet it was only after the fall of the socialist regime that Mongolia became involved in and influenced by the popular music activity of other parts of East Asia. Canto-pop, the popular music of Hong Kong, grew in popularity in Mongolia during the 1990s, and by the early 2000s Mongolia embraced the Korean Wave (Korean: *hanryu*), a musical phenomenon in which K-pop (Korean popular music) became hugely popular and influential across East Asia.

The music genres that were prominent during the Socialist era continued to exist in Mongolia after 1990 but have become somewhat overshadowed by the developments in local and incoming popular music, especially amongst younger people, who make up the majority of the population. The Mongolian Military Song and Dance Academic Ensemble and the State Symphony Orchestra have continued to operate after 1990, although their output has been significantly reduced, in particular their tours to the countryside. The post-1990 repertoire of the opera and ballet theatres is similar to that of the Socialist era in that Mongolian national operas and Russian ballets are performed regularly, but audiences attend by choice rather than being escorted by bosses and school teachers. Although the Mongolian National Song and Dance Academic Ensemble remains the largest ensemble of folk music (*yazguur khögjim*), several private ensembles have appeared in Ulaanbaatar since 1990, such as the Saryn Chuluun (Moonstone) and Tümen Ekh (Mother of the Ten Thousand) ensembles. These are full-time professional folk music troupes, consisting of musicians trained at the State College of Music and Dance, and with audiences largely made up of tourists and foreign visitors. Both the Saryn Chuluun and Tümen Ekh ensembles rehearse for six months of the year during the winter and perform daily for the other six months, when there are more foreign visitors and tourists in Mongolia. Nyamsüren (INT), *yoochin* player in the Tümen Ekh ensemble, told me that on evenings when the audience comprises mostly foreigners they play new Mongolian folk pieces whereas they tend to perform adaptations of Western pieces such as Mozart's *Rondo Alla Turca* for Mongolian audiences. During the Socialist era, folk music developed to cater to governmental ideas; the cessation of state support for folk music troupes after 1990 and the consequent dependence on foreign revenue through ticket sales led to musicians adjusting their repertoire to suit the tastes of foreign visitors.

Immediately after 1990, there was an upsurge in Mongolian patriotism, as the country came to terms with its dissociation from the Soviet Union. Traditional Mongolian systems of belief such as shamanism and Buddhism were practised once more with greater freedom, *Tsagaan Sar* (Mongolian New Year) was celebrated openly as the main event in the Mongolian calendar along with the *Naadam* festival, and the horse-head fiddle became an iconic figure. Horse-head fiddle maker Ulambayar (INT), who established a horse-head fiddle factory in Ulaanbaatar in 1990, told me, 'Lots of people wanted to do something traditionally Mongolian at this time [1990] so I decided to make horse-head fiddles. I wanted to change life [for Mongolians], to move away from the Soviet Union, so I established the horse-head fiddle factory in the same year as the Democratic Revolution.' Ulambayar has worked continuously to develop the instrument but says that he always combines his innovations with what he describes as traditional craft. He has recently made a horse-head fiddle with machine heads rather than tuning pegs, since they make it easier to tune the instrument.[5]

In 1991, Jantsannorov composed concerti for the *shanz* and *yoochin*. His reasons for doing so were partly due to the economic problems in Mongolia, which made it too expensive for larger-scale symphonic works to be performed, and partly because 'people at this time wanted to listen to this kind of music, music with traditional instruments' (Jantsannorov, INT). In 1992, the Mongolian Horse-Head Fiddle Ensemble was established officially. Its repertoire consists of adaptations of traditional Mongolian pieces, European classical pieces by composers such as Mozart and Bach, and new compositions by Jantsannorov and Sharav. Throughout the Socialist era, the government had steered Mongolia towards an idealistic future, whilst the embracing of popular music after 1990 symbolised a desire for a more global future. In contrast, after 1990 many Mongolians looked back to the traditions of their past but, as is the case with Ulambayar's horse-head fiddle with machine heads, a traditional past with a modern twist.

Developments in the Film Industry

Since 1990, the state film studio, renamed Mongol Kino in 1991, has continued to operate and to receive government funding, albeit reduced, and much of its output has consisted of short documentary films both for archive purposes and for public broadcast. After the withdrawal of Soviet aid, the studio had very little money to update its filmmaking technology so many of these documentaries were filmed in black and white, and of the twenty feature films produced between 1991 and 2000, five were filmed in black and white. Mongol Kino's output of feature films diminished throughout the decade: it produced four feature films in 1991, eight in 1992, four in 1993, two in 1994, only one the following year and then, after a four-year hiatus, one in 2000. A number of independent studios were established quickly after 1990 and very few of them were commercially successful. Certain studios such as Orchlon Film, Batkhaan and Khiimori Film prospered whilst others suffered from lack of funds and inexperienced management, and produced only one or two films with limited distribution before going out of business. Unlike

---

[5] The use of machine heads on the horse-head fiddle is not an isolated phenomenon. Some West-African koras (21-string harps), for example, are now made with machine heads for ease of tuning and to help them stay in tune when played with other instruments.

122 *Mongolian Film Music*

films of the state film studio, which were stored at the Mongolian Film Archive, films by other studios were not stored anywhere, so they often faded into obscurity soon after being released.

It was not only film production that changed in Mongolia after 1990 but also film viewing. It was not uncommon in the 1990s for people to create makeshift cinemas in their homes with televisions and charge people a few tugriks to watch a film. Government initiatives to disseminate films to the rural population ceased after 1990, so going to the cinema became an urban activity very much based in Ulaanbaatar. The decline in the rural population set against the rising urban population accounted for the increased output of films with urban themes, which were produced to cater to the majority of film viewers. Between 1995 and 2000, the rural population decreased from approximately 1,080,000 to 1,000,000 whereas the Ulaanbaatar population increased from approximately 650,000 to 800,000 (Sneath, 2005, p. 142). After 1990, parties of workers and school children were no longer escorted to the cinema *en masse* so it was the responsibility of filmmakers to attract audiences, and their lack of experience in doing so often resulted in low audience numbers. The sudden growth in the number of film studios and the more informal and small-scale methods of film dissemination had an effect on the quality of the films being produced.

After 1990, Mongolians had access to an increasingly wider range of films. Hollywood and Japanese films gained popularity and, in a similar manner to the trends in popular music, films from Hong Kong became widespread in the 1990s and those from Korea in the 2000s. Mongolian television channels had little funds to produce new programmes, so foreign films and drama serials were broadcast regularly. Mongolian filmmakers were influenced by the genres of these foreign films, in stark contrast to the Socialist era when film genres and themes were dictated by the five-year plan. Action, martial arts and horror films began to be made after 1990 in addition to dramas and comedies, which had been prominent genres of the Socialist era. Many of these independent films, however, were shot in black and white and produced with inexpensive equipment, making them appear somewhat old-fashioned compared to the films being made at the same time in countries such as Japan and Korea. This made it difficult for Mongolian cinema to compete in the international arena, so films that were successful within Mongolia were not distributed commercially elsewhere. The fall of the socialist regime enabled Mongolian filmmakers to be influenced by East Asian and Western films, but the reverse was not true.

Amongst the foreign-influenced action films and Mongol Kino documentaries, another kind of film emerged in Mongolia, films about Chinggis Khaan, and many of these attracted generous governmental funding and private sponsorship. The first of these, *Eternal Power of the Sky* (*Mönkh Tengeriin Khüchin Dor*), was made in 1992 by the newly established Chinggis Film studio, and such films provided the country with a national hero and a focus that had no links with socialism. The music was composed by Jantsannorov and is very similar in style to his score for *Mandukhai the Wise Queen* (*Mandukhai Tsetsen Khatan*, 1988).

Production of films about Chinggis Khaan peaked between June and December 2006 during the celebrations for the eight-hundredth anniversary of the Mongol State. Mongolians consider 1206, the start of the Mongol Empire (1206–1368), the beginning of the 'state' of Mongolia, or independent Mongolia. In 2006, the government provided Mongol Kino with a generous budget to produce *The Heritage of the Great Leader* (*Ikh Türiin Golomt*), which was the first Mongolian film to use surround sound. The state funding of such films helped to reinstate Chinggis Khaan as a national icon in much the same way as Sükhbaatar had been installed as national hero in the 1940s–1970s.

The 2006 celebrations also included the commissioning of a rock opera, *Chinggis Khaan*, composed by S. Taraa, traditional sporting matches, exhibitions, conferences, workshops, parades, beauty pageants, and theatre and poetry festivals. There were numerous traditional music performances, including one concert involving 800 horse-head fiddle players and 800 long-song (*urtyn duu*) singers on 11 July. A large statue of Chinggis Khaan was built outside the parliament building in Sükhbaatar Square (Figure 7.1)[6] and the airport formerly known as Buyant Ukhaa was renamed Chinggis Khaan International Airport. Many everyday places

Figure 7.1   Chinggis Khaan statue (built in 2006), Sükhbaatar Square, Ulaanbaatar

---

[6] Two years later in 2008, a huge 40-metre statue of Chinggis Khaan on horseback, commonly known as the Chinggis Khaan equestrian statue, was built in Töv province.

and items from streets and buildings to alcoholic beverages, sweets and boxes of matches have since been named after Chinggis Khaan. Numerous Mongolians told me that although they have deep respect for Chinggis Khaan, they believe there is an element of overkill in the trend for naming things after him, and his near deification since 1990 has resulted in the marginalisation of other important Mongolian historical figures. Yet in the immediate post-Socialist era, when the political system of the previous seven decades had proved inefficacious, it is understandable that the population focused on the thirteenth-century warrior. The Mongol Empire under Chinggis Khaan was the glorious empire the Soviet Union and its satellite states failed to become.

The dichotomous experiences of musicians and filmmakers in the wake of the Socialist era were felt equally by Mongolian film composers. New composers brought fresh ideas to film scoring and had more choice over what to compose due to the increased musical influences available in the country and the cessation of governmental control over filmmaking. On the other hand, they suffered similarly to musicians and filmmakers in terms of lack of money and training. Many film composers of the Socialist era failed to find work after 1990, since filmmakers did not have the budget to allow for the orchestral scores they were used to composing. Other film composers quit the profession not only because of a dearth of job opportunities but also because they were disconcerted by the quality of many of the films they were asked to score. Angirmaa, sister of music producer Dolgion and singer in his Socialist-era underground band Ineemseglel (Smile), composed the score for two films in the 2000s. I interviewed her in Ulaanbaatar in 2008, and her story is an example of the perceived poor quality of films discouraging celebrated musicians from working as film composers. She studied at the Tchaikovsky College of Music and Dance in Ulan-Ude in the Soviet Union in the late 1980s but has composed only popular music since graduating in 1990. She was commissioned to compose the scores for *Three Weeks* (*Gurvan Doloo Khonog*, 2001) and *Two Nights, Three Days* (*Khoyor Shönö, Gurvan Ödör*, 2007). On both occasions she began composing the scores with knowledge only of the genres of the films and the main plot lines, and she had neither seen the footage nor read the scripts. On watching the final cut of the films, Angirmaa was dismayed at the overall quality and, on the second occasion, decided to quit the film music business. Speaking about the 2007 film Angirmaa (INT) told me, 'My music would have been more suitable for a better-quality film. That film was so bad it was shameful! I will never compose film music again.' She has subsequently turned down further commissions.

Despite difficulties in Mongolian cinema and film scoring after the fall of the socialist regime, the situation started to improve around 2006 following the government funding of films about Chinggis Khaan. Since then, many films have been produced with increased budgets and newer technology and are comparable to films from Korea, Japan and Hong Kong, at least in terms of picture and sound quality. Films such as *Hello, My Life* (*Sain Uu, Amidral Mini*, 2008), *The Slave's Contract* (*Boolyn Geree*, 2008) and *Enemy of the State* (*Töriin Daisan*, 2009) were blockbusters within Mongolia and are in part responsible for an increased interest amongst Mongolians in films made in Mongolia. In 2008 I interviewed the well-respected Mongol Kino sound engineer Tomoo, who won the Pentatonic Academy Award, a prestigious annual Mongolian music award ceremony, for Best Sound Engineer in 2003 and 2005. He told me:

> The quality of feature films between 1990 and 2005 was not very good. We needed more money to make films; we needed more sponsorship. The quality of films was not as good as it was in the old days. But since 2006 the quality is getting much better. There is a revival of good quality films. People's lives have really changed now. Before, times were really hard, when we changed to a market economy. But now [after 2005] people are getting better educated and they want to watch films, especially Mongolian films. So now when we make a film it becomes popular very quickly. (Tomoo, INT)

Made in Mongolia for Mongolians: Three Trends in Post-1990 Film Scoring

The scoring of post-1990 films made in Mongolia for Mongolian audiences falls broadly into three categories: popular music scores, orchestral scores like those of the Socialist era, and music written for orchestra but scored and produced on computers.

Unlike the Socialist era, when films were produced largely for purposes of propaganda, cinema since 1990 has been a commercial endeavour and filmmakers have had to make shrewd decisions to utilise in-vogue music genres within their soundtracks to help their films gain popularity and consequently make money. As a result, film soundtracks comprising pop, rock and hip-hop music have flourished. As far back as the 1960s, film composers such as Luvsansharav wanted access to popular music even though it was discouraged by the state. After 1990, film composers had both the freedom and commercial incentive to listen to and compose popular music. The soundtracks of the Socialist era had echoed the contemporary political environment in that they comprised Soviet-influenced symphonic music and rousing patriotic revolutionary songs (*khuvsgalyn duu*) advocated by the government. Similarly, after 1990 soundtracks became emblematic of the new market economy in Mongolia in that music was often chosen on the basis of consumer demand. Since pop, rock and hip-hop were becoming fashionable, it made commercial sense for filmmakers to incorporate these genres in their films in order to attract and appeal to audiences.

The popular music used in post-1990 films was a combination of newly composed pieces and pre-existing songs, sometimes Western popular songs released on major record labels. Artistic works created in Mongolia during the Socialist era automatically became the property of the state rather than belonging to the individual artist. The Law of Mongolian Copyright came into force on 22 June 1993, and the copyright of music was included in an amendment of 1999.

Nonetheless, filmmakers throughout the 1990s were not yet in the habit of seeking permission to use music; many failed to adhere to copyright law and numerous songs were used without permission or without royalties being paid to the rightful composers and songwriters. In the context of the economic difficulties in Mongolia in the immediate post-Socialist era, it was considerably cheaper for filmmakers to use pre-existing songs in their soundtracks, unpaid copyright fees notwithstanding, than to commission composers to write original scores.

The use of popular music in film soundtracks was not always a cost-cutting exercise or the result of commercial canniness but often an artistic decision on behalf of the filmmaker. Although popular music was used in all types of films, a variety of rock, pop and hip-hop styles became especially associated with the new film genres, including horror and action films. The 1993 ghost story *Golden Resurrection (Alt Amilakh Tsagaar)* has a score of pop-type ballads composed by veteran film composer Natsagdorj (b. 1951), and the 2006 horror film *The Wall (Khana)* is scored with heavy metal music.[7] Popular music was also used frequently in Mongolian films marketed at younger audiences, such as the 1991 Mongol Kino film about a teenagers' summer camp, *The Wooden Snake (Modon Mogoi)*. Canto-pop and K-pop music was used frequently in the Hong Kong and Korean films that influenced Mongolian filmmakers. Due to the Soviet influence during the Socialist era, the symphony orchestra came to be viewed as the most appropriate instrumentation for film scoring. After 1990, partly due to the Hong Kong and Korean influence, popular music became accepted as a fitting genre for film soundtracks. Modern scoring techniques have become increasingly popular since 2006, and action blockbusters such as *Enemy of the State (Töriin Daisan, 2009)* have utilised state of the art sound design and surround sound.[8]

Orchestral film scores have been composed since 1990, although they are in the minority and have generally been written by veteran film composers of the Socialist era, primarily Jantsannorov and Sharav. The lack of money necessary to produce lavish film scores is the major reason for this decline, although there are a number of other contributory factors. Mongolian composers are no longer obliged to promote socialist ideology by means of music genres advocated by the state. Symphonic music is used infrequently in the soundtracks of the Hong Kong and Korean films that have influenced Mongolian filmmakers since 1990, therefore the symphony orchestra is no longer viewed as the most appropriate instrumentation for film scoring. Furthermore, following the trends in soundtracks of the urban dramas of the 1980s, many composers since 1990 have deemed popular music a better match for modern film topics than the sounds of a symphony orchestra.

---

[7] There are no musicians or composers credited to *The Wall (Khana*, 2006) although the languages of the heavy metal songs in the soundtrack are Mongolian and German.

[8] Sound design is the electronic manipulation of recorded audio to be used in film soundtracks to provide a function similar to that of underscoring. I was present as an observer at the Mongol Kino studios during an editing session on the *Enemy of the State* soundtrack on 29 April 2009.

New Directions 127

The state film studio destroyed its collection of historical film sets and costumes before the end of the Socialist era in order to create storage space. As a result, very few historical films have been made since 1990 because the sets and costumes are too expensive to recreate, thereby making the tradition of scoring historical films with symphonic music redundant. There may be instances of modern film composers wishing to compose for orchestra but lacking the necessary skills, knowledge and opportunity to do so, not to mention the finances or resources, since composers are no longer trained in well-equipped Eastern European conservatoires.

In the context of the resurgence of traditions after 1990, a small number of films were made that celebrated Mongolia's heritage and customs. Similar expressions of patriotism were to be found soon after the dissolution of the Soviet Union in the former Soviet Central Asian Republics, where films were produced in languages such as Kazakh (Dönmez-Colin, 2006, p. 159). Since Mongolia had never been part of the Soviet Union, it had always retained its language, and so the country sought other ways to express its patriotism, including its cinema and film scores. The patriotic Mongolian films that depicted traditions and heroes of the country's pre-socialist past, including the films about Chinggis Khaan, tended to have larger budgets and orchestral scores.

Jantsannorov composed the music for *Champion Horse* (*Tod Magnai*, 1993) and *The Archer* (*Tsets Magnai*, 1995), thereby completing the trilogy on Mongolia's three manly sports, following *The Wrestler* (*Garid Magnai*, 1983). Jantsannorov's music utilised both symphonic and traditional Mongolian instruments, continuing the new style of professional music (*mergejliin khögjim*) he had developed in *Mandukhai the Wise Queen*. The other leading composer of symphonic film scores, Sharav, was born to a musical family in Khentii province in 1952 and studied composition at the Ural Conservatoire in the Soviet Union between 1975 and 1983, after studying in Ulaanbaatar with Gonchigsumlaa. He scored four films before 1990, *Ayuush of the People* (*Ard Ayuush*, 1984), *Duties of War* (*Baildaany Daalgavar*, 1985), *An Extended Summer* (*Ilüü Sartai Zun*, 1987), and *The Forgotten Tale* (*Martagdsan Duuli*, 1989), and continued composing orchestral pieces after this date. Examples include his monothematic score for the 1992 film *Maternal Bonding* (*Khüin Kholboo*) about a blind herdswoman, and his rousing orchestral cues for the 1993 film *Inadequate Fate* (*Kheltgii Zayaa*), based on the legend of Mongolia's only female champion wrestler.[9]

In the context of revitalising traditions such as the three manly sports and the re-establishment of Chinggis Khaan as a national icon, it could appear contradictory that the symphony orchestra rather than traditional instruments was

---

[9] The legend of Mongolia's only female champion wrestler is as follows. In the seventeenth century, a female wrestler disguised herself as a man in order to compete in wrestling competitions. After she won an important competition, it was revealed that she was in fact a woman. From that point forth, wrestlers were obliged to wear cropped open shirts (*zodog*), to make it clear to all that they were indeed men. The legend explains the origin of the wrestler's uniform that is worn to this day.

128   *Mongolian Film Music*

chosen to score the few films produced on these topics. Yet symphonic music is the earliest tradition of Mongolian film scoring, and professional music became a new tradition that developed concurrently with the film industry, so the relatively new tradition of symphonic music is more fitting to the traditional subject matter of these films than it may at first appear. Furthermore, symphonic music was used to score many of the historical epics made in Hollywood and elsewhere in the world to which Mongolian filmmakers and viewers now had greater access. After the fall of socialism and the golden age (*Altan Üye*) of Mongolian film music, there were still composers and filmmakers who considered symphonic music to be the most appropriate means to score high-quality, well-funded films. This is especially relevant given that, since 1990, the emergence of popular music in modern film soundtracks has attracted some negative associations on account of the large number of low-budget films produced featuring pop, rock and hip-hop styles. Despite the rise of popular music and the use of music technology, many composers still prefer the sound of a symphony orchestra, whether it is recorded live or produced on a sequencer or electronic keyboard.

It would be erroneous to think that all Mongolian film composers who reproduce the sound of an orchestra with MIDI (musical instrument digital interface) or electronic keyboards do so because there are insufficient funds to record a live orchestra, although this is often the case. The majority of Mongolian composers I interviewed composed computer-generated orchestral scores due to financial constraints, although many saw several advantages to these modern compositional methods. Furthermore, instrumental sounds generated by computers are commonplace in the soundtracks of the Korean films and television dramas with which contemporary Mongolian film composers are familiar.

Film music since 1990 has been composed and recorded on a much smaller scale than that of the Socialist era, with the thin textures of computer-generated soundtracks and the occasional added live solo instrument replacing the earlier rich textures of the full symphony orchestra. Many contemporary Mongolian film composers are not able to fulfil their creative and musical potential due to the lack of instrumental resources at their disposal. Professor Chinbat (INT) of the State College of Music and Dance told me, 'Film composers now are not well paid and that is why they compose small-scale works. Poor-quality soundtracks are nothing to do with the ability of the composer; the problem is lack of money.' Film composer and songwriter Balkhjav (INT) reinforced this sentiment when he said, '[Composers] cannot afford to hire a symphony orchestra. If they had the opportunity to compose for symphony orchestra rather than computer, their music would be so much better.'

Geserjavyn Pürevdorj (b. 1954) was the only composer I interviewed who expressed a firm preference for composing orchestral scores on the computer, whether or not live orchestras were available, although it is possible he is not an isolated case. Pürevdorj was trained at the Yekaterinburg Conservatoire, and used to write scores and parts by hand to be recorded by a live orchestra. When I interviewed him, he told me, 'Nowadays we don't need orchestras. We can play all the instruments of the orchestra ourselves on the computer.' He now uses the software sequencer Cubase for all his compositions. He gave me several reasons why he actively chooses to work alone with a computer. He is more in control of the outcome when he plays all parts himself rather than relying on individual orchestra members' interpretations of his music. Working alone has the advantage of avoiding potential personality clashes with orchestra members, conductors or technicians. He also told me that working on the computer allows him to make changes to the music after it has been synchronised to the film, which was impossible during the days when the score had to be completed before the recording session during the postproduction stage of filmmaking. Despite Pürevdorj's preference for working alone, he told me, 'the sound [would be] better with a live orchestra rather than a sequencer'. Occasionally, he combines single tracks of solo live instruments with sequenced tracks, especially when his music requires traditional instruments such as the horse-head fiddle, because traditional Mongolian instruments are not available in the sound banks of most sequencers and he does not have access to a sampler.

Whether composers, filmmakers and film viewers prefer the symphonic sounds of Socialist-era film scores to the computed-generated sounds of many post-1990 film soundtracks comes down to a matter of taste. Composers such as Pürevdorj choose to use computers rather than record a live orchestra whilst others do so because of lack of funds. Regardless of the preferences of film composers and listeners in Mongolia, it is a fact that technology and composing on the computer has become as prominent a force in modern Mongolian film composition as it has around the world.

Mongolian–Foreign Collaborations

From the mid-1990s, Mongolia and Mongolian music started to gain recognition worldwide through the medium of film; however, it was films produced by foreign film studios or made by foreign filmmakers that had international exposure rather than those made entirely by Mongolian studios and crews. These included makers of documentary and feature films, who could cater to the tastes of audiences in their home countries that were fascinated by the mystery and erstwhile inaccessibility of this remote country. The feature films *Khadak* (2006)[10] and *Mongol: The Rise to Power of Genghis Khaan* (2007), also known as *Mongol*, to give two examples, have been released internationally and both feature the music of Mongolian folk rock band Altan Urag.[11] The band is made up of two horse-head fiddles, *ikh khuur*

---

[10] *Khadak* is the international release title and refers to the Mongolian sacred blue scarf (*khadag*), which features in this film.

[11] Folk rock bands are rock bands that incorporate folk instruments and influences. Examples include The Oysterband or The Levellers in the UK and Yat-Kha or Hanggai in Central Asia. These bands may also be labelled ethnic rock or roots rock.

130   *Mongolian Film Music*

and *yoochin*, all amplified and with added distortion, *bishgüür, khöömii* and drum kit. Altan Urag's horse-head fiddles were specially designed for the band and feature a goat's rather than a horse's head, since members of the band believe the goat to be the 'mother of rock music' (Altan Urag, INT).

    Khadak was produced in Belgium and directed by Peter Brosens and Jessica Hope Woodworth, both of whom had previously directed short films about Mongolia. Woodworth directed the 18-minute film *Urga Song* (1999) and Brosens directed the 'Mongolia Trilogy' *City of the Steppes* (1994), *State of Dogs* (co-directed by Dorjkhandyn Törmönkh, 1998) and *Poets of Mongolia* (1999). *Khadak* tells the story of Bagi, a young herder whose family is relocated to a nearby town following a mysterious plague that inflicts their livestock, and through his shamanic visionary powers, discovers the plague was a cover story for a governmental ploy to eradicate nomadism. Aimed at art-house cinema or festival audiences rather than commercial consumption, the story is told through a mixture of dream sequences, visions, and scenes of realism and relies heavily on symbolism and imagery, leaving the audience to piece together the story. It is very different in style to the linear plots and realism of films produced by Mongolian studios. The soundtrack features original compositions by Dominique Lawalrée, Bach's Double Violin Concerto, and one cue taken from Altan Urag's first album *Foal's Been Born*. This is used during the most surreal, dreamlike sequence, and the band members themselves appear in the scene as extras. Altan Urag's *yoochin* player, Erdenebat, says of the scene, 'That scene is all about the social problems facing Mongolians today. Our music complements this. It is different to all the other music used in the film' (Altan Urag, INT). The use of Mongolian folk rock solely in this scene highlights the societal problems in question and helps locate them specifically in Mongolia.

    Five excerpts from Altan Urag's second album, *Made in Altan Urag,* are used in the 2007 feature film *Mongol*, which charts the early life of the boy Temujin until he becomes known as Chinggis Khaan in 1206. The remaining 43 cues were composed by the Finn Tuomas Kantelinen and feature orchestra, *yoochin*, vocals and a violoncello soloist imitating the sound of a horse-head fiddle. The final cue of the film, which accompanies the caption, 'It is 1206. Temujin becomes Khaan', is scored for orchestra and *khöömii*, then blends into a song by German rock band Magnetissimus Elektro followed by a final song by Altan Urag during the credits. Unlike *Khadak*, which was aimed at film festival audiences, *Mongol* is a commercial endeavour and targets the widest possible audience. The use of *khöömii* and a simulated horse-head fiddle provides the score with a quintessential Mongolian sound. In combination with rock songs and a symphony orchestra, the score appeals to a broad range of twenty-first-century audience members whilst maintaining an element of traditional Mongolian music.

    The members of Altan Urag support the notion that neither *Mongol* nor *Khadak* was popular amongst Mongolians. *Mongol* was unpopular for various reasons including its usage of non-Mongolian horses, Chinggis Khaan being played by a Japanese actor and portrayed as somewhat weak, and extras speaking Mandarin

New Directions 131

Chinese when in reality they would have spoken Turkic languages and dialects. The band's horse-head fiddle player and *khöömiich* Oyunbileg says, 'Mongolian people don't like the film *Mongol*. We don't like the way we are portrayed in that film' (Altan Urag, INT). Discussing *Khadak*, *yoochin* player Erdenebat says, 'Foreigners make films about our country from a different perspective, a different point of view. Sometimes this causes problems' (Altan Urag, INT). The problems Erdenebat refers to include the portrayal of Mongolians in films made by foreigners that may appear accurate to foreigners but cause objections amongst those being portrayed.

Some Mongolian–foreign collaborations made since the mid-1990s are in a quasi-documentary style with a content that is a combination of fact and fiction, and are therefore classed as semidocumentaries. Many are in the Mongolian language, are set in rural parts of the country, are about the daily lives of nomadic families and feature traditional Mongolian music. Two well-known examples are Byambasüren Davaa's award-winning and widely distributed films *The Story of the Weeping Camel* (2003) and *The Cave of the Yellow Dog* (2005).[12] A lesser-known example is Chris McKee's short film *Mujaan* (lit. *The Craftsman*, 2004), which met with some success in North American film festivals and was released independently on DVD. These three semidocumentary films are set in rural Mongolia and portray nomadic traditions that may soon become obsolete, and the target audiences are foreigners, predominantly Europeans and Americans. The depiction of Mongolians in these films did not receive the same negative reaction in Mongolia as their feature film counterparts; however, the portrayals are to a certain extent romanticised.

Davaa (b. 1971) was born in Mongolia, studied at the University of Film Arts in Ulaanbaatar between 1995 and 1998, then at the HFF (*Hochschule für Fernsehen und Film München* or University of Television and Film in Munich) in Germany, where she still lives. *The Story of the Weeping Camel* and *The Cave of the Yellow Dog* were produced in Germany by the HFF in association with other German studios. They were screened and won awards at numerous international film festivals, and have been distributed in North and South America, Europe and East Asia with subtitles in English and other widely spoken languages. These two films depict traditional rural Mongolian life seemingly untouched by seven decades of socialism and industrialisation. Davaa produced a film treatment for each and allowed the participants to improvise around the script, which she filmed and subsequently edited into a coherent narrative. Due to the films' widespread commercial release with subtitles, they are two of the most accessible Mongolian films worldwide. The semidocumentary style of these films could lead audiences to believe they are actual documentaries and that the nomadic lifestyle depicted is indicative of life throughout Mongolia, and the lack of Mongolian films available

---

[12] Davaa also directed the 2009 film *Two Horses of Genghis Khan*, although the DVD release has only German subtitles, giving it limited distribution amongst English-speaking people.

132   *Mongolian Film Music*

worldwide that portray modern urban living enhances this notion. The success of Davaa's films worldwide can be attributed, at least in part, to the fact that it is the disappearing traditions of rural life that non-Mongolians are most interested in viewing.

The Story of the Weeping Camel portrays a family of camel herders from the Gobi, who try to encourage one of their camels to accept her new calf following a difficult birth. The film contains very little music, all of which is diegetic traditional song, including a lullaby (*büüvee büüvee*), a children's song and the grandmother singing whilst milking the sheep. There are hints of modernity in that the children watch television and nomads travel by motorbike, although both motorbikes and television could be seen in rural areas throughout the Socialist era and were a sign of a prosperous collective. The film drives gently towards the final scene in which a horse-head fiddle player is invited to accompany the mother of the family as she sings the *botgo duu* (a song for a baby camel), a traditional ritual song used to coax camels to bond with their rejected young. Former Film Factory director and television producer Gombojavyn Jigjidsüren (INT) told me that in the early 2000s, a number of documentaries about the *botgo duu* ritual were aired on Mongolian television aimed at young people to help reacquaint them with old traditions, and these were usually scored with traditional Mongolian music. He believes it is very important for young Mongolians to keep their traditions and to avoid the 'bad influence of pop and rock music and globalisation'. *The Story of the Weeping Camel* helps bring this traditionalist view of Mongolian culture to the wider film-viewing world.

Davaa's second film *The Cave of the Yellow Dog* is about a family from west Mongolia who tries to persuade the young daughter Nansal to leave behind a dog she has found when they move their *ger* to new pastures. Nomads on motorbikes are also present in this film, and there are scenes of men discussing the possibility of moving to the nearest town in order to find work. Through presenting motorbikes, Davaa has challenged the idea that all nomads travel on horseback, and by portraying a lack of rural prosperity, she has painted a more realistic picture of modern nomadism. Unlike Davaa's first film, this film contains a score, composed by D. Ganpürev. The instrumentation is the horse-head fiddle, *ikh khuur, khuuchir, yatga, yoochin* and *limbe*. The melodies are based on the pentatonic scale, and some European classical harmonic devices that would not normally be found in traditional Mongolian music are utilised, such as chromaticisms and suspension figures. The predominantly traditional music soundtrack with a hint of outside influence and modernism in the form of chromaticisms and suspension figures is fitting to the atmosphere of *The Cave of the Yellow Dog*, in which tradition meets modernity.

Mujaan is a 25-minute semidocumentary by the American first-time director Chris McKee, produced by his own production company, Ragcha Media, based in California, USA. In *Mujaan*, he too intended to present a nomadic lifestyle that is virtually unknown in the West and that may soon be lost. The film depicts the working life of Mongolian carpenter Sükhbaatar as he builds a *ger.* Unlike

New Directions 133

Davaa's films, however, images of modernity such as motorbikes and televisions were altogether avoided. In the DVD commentary, McKee explains that he asked Sükhbaatar to put away his modern electric tools and to use old-fashioned manual tools during filming. McKee goes on to say that Sükhbaatar was at first reluctant since the craftsman did not want his community to be portrayed as 'savages'. McKee intended to portray some long-established carpentry methods that are still operational in some parts of Mongolia, yet the fact that modern electric tools and Western dress are not presented could lead non-Mongolian audiences to believe that all Mongolians wear a *deel* daily and use these outmoded working methods.

There are nine cues in *Mujaan*: two diegetic songs sung by Sükhbaatar, four traditional songs recorded by McKee for the film, one piece of sound design and two cues of traditional singing with added instruments composed by Daniel David Feinsmith. The traditional vocal cues are used to accompany landscape shots and scenes of Sükhbaatar working. Instruments are not heard until the 14th minute, when Sükhbaatar slaughters a sheep. For this cue, composer Feinsmith took an excerpt from his earlier solo violoncello piece *Raziel*, sped it up digitally and added further effects, then mixed it with McKee's field recordings of *khöömii* and long-song. The slaughter of the sheep could be an uncomfortable scene for Western audiences to watch, especially given the traditional Mongolian method of doing so by slitting open the chest and plunging a hand in to remove the heart, and this is the only point in the film when Western instruments are added to the score. McKee had asked Feinsmith to add emotional intensity to the scene and to create a different mood (Feinsmith, INT). The use of music and the deliberate depiction of old-fashioned tools reinforce an exotic image of modern Mongolia that would appeal to many Western audience members.

Although it was Davaa and McKee's intention to present disappearing traditions rather than an accurate overview of contemporary Mongolian life, their portrayal is somewhat idyllic, since neither highlights the inherent hardships of nomadism. At no point in these films, for example, do we see nomadic Mongolian life during the winter, when temperatures plummet regularly to below minus 30 degrees Celsius and hundreds of livestock perish annually. These films present waning traditions to the rest of the world successfully, but they do so with nostalgia and romanticism. Films produced entirely in Mongolia that portray modern urban life with popular music soundtracks do not have the international distribution of these foreign co-productions. Since the only access most non-Mongolians have to contemporary Mongolian films are these foreign collaborations, and especially given the trend for semidocumentary style and the use of traditional instruments and vocal styles, audiences can be left with a romanticised and inaccurate idea of life and filmmaking in contemporary Mongolia. In 2012, Australian director Benj Binks produced the documentary film *Mongolian Bling*, about the current thriving hip-hop scene in Ulaanbaatar, and in 2014 American Lauren Knapp produced the documentary *Live from UB*, about the city's rock music scene. These films should contribute to a clearer understanding of contemporary urban Mongolia

134 *Mongolian Film Music*

to international audiences who can gain access to them, and help create a more rounded picture of the current cultural scene in Mongolia.

During the Socialist era, the professionalisation of Khalkha music and the modification of Khalkha musical instruments, tuning systems and performance practices helped the government strive towards creating a uniform socialist identity throughout Mongolia. This intended homogenisation of music, arts and culture resulted in the depletion of musical and cultural practices of Mongolia's numerous ethnic minorities, the 1956 musical film *Our Melody* (*Manai Ayalguu*) being the main exception. After 1990, ethnic minorities began once more to celebrate their musical traditions and festivities freely, such as the Kazakh eagle festival held in Bayan Ölgii province every October and the Tsaatan ice festival held each February in Khövsgöl province. These festivals, however, have become popular tourist attractions, and Tsaatan and Kazakh populations may soon feel compelled to modify their traditions to cater to the predominantly Western tourists in much the same way as Khalkha Mongolian traditions were adapted to suit Soviet tastes during the Socialist era. After 1990, songs and instruments of Mongolia's numerous ethnic minorities began to be featured in the performances of the Mongolian National Song and Dance Academic Ensemble. In the former Soviet Central Asian Republics, Uzbek, Kyrgyz, Kazakh, Tajik and Turkmen folk music traditions were similarly promoted after the fall of socialism.

Despite this revival of the music of ethnic minorities in performance contexts, it is largely absent from the film soundtracks produced in Mongolia. This is partly due to the film industry being based in Ulaanbaatar, where very few ethnic minority communities exist. Film studios, equipment, funding and expertise are not present where these communities live, which tends to be remote rural areas and borderlands. The rising number of foreign visitors to Mongolia since 1990 has led to an increasing interest in the culture of the country's ethnic minorities, especially by the foreign filmmakers who have come to Mongolia to document these cultural practices on film.

Amongst Mongolia's ethnic minorities, it is the Kazakhs who have attracted the most attention from foreign filmmakers, especially their tradition of hunting with eagles. Foreign-produced films about Kazakh eagle hunters accommodate the rare appearances in film soundtracks of traditional Kazakh instruments such as the two-stringed lute, the *dombra* (Figure 7.2), and the overtone flute, the *sybyzgy*. American-Iranian filmmaker and photographer Hamid Sardar-Afkhami made two documentaries in Mongolia, the first of which, *Balapan: Wings of Altai* (2005), is the story of a father training his son to hunt with eagles. Amongst the orchestral and *khöömii* cues, there are two solos played on the *dombra*. Sardar's second documentary, *Tracking the White Reindeer* (2008) is about the Tsaatan reindeer herders of northern Mongolia, yet the score by French composer Olivier Bernet is scored for the distinctly non-Tsaatan sounds of the tuba, trombone, mandolin and guitar. The Swedish–German co-production *The Eagle Hunter's Son* (2009) is a semidocumentary about a Kazakh boy who dreams of moving to Ulaanbaatar but unintentionally rediscovers his Kazakh heritage on the way. Of the films that

Figure 7.2   A *dombra* on a hand-woven Kazakh rug, Töv province, Mongolia

portray Kazakh eagle-hunting traditions, traditional Kazakh music is utilised most widely is Joseph Spaid's 2005 semidocumentary *Kiran Over Mongolia.*

Unlike *The Story of the Weeping Camel, Mujaan* or *Balapan: Wings of Altai*, which are set wholly in nomadic communities and generally eschew portraying modernity, *Kiran Over Mongolia* is placed in a modern context. The story begins in Ulaanbaatar, where the young Kazakh man Kuma decides to travel to Bayan Ölgii in western Mongolia to discover his Kazakh heritage. The opening montage, which is accompanied by techno music, shows Kuma shopping, walking past an industrial estate, playing billiards and dancing in an Ulaanbaatar nightclub. The bulk of the story is set in Bayan Ölgii, where Kuma improves his Kazakh language skills and learns the art of hunting with eagles from eagle master Khairatkhan. During his journey to Bayan Ölgii, popular music is played on the jeep radio, and villages where he stops *en route* are depicted realistically with a mixture of people in traditional dress, and baseball caps and jeans. Nostalgia and romanticism are avoided through portraying the disappearing traditions of Mongolia's Kazakh communities in a realistic contemporary context, including the use of traditional Kazakh music and modern popular music.

Like Davaa's films, *Kiran Over Mongolia* is semiscripted and styled as a documentary. Davaa met and auditioned several people before choosing the families featured in her first two films. Likewise, the American director Joseph Spaid chose Kuma from a group of young Kazakh men at an informal audition

136 *Mongolian Film Music*

in Ulaanbaatar. Khairatkhan is an eagle hunter and was chosen after the initial eagle hunter pulled out of production because he did not want to repeat actions for filming. Neither Kuma nor Khairkhatan is a professional actor or has appeared in other films.

In addition to the techno music at the nightclub and the popular song in the jeep, the soundtrack features four pieces for frame drums, drum kit and sound design during scenes when the eagles chase their prey. The remaining 16 cues comprise 8 *dombra* solos, 4 *sybyzgy* solos, and 4 Kazakh folk songs accompanied by the *dombra*. The first song is played and sung by Oral Esemgul, a young girl whom Spaid came across one day as she sang and played the *dombra* outside her home for her own entertainment. The song appears at the point in the film when Kuma captures his own eagle and the lyrics are about Kazakhs retaining their traditions. Another song demonstrates the Kazakh tradition of improvising lyrics about a fellow guest at a dinner party. Khairatkhan sings the song diegetically during a dinner party held for Kuma before he leaves Bayan Ölgii to return to Ulaanbaatar with his new eagle. The improvised lyrics tell of Khairatkhan's bond with Kuma and how they are now nominal brothers. The notion of disappearing traditions is presented in *Kiran Over Mongolia* juxtaposed against images of modernity, resulting in a representational picture of the contemporary situation in Mongolia. The tradition–modernity dichotomy is echoed in the music: solos on Kazakh instruments and traditional songs set against pop songs broadcast on the radio and techno in an Ulaanbaatar nightclub.

Since the film music of Mongolian–foreign collaborations often accompanies scenes of an historical, nomadic or pastoral nature, or of life untouched by socialism, international and younger Mongolian audiences would be forgiven for thinking that the music is folk music unaffected by socialist policy. What Mongolian folk music actually sounded like before the Socialist era is difficult to infer, and impossible for current filmmakers and composers to know. Recordings of Mongolian music have been made only since the 1930s and there is very little documented evidence of music before this date. Details of how music was modified under the socialist regime, such as retuning and redesigning instruments, can only hint at what music sounded like before this time. Composers generally intend to create music that complements the action of a particular film and they are not obliged to educate viewers on the cultural context of the music they present. Nonetheless, audiences of *The Cave of the Yellow Dog* or *Mujaan* may be unaware of the professionalisation of folk music under the socialist regime, and viewers of *Mongol* or *Khadak* might not know that Altan Urag's folk rock developed as recently as the 2000s.

Although films on a range of topics presenting a broad spectrum of lifestyles in Mongolia are produced annually in the country, it is mostly those that depict nomadic traditions that are presented internationally, namely the foreign co-productions. The same cannot be said of the films of other East Asian countries. The 2003 Korean film *Spring, Summer, Autumn, Winter ... and Spring*, for example, portrays the isolated life of a tiny traditional Korean monastic community, and was met

New Directions 137

with critical acclaim in Europe and the USA. Yet there are numerous Korean films with equivalent international distribution and commendation that portray modern urban life, such as Park Chan-Wook's *Vengeance Trilogy*.[13] Similarly, Japanese and Chinese films that are available internationally portray the broad spectrum of lifestyles and environments in these countries, from remote rural communities to busy city life. International audiences who have never visited East Asia, therefore, have a more complete picture of the output of the film industries of Korea, Japan and China in comparison to Mongolia, and consequently a more realistic impression of contemporary life. Mongolia's increased political and cultural freedom from 1990 coincided with the withdrawal of Soviet funding, severe economic problems and widespread release of films produced by inexperienced filmmakers on inexpensive or old-fashioned equipment. After 1990, it was only foreign studios and directors that had the financial resources to produce and distribute Mongolian films internationally, and so the topics covered tended to be those desired by non-Mongolian audiences, namely rural Mongolian traditions.

Film and Film Music in Democratic Mongolia

Since 1990, Mongolian films have been produced either wholly in Mongolia or in collaboration with foreign filmmakers and studios, and there are significant differences in the outcomes of these two trends. Stylistically, solely Mongolian-produced films tend to have linear fictional plots and dramatic performances, whereas amongst foreign collaborations the semidocumentary style starring real-life people rather than actors is more prevalent. The dichotomy seen in solely Mongolian-produced films that either glorify a traditional past or anticipate a modern future follows on from *Mandukhai the Wise Queen* and *Whirlpool* respectively in the late 1980s that foreshadowed the end of socialism. The majority of solely Mongolian-produced films are either modern urban stories with popular music soundtracks or films depicting ancient traditions or Chinggis Khaan with symphonic scores either produced on the computer or by recording a live orchestra. Whilst the Chinggis Khaan films are clearly patriotic, the urban dramas are no less patriotic, since they portray the forward-looking life desired by many young Mongolians as they move towards new Mongolian capitalism. Foreign collaborative films, on the other hand, often portray a romanticised picture of a disappearing traditional rural Mongolian lifestyle that may soon become fascinating not just to foreign audiences but also to modern urban Mongolians.

The significance of the resurgence of traditional symbolism in post-1990 films and film scores should not be overemphasised. The Chinggis Khaan films and foreign collaborations about nomadic life form only a part of the post-1990 film and film music scenes. Mongolia has since established new connections with the

---

[13] *Sympathy for Mr Vengeance* (2002), *Oldboy* (2003) and *Sympathy for Lady Vengeance* (2005).

West and East Asia through embracing the Hollywood, Korean and Hong Kong filmic influences to which Mongolians had direct access, in addition to scores featuring rock music, hip-hop and orchestral sounds produced on the computer. Despite the justifiable optimism shown by certain film professionals regarding recent improvements in film and film-score quality, there are still numerous low-budget films being made. There are also numerous former filmmakers and film composers of the golden age who would like to see a return to socialism, since they had greater job stability and financial freedom when the state film studio had exclusive rights over filmmaking and film scoring. Many of these Mongolians who would welcome a return to socialism were trained in the Soviet Union and became accustomed to Soviet methodologies, whereas younger Mongolian film composers have been trained in Ulaanbaatar without a strong Soviet influence. Nonetheless, whether or not the filmmaking and film-scoring environment during the Socialist era is considered a sad loss or a welcome departure, Mongolian filmmaking and scoring since 1990 have developed in various and varied directions, and have embraced a mixture of tradition and modernity.

Chapter 8

Tradition, Revolution, Propaganda and Consolidation: A Brief Conclusion

The Mongolian film industry was established to fulfil a political agenda and music was needed to accompany and enhance the message of the films. This relationship between politics and film music began as an elder-brother / younger-brother relationship with the Soviet Union and was cultivated for over five decades until the late 1980s, when film composers became the voice of the disillusioned population. Throughout the Socialist era, film music developed in a manner that both fulfilled political obligations and nurtured certain Mongolian traditions. The dual musical background of the majority of state film composers, as well as the subject matter of the films they had to score, were crucial in bringing together tradition and socialist progress in the form of music. The result was a rich collection of film scores comprising a variety of genres, which maintained traditions, promoted socialism and, in some cases, literally combined these juxtaposed influences. After 1990, Mongolian film composers still embraced pre-1921 Mongolian traditions as well as foreign political and artistic influences, although the way traditions have been expressed and the foreign influences in question have differed significantly from those of the Socialist era.

Elder Brother, Younger Brother, Politics and Film Music

There were strong links between politics and cinema, and politics and music throughout the Socialist era. It was the MPRP that decreed the founding of the Mongolian film industry and there was a closed community of personnel who worked therein. The five-year plan determined everything from the number of films made to the topics they should address, and films and new music were disseminated to the entire population through political initiatives rather than commercial enterprise. All of this was done in the name of socialist propaganda and influenced by the film and music industries in the Soviet Union.

Since the Soviet Union served as a model for a number of socialist nations including Mongolia, Mongolians were encouraged to emulate certain characteristics of a (good) Soviet citizen that the CPSU promoted. For this to happen in Mongolia, the MPRP had to suppress certain characteristics relating to religious, feudal and nomadic culture that were not compatible with the socialist ideal. Frederik Barth (Barth, 1969, p. 3) explains that 'political innovators' – the MPRP in the case of Mongolia – pinpoint characteristics of identity within

140 *Mongolian Film Music*

a certain culture and then suppress them in order to assert their own power. The swift suppression of pre-twentieth-century Mongolian heritage was replaced with adherence to Marxist–Leninist doctrine, loyalty to the state, solidarity with neighbouring socialist nations and the rejection of principles that threatened the struggle towards the ultimate goal of communism. The state promoted a sense of equality regarding social status and distribution of wealth by substituting feudal structures with collectivisation. Socialist ideals were nurtured from an early age through formal education and membership of organisations such as the Pioneers and the Revolutionary League of Youth through to red corners, trade unions, propaganda cinema and large-scale music ensembles. This was, of course, the ideal, and the anti-socialist protests in Mongolia in 1989–90 demonstrate that the reality of socialism for many Mongolians did not correspond with this vision.

From 1921, Mongolia adopted not only Soviet-inspired politics but also Soviet and Russian culture and lifestyle, incorporating everything from agriculture and industry to the arts and the Cyrillic alphabet, and many Mongolians welcomed these changes. The younger-brother nation benefitted from Soviet training in everything from railway mechanics and veterinary science to film composition. Whilst these processes of cultural adoption and professional training were underway, Mongolia was to all intents and purposes closed off from nations that were not members of COMECON, particularly after it became a full member in 1962. Since COMECON was led from Moscow, the Soviet influence extended throughout all member states. This geographical and political isolation meant, for Mongolian film composers as well as other professionals, that the only influences readily available to them were those from the Eastern Bloc and the Mongolian traditions into which they were born.

Composers' Dual Musical Backgrounds

Although the MPRP tried to encourage every citizen to relate to a unified ideal, many filmmakers and composers identified with a range of cultural traditions, whether or not they were free to do so. Luvsansharav (INT), for example, stated that he wanted to listen to Western music but was not allowed, whereas the composer Gonchigsumlaa and director Erdenbatyn Oyuun clearly identified with the range of musical traditions from Mongolia's ethnic minorities that they presented in the 1956 film *Our Melody* (*Manai Ayalguu*). Whilst the Soviet Union was a strong influence, Mongolians still had a rich and separate cultural heritage on which to draw.

The majority of Mongolian film composers of the Socialist era came from the countryside rather than the capital city, which, even then, contained a sizeable portion of the population. Of course this could be merely coincidence and there is the possibility that musicians from the countryside were, or were perceived to be, more musically talented than their urban counterparts. A more likely explanation as to why the MPRP chose to send promising musicians from rural areas for formal musical training in preference to those from Ulaanbaatar is one that is connected to socialist ideology. It is in keeping with Marxist–Leninist theory to exalt the proletariat and glorify the common man. Musicians from poor rural backgrounds becoming state-honoured film composers represented the journey of socialist progress the MPRP wanted Mongolian citizens to follow. Film music had to appeal to the rural as well as urban population, so composers were compelled to combine the musical skills they had learned in Soviet conservatoires with the musical traditions of their own childhood and of the Mongolian population for whom they composed. This dual musical background gave composers experience in both symphonic and traditional music, and – maybe more importantly – only in these two areas of music.

The relatively few film composers from Ulaanbaatar were also knowledgeable about traditional Mongolian music, although they lacked the nomadic upbringing and lifestyle as experienced directly by composers such as Luvsansharav, Sharav and Jantsannorov. Hiring film composers with a dual musical background, whether they were born in the countryside or the capital, had an inevitable impact on the music. When composing symphonic music, film composers utilised some of the sounds and characteristics of the traditional Mongolian music with which the population was familiar, from the string ostinati reminiscent of a horse's hooves heard in Mördorj's scores of the 1950s to Jantsannorov's use of symphonic instruments that sounded like traditional Mongolian instruments in the late 1980s.

The main elements of European symphonic music Mongolian composers adopted included instrumentation, performance practice, performance spaces, staff notation, and musical structures and harmonies. From Mongolian composers' own traditions, they utilised instrumental sounds, scales, melodic structures and music with an improvisatory feel. These two sets of characteristics complement each other well and made musical syncretism possible. This syncretism developed into professional music (*mergejliin khögjim*), and the term gave this music a certain status by its being associated with the new professional music industry and film industry for which it was composed.

Complementing the Message of the Film

Despite the influences to which Mongolian film composers were subject, their principal obligation was to complement the action and message of the films. Ultimately, they had to produce scores appropriate to the ideology and cultural policies that were at the core of the music and film industries. Since film composers had to complement the blend of traditional Mongolian and Soviet characteristics present in the films they scored, many did this by composing some traditional cues, some symphonic cues, and other cues that were literally a combination of the two.

Film composers became involved in the filmmaking process during the postproduction stage, when the film had already been shot and a rough cut was available, namely when the message of the film had already been established and

142   *Mongolian Film Music*

fully explored. If the topic of the film was the 1921 Revolution, for example, then the score had to reflect this through its musical genres, styles and atmosphere. Different genres and styles came to be associated with different types of scenes, such as rousing symphonic music with full textures and march-like rhythms for battle scenes, or diegetic cues featuring traditional instruments and vocal styles for scenes set before 1921 that depicted the lifestyle socialism was meant to replace. Rousing, anthem-like cues for full orchestra became associated with Sükhbaatar, which helped the government's aim to present him as the new national hero of socialist Mongolia. Professional music tended to be composed for film scenes depicting Mongolian life that had been improved by the adoption and implementation of socialism.

The portrayal of socialist Mongolian citizens in films is likely to have differed from the way audiences – as well as filmmakers and film composers – viewed themselves. The relatively large proportion of the population who identified with films such as *Whirlpool* (*Ergüüleg*) in 1989 and who participated in the 1989–90 protests suggests strongly that people did not view their reality in the way it had been portrayed in the propaganda films. It is possible to identify the on-screen portrayal of socialist citizens by watching the films, yet it is more difficult to determine how people viewed themselves, since documentary evidence of audience reception produced during the Socialist era is sparse and, on the whole, as imbued with propaganda as the films. There is little or no first-hand evidence in the form of personal memoirs, books or independent film reviews from the Socialist era that provide information on audience reception other than articles printed in official publications, such as *Ünen*.

When interviewing Mongolians on this matter, I discovered a divide in opinion between older and younger people regarding their identification with socialism and the Soviet Union and whether they approved of the way Mongolians had been portrayed on screen. Many of the older Mongolians I spoke to viewed the Socialist era favourably, albeit with a hint of nostalgia, whilst the majority of younger Mongolians with whom I had contact had had no direct experience of living under a socialist regime. I rarely encountered Mongolians who deemed the Soviet Union a wholly oppressive influence over its satellite states, which was an image frequently portrayed by Western media throughout the Cold War. Although professional Mongolians were obliged to follow governmental plans and guidelines, many saw this as an opportunity to learn and improve their work.

Filmmakers and composers were obliged to promote socialist ideology, particularly before the 1980s when some of the problems of socialism began to be publicised. Of course, this does not mean that the filmmakers and composers in question did not genuinely sympathise with socialism, although it certainly does not prove that they did. Official reports on film viewing published during the Socialist era were also propaganda, and the touch of nostalgia with which many contemporary Mongolians remember the era make it difficult to determine whether the life portrayed in films before the 1980s matched that experienced by ordinary citizens. Whilst composers were often successful in complementing the

Tradition, Revolution, Propaganda and Consolidation 143

topics, themes and action of the films, particularly in the early to mid-Socialist era, it is less certain whether composers successfully echoed the true sentiments of the Mongolian population, the filmmakers or even themselves.

The Development of Film Music

Composing film music was a brand new concept in Mongolia from 1936, when the film industry was established. Its development was rapid and varied, particularly regarding the assimilation of music genres introduced by the Soviet Union. Furthermore, film music developed in certain directions the socialist government may not have anticipated, namely the introduction of popular music later in the Socialist era and the fact that film was in part responsible for the preservation of Buddhist and shamanic music. Musical development was strongly linked with developments in politics, and certain political events triggered musical innovation. Furthermore, the government had control over what music the public listened to, since music was available only through film screenings, concerts, and radio and television broadcasts, and this limitation of public consumption helped the government to promote only state-approved music.

Since the film industry was influenced by that of the Soviet Union, early film music was based on Soviet film-scoring conventions until Mongolian film composers started to develop their own compositional styles. With very few exceptions, Film Factory films were scored for symphony orchestra on account of the influence of Soviet film-scoring traditions and also because the State Symphony Orchestra became the official orchestra of the studio and was therefore utilised whenever possible. Before 1921, symphonic music had barely been heard in Mongolia whereas by the 1950s, orchestral cues were present in almost every Film Factory soundtrack. The speed at which symphonic music became embedded into Mongolian musical and filmic traditions reflects the swift process by which the country adopted Soviet culture and socialist politics.

The series of five-year plans included initiatives that led to composers combining the art music they studied in the Soviet Union with traditional Mongolian music. This process had already begun in the 1930s in the Soviet Central Asian Republics with the practice of harmonising folk tunes, and was echoed in Mongolia from the 1940s, suggesting strongly that the state intended a Soviet–Mongolian musical union to occur. As soon as Mongolian composers started to receive formal training in composition and orchestration, they were able to harmonise melodies themselves, and this process became one of the most significant developments in Mongolian music of the twentieth century. The MPRP further encouraged the development of professional music by bestowing state awards upon composers, thereby publicly celebrating compositions that combined Mongolian and Soviet musical influences.

Another development was the adoption of Soviet musical genres and ensembles, such as revolutionary songs, accordion music and brass bands, which

144   *Mongolian Film Music*

were associated with particular groups of people, largely on account of their appearance on screen. Revolutionary songs, for example, became associated with the Revolutionary League of Youth, the Pioneers and with soldiers, and these songs became part of the unity of these groups of people as well as new musical traditions in Mongolia.

The musical heritage of the pre-1921 era, on the other hand, was discouraged. Folk music of ethnic groups other than the Khalkha was mostly ignored and unmodified Khalkha music and religious music were usually given negative associations, especially in comparison with other genres such as revolutionary songs or symphonic music. The eschewal or unfavourable portrayal of these genres on screen suggests that audiences were not intended to view such music positively. If a *shanz* solo was portrayed as decadent and reminiscent of the days of feudalism, as in the party scene in *The Clear River Tamir* (*Tungalag Tamir*, 1970–73), or if a rendition of *uukhai* at a *Naadam* festival was presented as old-fashioned, then audiences would receive the music in this way, particularly if it was diegetic and therefore more verisimilar. Furthermore, traditional and religious music was afforded less prominence overall than symphonic music, which formed the majority of cues. Representing 'old' traditional and religious music negatively or sparsely within films blemished the image of pre-1921 traditional culture, although ultimately it helped preserve such music since it was not performed regularly elsewhere.

Despite the convention for using the symphony orchestra and the eschewal of pre-1921 musical traditions, film composers had to produce scores that appealed to the entire Mongolian population. One way of doing this was to use symphonic instruments that sound similar to certain traditional Mongolian instruments, which would have added an element of familiarity to the music. Jantsannorov (INT) believes that using symphonic instruments that sound like traditional Mongolian instruments 'makes the music more powerful'.[1] There are numerous examples in Film Factory soundtracks of violoncello solos sounding like the horse-head fiddle or the oboe sounding like the *bishgüür*. Symphonic music was combined with traditional Mongolian music also through performance practice, such as Western bowing techniques being used on the horse-head fiddle, or through harmonising pentatonic and improvisatory melodies with diatonic chords. The development of professional music became an appropriate method of scoring scenes depicting the new socialist Mongolia, such as the opening cue to Part 3 of *The Clear River Tamir*. The range of characters associated with this music was very broad, from important historical figures such as Sükhbaatar to fictional ordinary Mongolians such as Erdene and Tömör. Professional music became an archetypal socialist music genre not only because it utilises traditional Mongolian and Soviet musical elements, but also because, in keeping with socialist ideology, it came to be associated with the widest possible spectrum of Mongolian citizens.

---

[1]   See Chapter 3, p. 45, for Jantsannorov's full quotation.

Developments were seen not only in the actual music but also in the function of the cues. In early films, the usage of music was straightforward: rousing symphonic cues accompanied battle scenes, softer cues were used for more tender moments, such as the scene in *Tsogt Taij* (1945) in which Tsogt Taij bids farewell to his mother, and traditional music was used when musicians or vocalists were incorporated into the action, such as the numerous examples of *uukhai* in scenes of *Naadam* festivals. By the 1960s, there are examples of music being used ironically, as heard in *The Obstacles We Confront* (*Bidend Yuu Saad Bolj Baina*, 1956), and symbolically, such as the harmonica cue in *The Harmonica* (*Aman Khuur*, 1963), which served as a symbol for progress in the construction industry. This latter cue is particularly significant regarding its function, since it also enhanced the ideological and comedic elements of the film simultaneously by drawing attention to the protagonist's changing attitudes towards progress. From the 1970s, when characterisations were developed to cater to audience members with more experience in film viewing, music was used to highlight certain character traits. A notable example is the cue used to underpin Tügjil's deviousness in *The Clear River Tamir* when he befriends Tömör only to stab him and steal his horses. Namsraijav achieved this by borrowing a technique common within comedy film scoring, namely the matching of hit-points.

Notable films that were considered unusual or rebellious within the context of the output of the Film Factory and that led to musical innovation were generally triggered by significant political events of the Socialist era. The production of *Tsogt Taij*, the first film to celebrate a pre-1921 Mongolian hero, was sparked by the end of the Great Patriotic War. The controversial *The Obstacles We Confront* and the unusual *Our Melody* were released in 1956 after the deaths of Choibalsan in 1952 and Stalin in 1953 in the midst of the Khrushchev Thaw, when censorship became more relaxed. Glasnost and perestroika in the 1980s directly influenced Jantsannorov's innovative score for the historical epic *Mandukhai the Wise Queen* (*Mandukhai Tsetsen Khatan*, 1988) and Jumdaan's controversial *Whirlpool*. These films are considered great achievements in filmmaking not only because of their technical and artistic mastery and innovative scores but also because of their timely release. Important political events provided the catalyst for innovative films and film scores, at least in part because they provided filmmakers and composers with the inspiration and freedom to experiment and create new musical ideas and styles. The biggest changes in Mongolian film scoring, notably the introduction of music generated on computers and the widespread use of popular music, were introduced directly after one of the most momentous political events in modern Mongolian history: the Democratic Revolution in 1990.

After the 1990 Democratic Revolution

The opening up of Mongolia to worldwide influences after 1990 led to a diversification of film music genres. After 1990 and almost seventy years of

146 *Mongolian Film Music*

political isolation, the democratically elected government (although this was still the MPRP) was keen for Mongolia to become more involved in the wider world. Although diplomatic relations had opened with Japan in 1972, with the USA in 1988 and with South Korea in March 1990, ordinary Mongolians had regular access to the popular culture of these nations only after July 1990. The musical influences from these countries soon became apparent in Mongolian post-1990 film soundtracks.

Mongolia's sudden transition into democracy and a market economy was echoed in its cinema. Small independent businesses began to replace state-controlled industry, and small independent film studios emerged, thereby putting an end to the state film studio's monopoly over Mongolian filmmaking. The freedom for anyone to make films was coupled with freedom of speech, so filmmakers could produce films on whichever topics they chose. In comparison to the early days of the Socialist era, the population after 1990 was relatively young and urbanised, so filmmakers produced films that appealed to this demographic, such as ghost stories, martial arts, and gangster films. Film soundtracks followed the same route, with genres such as heavy metal and hip-hop being widely utilised.

Despite embracing post-1990 modernity, many Mongolians felt a sense of nostalgia for lost traditions. Jantsannorov (INT) told me he had collected 560 hours of recordings of traditional Mongolian music, which he had archived for posterity and wished to be used 'in the distant future to keep the music alive'.[2] Jantsannorov's desire to preserve traditional music demonstrates his identification with pre-revolutionary Mongolia, and recording this music rather than performing it live gives it a modern twist. His celebration of traditional music began publicly within the first few minutes of his score to *Mandukhai the Wise Queen*, when traditional music, costume and customs were presented in a positive light during the scene of Mandukhai's wedding.

Other film composers expressed their connection to pre-revolutionary Mongolia by combining traditional Mongolian musical elements with the new popular music genres to which they had recently gained access such as K-pop, hip-hop and rock. Since 1990, the process of combining traditional Mongolian and foreign musical influences has seen similarities with that of the Socialist era, even though the contexts of film production are different and the foreign influences are from elsewhere.

Although Mongolia's borders have been more open to foreign visitors since 1990, it is traditional Mongolia (or a reimagination of traditional Mongolia) with which many foreign visitors identify. This is a two-way process. Foreign visitors often seek out traditional Mongolian culture by attending cultural shows performed by professional folk music ensembles or by watching films such as *The Story of the Weeping Camel* (2003) and *The Cave of the Yellow Dog* (2005).

---

[2] This music was recorded between 1997 and 2006 as part of a Japanese-funded project with the Mongolian Centre for Intangible Culture, of which Jantsannorov is a key member.

Tradition, Revolution, Propaganda and Consolidation 147

On the other hand, traditional music and professional music, particularly Jantsannorov's compositions, have been used widely within the tourist industry, such as the soundtrack to a documentary played to visitors at Hustai National Park, one of Mongolia's major tourist attractions, and during the flights of Mongolia's national airline, MIAT. Tourist attractions and the national airline are bowing to consumer demand as well as deliberately presenting traditional music to non-Mongolians.

Throughout Mongolia's filmmaking history, film composers have identified with the music and culture of the foreign nations to which they had access whilst consistently maintaining their cultural traditions, albeit in a modified form. Numerous examples are evident, from composers developing professional music during the Socialist era to contributing to the re-establishment of Chinggis Khaan as a cultural icon after 1990 and combining the characteristics of their traditional music with the popular music of other nations. Horse-head-fiddle maker Ulambayar (INT) sums up a common feeling in the post-Socialist era regarding Mongolian film and music: 'We [Mongolians] like to be involved with what is happening in the world, with globalisation, but we like to keep our traditions too.'

Appendix A

Feature Films Produced by the State Film Studio, 1938–1990[1]

1938
Norjmaa's Way[2] (*Norjmagiin Zam*). B&W (black and white). Silent. Director: Natsagdorj.

1939
Pack of Wolves, A (*Süreg Chono*). B&W. Silent. Director: Natsagdorj.

1940
Bubonic Plague (*Tarvagan Takhal*). B&W. Silent. Director: Natsagdorj.
First Lesson, The (*Ankhdugaar Khicheel*). B&W. Director: Natsagdorj. Composer: Mördorj.

1941
Life's Enemy (*Amidralyn Daisan*). B&W. Silent. Director: Natsagdorj.

1942
Brave Patriot, The (*Aimshiggüi Ekh Oronch*). B&W. Director: Luvsanjamts. Composer: S. S. Galiperin.
Conflict on the Border (*Khil Deer Garsan Khereg*). B&W. Directors: Luvsanjamts and Bold. Composer: S. S. Galiperin.
Leader of the Horse Battalion (*Morin Tsereg Tankist*). B&W. Directors: Luvsanjamts and Bold. Composer: S. S. Galiperin.

1945
Tsogt Taij (*Tsogt Taij*). B&W. Directors: T. Yuri and Rinchen. Composers: Damdinsüren, Mördorj and Smirnov.

---

[1] *Source:* Jigjidsüren and Tsetseg, 2005, pp. 10–292.
[2] English translations by Lucy M. Rees and Tümenjiin Bekhbat (January 2009). Film titles have been translated as close as possible to the original Mongolian. Some are literal translations whereas others have been altered to express the theme of the film (e.g. *Niislel Khüü* has been translated as *City Slicker* rather than its literal translation 'Son of the Capital').

150 *Mongolian Film Music*

1954
New Year (Shine Jil). B&W. Director: Zandraa.

1955
Mistake in the South (Gem Ni Urdaa). B&W. Director: Oyuun. Composer: Dugarsüren.

1956
Obstacles We Confront, The (Bidend Yuu Saad Bolj Baina). B&W. Director: Dorjpalam. Composer: Mördorj.
Our Melody (Manai Ayalguu). B&W. Director: Oyuun. Composer: Gonchigsumlaa.

1957
Awakening (Serelt). B&W. Director: Genden. Composer: Gonchigsumlaa.

1958
Three Friends (Gurvan Naiz). B&W. Director: Dorjpalam. Composer: Namsraijav.

1959
If Only I Had a Horse (Moritoi Ch Boloosoi). B&W. Director: Dorjpalam. Composer: Mödorj.
Messenger of the People (Ardyn Elch). B&W. Director: Jigjid. Composer: Mödorj.

1960
Oversized Coat, The (Elbeg Deel). B&W. Director: Jamsran. Composer: Mödorj.
Taste of Wind, The (Salikhny Amt). B&W. Director: Dorjpalam. Composer: Tümenjargal.

1961
Before Dawn (Üüreer). B&W. Director: Jamsran. Composer: Namsraijav.
*Golden Palace (Altan Örgöö). Colour. Directors: Dorjpalam and G. Kolditz. Composers: Mödorj and P. Werner (in association with DEFA Film, East Germany).[3]
My Father is in Ulaanbaatar (Ulaanbaatart Baigaa Minii Aavd). B&W. Director: Jigjid. Composer: Gonchigsumlaa.
Unwanted Lady, The (Gologdson Khüükhen). B&W. Director: Chimed-Osor. Composer: Tserendorj.

1962
Bayasgalan (Bayasgalan). B&W. Director: Khishgit. Composer: Luvsansharav.
Khökhöö Almost Gets Married (Khökhöö Gerlekh Dökhlöö). B&W. Director: Jamsran. Composer: Birvaa.

---

[3] An asterisk denotes films co-produced with another studio (named in brackets).

Appendix A 151

One of the Ten Thousand (*Tümnii Neg*). B&W. Director: Jigjid. Composer: Namsraijav.
Secret of the Dirty Hands, The (*Bokhir Garyn Nuuts*). B&W. Director: Tserendorj. Composer: Birvaa.
Stained Rug, The (*Tolbot Khivs*). B&W. Director: Sumkhüü. Composer: Birvaa.

1963

Harmonica, The (*Aman Khuur*). B&W. Director: Jamsran. Composer: Luvsansharav.
Oh, Those Ladies! (*Ene Khüükhnüüd Üü?*). B&W. Director: Dorjpalam. Composer: Mördorj.
Sin and Virtue (*Nügel Buyan*). B&W. Director: Chimed-Osor. Composer: Luvsansharav.
Two Friends (*Khoyor Naiz*). Colour. Director: Zandraa. Composer: Birvaa.

1964

Disaster in Khovd (*Khovdgiin Gai*). B&W. Director: Genden. Composer: Namsraijav.
Unreciprocated Favour, An (*Tus Bish Us*). B&W. Director: Khishgit. Composer: Mördorj.

1965

Before the Enthronement (*Zereg Nemkhiin Ömnö*). B&W. Director: Chimed-Osor. Composer: Mördorj.
Footprints (*Khünii Mör*). B&W. Director: Jigjid. Composer: Namsraijav.
Good Intentions (*Setgeliin Duudlagaar*). B&W. Director: Dorjpalam. Composer: Dashzeveg.
Regret (*Gemshil Zemlel*). B&W. Director: Zandraa. Composer: Dashzeveg.
Water (*Us*). B&W. Director: Ariyaa. Composer: Dashzeveg.

1966

Echo of Nömrög Rock, The (*Nömrög Khadny Tsuurai*). B&W. Director: Dorjpalam. Composer: Damdinsüren.
Flood, The (*Üyer*). B&W. Director: Jigjid. Composer: Mördorj.
Lost Finds His Way, The (*Töörsöör Töröldöör*). B&W. Director: Sumkhüü. Composer: Luvsansharav.
Soldier's Son, The (*Tsergiin Khüü*). B&W. Director: Tserendorj. Composer: Banid.

1967

*End, The (*Tögsgöl*). Colour. Directors: Buntar and A. Bobrovsky. Composers: Mördorj and N. Sidelnikov (in association with Mosfilm, Soviet Union).
On the Border (*Khil Deer*). B&W. Director: Sumkhüü. Composer: Dashzeveg.

1968

City Slicker (*Niislel Khüü*). B&W. Director: Jamsran. Composer: Birvaa.

152 *Mongolian Film Music*

Morning (Öglöö). B&W. Director: Jigjid. Composer: Luvsansharav.
Respected Mother (Öndör Eej). B&W. Director: Dorjpalam. Composer: Tserendorj.

1969

Secret of the Cave, The (Agüin Nuuts). B&W. Director: Sumkhüü. Composers: Khayankhyarvaa and Mendbayar.

1970

Bridegroom, The (Khürgen Khüü). B&W. Director: Jigjid. Composer: Choidog.
Echo of the Steppe (Talyn Tsuurai). B&W. Director: Tserendorj. Composer: Dashzeveg.
First Step, The (Ankhny Alkham). B&W. Director: Jigjidsüren. Composer: Mördorj.
Tales of War (Dainy Tukhai Ögüüllegüüd). B&W. Part 1: *A Sip of Water (Balga Us)*. Director: Nyamdavaa. Composer: Birvaa; Part 2: *Small Savings Make Big Profits (Daliad Dusal Nemer)* Director: Buntar. Composer: Birvaa; Part 3: *The Two of Us (Khoyolaa)*. Director: Nyamdavaa. Composer: Tserendorj.

1971

*Attention, Soldiers! (Daisny Tsergüüdee). Colour. Directors: Sumkhüü and Boris Yermolayev. Composers: Choidog and B. A. Ovchinnikov (in association with Mosfilm, Soviet Union).
Battle, The (Temtsel). B&W. Director: Jigjid. Composer: Luvsansharav.
Red Flag (Ulaan Dartsag). B&W. Director: Khaltaryn. Composer: Birvaa.

1972

Before the Battle (Tulaldaany Ömnö). B&W. Director: Jamsran. Composer: Musaif.
In the Beginning (Ekhlelt). B&W. Director: Jigjidsüren. Composer: Mördorj.
In the Nest (Icheend Ni). B&W. Director: Sumkhüü. Composer: Luvsansharav.

1973

Clear River Tamir, The (Tungalag Tamir). (1970–73). B&W. Director: Dorjpalam. Composer: Namsraijav.
Community of Bayan Bulag, The (Bayanbulgiinkhan). B&W. Director: Jigjid. Composer: Birvaa.
New Acquaintances (Shine Taniluud). Colour. Directors: Tserendorj and Nyamdavaa. Composers: Birvaa and Janchiv.
Sound of the Engine, The (Motoryn Duu). B&W. Director: Sumkhüü. Composer: Luvsansharav.

1974

Daughter of the River Tamir (Tamiryn Okhin). B&W. Director: Chimed-Osor. Composer: Janchiv.
Happiness in the Countryside (Khödöögiin Bayasgalan). B&W. Director: Jigjid. Composer: Birvaa.

Appendix A 153

Meeting, The (*Uulzalt*). B&W. Director: Nyamdavaa. Composer: Namsraijav.
Treasure of the Gobi (*Goviin Nüden*). Colour. Director: Jigjidsüren. Composer: Mördorj.
Two Classmates (*Neg Angiin Khoyor*). B&W. Director: Damdin. Composer: Birvaa.
Year of the Eclipse. (*Nar Khirtsen Jil*). Colour. Director: Buntar. Composer: Choidog.

1975
Beloved, The (*Khani*). B&W. Director: Sumkhüü. Composer: Luvsansharav.
Egg, The (*Öndög*). Colour. Director: Dashdorj. Composer: Sangidorj.
Legend of Ekh Bürd, The (*Ekh Bürdiin Domog*). Colour. Directors: Buntar and Jigjidsüren. Composer: E. Choidog.
Story of the Golden Soyombo[4] (*Altan Soyombyn Duulal*). Colour. Director: Dorjpalam. Composer: Chuluun.
Sükhbold's Conversation (*Sükhboldyn Yaria*). B&W. Director: Nyamdavaa. Composer: Chimiddorj.
Tales of First Love (*Ankhny Khairyn Duuli*). Colour. Director: B. Sumkhüü. Composers: Luvsansharav and Batsükh.
Unforgettable Autumn, An (*Martagdashgüi Namar*). B&W. Director: Damdin. Composer: Janchiv.

1976
Human Soul (*Khünii Ami*). B&W. Director: Jigjidsüren. Composer: Mördorj.
New Beginning, The (*Shine Khotyn Gerel*). Colour. Director: Dorjpalam. Composer: Janchiv.
Philanthropist, The (*Khünii Tölöö*). B&W. Director: Jigjid. Composer: Birvaa.
Sheep's Feast, The (*Khoniny Nair*). B&W. Directors: Chimed-Osor and Tserendorj. Composer: Chuluun.

1977
Blue Mist (*Khökh Nogoony Uniar*). B&W. Director: Jigjid. Composer: Birvaa.
Childhood (*Degdeekhei Nas*). Colour. Director: Nyamdavaa. Composer: Khangal.
Friends from Summer Camp (*Zuslangiin Naizuud*). Colour. Director: Damdin. Composer: Janchiv.
Rolling Hills, The (*Davaany Tsaana Davaa*). Colour. Director: Buntar. Composer: Chuluun.

1978
After the Storm (*Tengeriin Muukhai Arildag*). Colour. Director: Dorjpalam. Composer: Janchiv.
Beautiful Blue Mountains (*Suvargan Tsenkher Uuls*). B&W. Director: Jigjidsüren. Composer: Khangal.

---

[4] The *Soyombo* is the symbol that appears on the national flag of Mongolia.

154   *Mongolian Film Music*

Five Colours of the Rainbow (Solongyn Tavan Öngö). Colour. Director: Nagnaidorj. Composer: Damdinsüren.

Scent of the Land, The (Gazryn Üner). Colour. Director: Damdin. Composer: Janchiv.

Start of the Journey, The (Ikh Zamyn Ekhend). B&W. Director: Sumkhüü, Composer: Namsraijav.

*Where are the Khairkhan Öndör Mountains? (Khairkhan Öndör Khaana Baina). Colour. Directors: Nyamdavaa and T. Iva. Composers: Mördorj and S. Irji (in association with Barrandov Studio, Czechoslovakia).

Wings of the Land (Gazryn Jigüür). B&W. Director: Jigjid. Composer: Luvsansharav.

1979

Aurora of Venus (Üüriin Tsolmon). B&W. Director: Buntar. Composer: Batsükh.

Letter of Notice (Toirokh Khuudas). B&W. Director: Selengesüren. Composer: Chuluun.

Naidan the Shepherd (Khonichin Naidan). B&W. Director: Nyamdavaa. Composer: Mördorj.

Nomads on the Move (Tuuvryn Zamd). B&W. Director: Jamsran. Composer: Birvaa.

Story of Bushkhüü, The (Bushkhüügiin Ülger). Colour. Director: Tsogzol. Composer: Namsraijav.

1980

Beginning, The (Ekhlel). B&W. Director: Selengesüren. Composer: Altankhuyag.

Big Family, A (Önör Bül). Colour. Director: Jigjid. Composer: Damdinsüren.

Broken Trust (Itleg Gomdol). B&W. Director: Nyam-Ochir.

Difficult Decision, A (Shiidverlekh Alkham). B&W. Directors: Ichinnorov and Nyam-Ochir. Composer: Natsagdorj.

Mirage in the Gobi (Goviin Zereglee). Colour. Director: Dorjpalam. Composer: Janchiv.

Person with Good Intentions, The (Khünii Saikhan Setgel). B&W. Director: Natsagdorj. Composer: Damdinsüren.

Re-evaluation (Ergej Bodokh Bodol). Colour. Director: Damdin. Composer: Janchiv.

1981

Aranjin the Swindler (Gul Aranjin). B&W. Director: Tserendorj. Composer: Chuluun.

*Battle in Gobi Khyangan (Govi Khyangand Tulaldsan Ni). Colour. Director: O. Vasily. Composer: Damdinsüren (in association with Mosfilm, Soviet Union).

Khatanbaatar (Khatanbaatar). Colour. Director: Jigjidsüren. Composer: Khangal.

Not Yet Married (Gerlej Amjaagüi Yavna). Colour. Director: Buntar. Composer: Khangal.

Soldiers' Days (Tsereg Ersiin Jiriin Ödrüüd). B&W. Director: Nyamdavaa. Composer: Namsraijav.

Appendix A 155

1982

Happiness Taken for Granted (*Jargal Daakhgüin Zovlon*). Colour. Director: Jigjid. Composer: Luvsansharav.

Old Temple (*Khuuchin Sum*). Colour. Director: Selengesüren. Composer: Altankhuyag.

Spark of the Battle (*Temtsliin Och*). Colour. Director: Dorjpalam. Composer: Khangal.

1983

Before Sunrise (*Üür Tsaikhyn Ömnö*). B&W. Director: Damdin. Composer: Natsagdorj.

Childhood Friends (*Bagyn Naiz*). B&W. Director: Tserendorj. Composer: Chimiddorj.

Five Fingers (*Garyn Tavan Khuruu*). Colour. Directors: Baljinnyam and Nyamgavaa. Composer: Jantsannorov.

Giddy-up! (*Giingoo*). Colour. Director: Ichinnorov. Composer: Natsagdorj.

*Guide, The (*Gazarchin*). Colour. Directors: Buntar and P. Konrad. Composer: Karl Ernest Sasse (in association with DEFA Film, East Germany).

Is It a Talisman or a Guard? (*Sakhius Uu, Sakhiul Uu?*). B&W. Director: Sumkhüü. Composer: Damdinsüren.

Prediction, The (*Ingekh Geed Baisan Yum*). Colour. Director: Jamsran. Composer: Birvaa.

Wrestler, The (*Garid Magnai*). Colour. Director: Buntar. Composer: Jantsannorov.

1984

Apple of the Gobi (*Zagiin Alim*). Colour. Director: Damdin. Composer: Jamsranjav.

Ayuush of the People (*Ard Ayuush*). B&W. Director: Jigjid. Composer: Sharav.

Colt of the Sun (*Narny Unaga*). Colour. Director: Jigjidsüren. Composer: Khangal.

Don't Forget Me (*Sanaj Yavaarai*). Colour. Director: Selengesüren. Composer: Altankhuyag.

Moving to Be With You (*Tani Ruu Nüüj Yavna*). B&W. Director: Baljinnyam. Composer: Khangal.

Prayer for the Broad Steppe (*Saruul Talyn Yerööl*). Colour. Director: Dorjpalam. Composer: Chuluun.

Sound of Victory, The (*Yalaltyn Duun*). Colour. Director: Dorjpalam. Composers: Jantsannorov and Khayankhyarvaa.

Tale of the Unannounced Battle (*Zarlaagüi Dainy Orshil*). Colour. Director: Jigjidsüren. Composer: Khangal.

1985

Application for the Front Line (*Frontod Yavakh Örgödöl*). Colour. Director: Jigjidsüren. Composer: Damdinsüren.

Dusty Road, The (*Ikh Zamyn Toos*). Colour. Director: Selengesüren. Composer: Namsraijav.

156 *Mongolian Film Music*

Duties of War (*Baildaany Daalgavar*). B&W. Director: Natsagdorj. Composer: Sharav.

Flickering Flames (*Galyn Ursgal*). B&W. Director: Buntar. Composer: Khangal.

Hot Autumn Day (*Namryn Khaluun Ödrüüd*). Colour. Director: Dolgor. Composer: Jantsannorov.

I Love You (*Bi Chamd Khairtai*). Colour. Director: Baljinnyam. Composer: Jantsannorov.

Silver Camel Herder's Tool (*Möngön Buil*). B&W. Director: Dorjpalam. Composer: Mördorj.

Spelling Mistake, The (*Atsag Shüdnii Zöröö*). B&W. Director: Baljinnyam. Composer: Damdinsüren.

We Didn't Forget You (*Bid Martakhgüi*). Colour. Director: Damdin. Composer: Jamsranjav.

1986

Dew (*Süüder*). Colour. Director: Baljinnyam. Composer: Jantsannorov.

Flower of Next Spring, The (*Irekh Khavryn Tsetseg*). B&W. Director: Selengesüren. Composer: Janchiv.

Future is Coming, The (*Irj Yavaa Tsag*). Colour. Director: Buntar. Composer: Khangal.

Precious Gems (*Nandin Erdene*). Colour. Director: Nyamgavaa. Composer: Pürevdorj.

Trees Grown in the Autumn (*Namar Nakhialsan Mod*). Colour. Director: Jigjidsüren. Composer: Khangal.

Zangi the Guard (*Kharuul Zangi*). B&W. Director: Dorjpalam. Composer: Chuluun.

1987

At the End of the Tale (*Ülger Duussan Khoino*). Colour. Director: Nyamgavaa. Composer: Altankhuyag.

Extended Summer, An (*Ilüü Sartai Zun*). Colour. Director: Selengesüren. Composer: Sharav.

I Like Flying (*Bi Nisekh Durtai*). Colour. Director: Sumkhüü. Composer: Khangal.

Reflection of Sunrise, The (*Mandakh Narny Tuyaa*). Colour. Director: Damdin. Composer: Janchiv.

Scarce People (*Khovor Khümüüs*). Colour. Director: Nyamdavaa. Composer: Bilegjargal.

Stranger, The (*Khünii Khün*). Colour. Director: Jumdaan. Composer: Chinzorig.

1988

Budding of Life, The (*Amidralyn Nakhia*). Colour. Director: Damdin. Composer: Jamsranjav.

Descendants of Nature (*Uul Usny Ür Sad*). Colour. Director: Nyamdavaa. Composer: Khangal.

Difficult Tasks (*Khetsüü Daalgavar*). Colour. Director: Dorjpalam. Composer: Chuluun.

Appendix A 157

Mandukhai the Wise Queen (*Mandukhai Tsetsen Khatan*). Colour. Director: Baljinnyam. Composer: Jantsannorov

1989

Deep Blue Övs Lake (*Khökh Övsnii Nuur Khölgüi*). Colour. Director: Sumkhüü. Composer: Damdinsüren.

Disaster at Serüün Temple (*Serüün Dygany Mökhöl*). Colour. Director: Damchaa. Composer: Damdinsüren.

Forgotten Tale, The (*Martagdsan Duuli*). Colour. Director: Selengesüren. Composer: Sharav.

Golden Hawk, The (*Altan Shonkhor*). Colour. Director: Jigjidsüren. Composer: Janchiv.

Musician, The (*Khögjimchin*). Colour. Directors: Nyamdavaa and Bold. Composer: Khangal.

Mysterious Person, The (*Khachin Khün*). B&W. Directors: Baljinnyam and Nagnaidorj. Composer: Jantsannorov.

Whirlpool (*Ergüüleg*). Colour. Director: Jumdaan. Composer: Altankhuyag.

Wilting Flower, The (*Dali Khagdrakh Tsagaar*). Colour. Director: Nyamdavaa. Composer: Khangal.

1990

Champion Horse, The (*Tod Magnai*). Colour. Director: Buntar. Composer: Jantsannorov.

Game Bell (*Alag Melkhiin Khonkh*). Colour. Director: Uranchimeg. Composer: Chinzorig.

Ganaa's Comedy Story (*Ganaagiin Payan*). Colour. Director: Tövsanaa. Composer: Khangal.

Milky White Palace (*Süün Tsagaan Örgöö*). Colour. Director: Damdin. Composers: Khangal and Mergejikh.

Shooting Star (*Odod Orchikh Khyazgaar*). Colour. Director: Sumkhüü. Composer: Batsükh.

Statue's Tears, The (*Khün Chuluuny Nulims*). Colour. Director: Jigjidsüren. Composer: Jantsannorov.

Warm Ashes (*Büleen Nuram*). Colour. Director: Jigjidsüren. Composer: Jantsannorov.

Appendix B
Glossary of Mongolian Words

Ail	An encampment of *ger*s, often belonging to one extended family
Aimag	Province
Airag	Fermented mare's milk (a traditional alcoholic beverage)
Altan Üye	'Golden age'
Aman khuur	Jaw harp; harmonica
Ardyn duu	Lit. public song, a new type of folk song developed during the Socialist era
Ardyn khögjim	Lit. music of the people, new folk music of the Socialist era
Bishgüür	A non-valved trumpet with a sound like a rich oboe
Bogino duu	Lit. short-song, a traditional Mongolian song/singing style, typically with one note to each syllable
Chinggis Khaan	Genghis Khan
Damaru	A small hand-held drum with two drumheads used in Buddhist and sometimes shamanic ceremonies
Deel	Traditional long-sleeved robe worn by both men and women
Dembe	A 'game song' in which singers/competitors improvise lyrics
Dombra	A Kazakh two-stringed lute
Domog	Legend
Dund khuur	Member of horse-head fiddle family, corresponds in pitch (and roughly in sound) to the violoncello
Eriin gurvan naadam	The 'three manly sports' of archery, wrestling and horse racing
Ever büree	A curly horn instrument with a sound similar to the clarinet
Gyaling	A Buddhist flute traditionally made from the thigh bone of a virgin

Mongolian Film Music

Ger	Lit. house or home, generally refers to a round felt tent (yurt)
Geriin khögjim	Lit. home music or domestic music, another term for folk music
Giingoo	A song sung by child jockeys before a horse race
Ikh büree	A large, low-pitched telescope trumpet used in Buddhist temples, originally from Tibet, common in Mongolia
Ikh khuur	Member of horse-head fiddle family, corresponds in pitch (and roughly in sound) to the double bass
Isgeree	Whistling, also used to describe the high-pitched style of *khöömii*
Khadag	Blue silk scarf used in rituals, given to people as a mark of respect
Khalkha	The largest ethnic group in Mongolia
Kharaal	Lit. curse, a genre of vocal music
Kharkhiraa	Low-pitched style of *khöömii*
Khögjim	Music
Khöömii	Overtone singing, also known as throat singing
Khöömiich	A singer of *khöömii*
Khuuchir	A two-stringed bowed fiddle similar to the Chinese *erhu*
Khuvsgalyn duu	Revolutionary song
Kino	Film, cinema
Limbe	A side-blown shepherd's flute
Magtaal	A song in praise of something or someone
Mergejliin khögjim	Lit. professional music, a genre or subgenre of symphonic music that utilises characteristics of traditional Mongolian music
Morin khuur	Horse-head fiddle, a two-stringed bowed spike fiddle decorated with a carved wooden horse's head at the top of the neck
Naadam	Festival; the main festival takes place every July and involves the 'three manly sports' of horse racing, wrestling and archery
Nauryz	Kazakh New Year, takes place in March
Niitiin duu	Lit. common song, a new folk music genre developed during the Socialist era

Appendix B   161

Nutag	Homeland, referring to an area a person was born, not the country
Ordony khögjim	Palace music, a traditional genre associated with the ruling classes
Ovog	A person's father's name, similar usage to a surname
Shanz, shudraga	A three-stringed plucked instrument similar to the banjo or Japanese *shamisen*
Songodog khögjim	Classical or art music
Sybyzgy	A Kazakh overtone flute (Kazakh equivalent of the *tsuur*)
Tögrög	The currency in Mongolia
Tovshuur	A Mongolian two-stringed fretless lute
Tsagaan Sar	Lit. white month/moon, Mongolian New Year, takes place in February
Tsam	A Buddhist masked dance accompanied by Tibetan music
Tsorj	A Buddhist title, roughly equivalent to 'abbot'
Tsuur	A traditional Mongolian herders' overtone flute
Tuuli	Epic (song or poetry) from west Mongolia
Ulaan bulan	'Red corners', provincial cultural centres during the Socialist era
Urtyn duu	Lit. long-song, a traditional, highly ornamented Mongolian song/singing style with many notes sung to each syllable
Uukhai	A traditional song genre sung at traditional sporting events, for example wrestling
Yatga	A zither (similar to the Korean *gayageum*, Chinese *guzheng* or Japanese *koto*)
Yazguur khögjim	Lit. music of ancestors, new folk music developed during the Socialist era, performed by professionals, usually in an ensemble
Yerööl	A prayer song or blessing, for example for a wedding or a birth
Yoochin	A stringed instrument similar to the hammer dulcimer
Zodog	A cropped open-fronted shirt worn by Mongolian wrestlers
Zokhiolyn duu	Lit. composed song, a new genre of popular folk music developed during the Socialist era

Appendix C
Glossary of Film and Film Music Terminology

Cinematographer	The lead member of the camera and lighting crews, responsible for technical and artistic decisions regarding the camera and lights
Cross-fade (verb)	One scene or one cue fades out whilst another fades in
Cue	An individual piece or fragment of music used in a film
Diegetic	Music in a film that the characters can hear, and when the source is shown: for example, musicians or a radio
Final cut	The final version of a film, ready for release
Film designer	The person in Mongolian filmmaking who draws the storyboard, designs the costumes and set, and often paints portraits of actors or film scenes
Film song	A song played at the end of a film, often used to promote the film before its release via radio broadcasts
Glue/gluing	When a cue enters at the end of one scene and continues into the start of the next scene to provide continuity
Hit-points	When music matches exactly the action on screen, such as a cymbal crash during an explosion
Rough cut	A 'complete' version of a film subject to further editing
Score (noun)	The music for a film, not its dialogue or sound effects
Score (verb)	To compose a film score
Screenplay	The script of a film or television programme (fiction)
Semidiegetic	Music of which the source is known but not seen on screen, such as music at a disco when the DJ is not visible
Semidocumentary	A fictional story featuring realistic events, presented in the style of a documentary
Sound design	Electronically manipulated audio, often used as underscoring

Soundtrack	The sound of a film, which includes three types of sound: the music, sound effects and dialogue
Spotting	The decision as to which scenes should have music, often decided during a meeting between the director and composer
Storyboard	A series of illustrations depicting scenes of a film, used before filming to help the director and crew visualise the film
Treatment	A sketch or outline of a film screenplay
Underscoring	Film music that is not meant to be part of the action

Appendix D
Timeline

c. 1162–1227	Chinggis Khaan (born Temujin, also known as Genghis Khan)
1206–1368	The Mongol Empire
1215–94	Khubilai Khan, Chinggis Khaan's grandson
c. 1449–1510	Mandukhai Khatan (known as the Wise Queen who reunited Mongolia)
1581–1637	Tsogt Taij (supported Ligden Khan and the Red Hat sect of Buddhism)
1644–1911	Qing (Manchu) Dynasty
Dec. 1911	Mongolia declares independence from Manchu (Qing/Chinese) rule
Dec. 1911	Buddhist leader the Bogd Khan becomes Head of State in Mongolia
1917	Russian Revolution; Bolsheviks and Red Army overthrow the Tsar
1917–24	Vladimir Lenin is creator and leader of the Soviet Union
25 Jun. 1920	Formation of the Mongolian People's Party
Oct. 1920	Baron Ungern-Sternberg attacks Urga (the name of the capital city in 1920)
Nov. 1920	First issue of Mongolian party newspaper *Ünen* printed in Irkutsk
Feb. 1921	Ungern-Sternberg captures Urga
27 Jun. 1921	1921 Revolution, when Sükhbaatar and Red Army claim victory
Sept. 1921	Ungern-Sternberg tried and executed in Novosibirsk
1921–90	The Socialist era in Mongolia
1921–90	Mongolian People's Revolutionary Party (MPRP) is the only party in Mongolia
1921	Mongolian Revolutionary League of Youth established
1921–40	Phase of 'democratic transition': Mongolia prepares for socialism
1924	The Bogd Khan dies; Mongolian People's Republic (MPR) declared
1924	The capital city of Mongolia, previously Urga, renamed Ulaanbaatar (lit. Red Hero)
1924	Mongolia joins Comintern (Communist International 1919–43)
1924–53	Joseph Stalin is leader of the Soviet Union
1925	Mongolian Pioneers established (subsidiary of Revolutionary League of Youth)

1925	Construction of the building for the Mongolian military music ensemble
1928–31	Cultural Revolution in the Soviet Union
1929–32	'Great Leap Forward': cultural revolution in Mongolia (see also 1959)
1931	Mongolian state radio and first theatre, Bömbögör Nogoon, established
1932	Mongolian Military Song and Dance Academic Ensemble established
1932	Composers' Union established in the Soviet Union
1933	Mongolian Ministry of Public Education establishes a cinema department
Oct. 1935	Governmental decree to establish a Mongolian film industry
1936	State film studio established (*Kino Üildver*, lit. Film Factory). Only studio until 1990
1936	First Mongolian–Soviet collaboration film, *Son of Mongolia* (*Mongol Khüü*)
1936–39	Khorloogiin Choibalsan is Minister of Internal Affairs in Mongolia
1937	School of Culture established in Ulaanbaatar
1937	Soviet troops stationed in Mongolia
Sept. 1937– Apr. 1939	'Great Purge', under Choibalsan's leadership
1938	First Film Factory (silent) feature film, *Norjmaa's Way* (*Norjmaagiin Zam*)
1939–52	Choibalsan is Prime Minister of Mongolia
1940	Tenth Congress of MPRP: Mongolia is considered ready to implement socialism
1941	Mongolia adopts Cyrillic alphabet, replacing Classical Mongol script
1941–45	The Great Patriotic War (the Soviet Union's involvement in World War II)
1942	Mongolia's first 'national opera' *Uchirtai Gurvan Tolgoi* produced
1945	Mongolian National Song and Dance Academic Ensemble established
1947–52	The first five-year plan in Mongolia
1950	Mongolian State Opera and Ballet Theatre established
1950	Mongolian state radio music department set up
1952–74	Yumjaagiin Tsedenbal is Prime Minister of Mongolia
1953	Central Committee of the MPRP takes control of process of collectivisation
1953–64	Nikita Khrushchev is General Secretary of the Communist Party of the Soviet Union (CPSU)
1956	Mongolian State Symphony Orchestra established

Appendix D 167

1957	Mongolian Composers' Union established
1957	Mongolian state radio music archive set up
1959	Mongolian 'Cultural Leap Forward' (see also 1929–32)
1959	School of Culture in Ulaanbaatar renamed State College of Music and Dance
1959	Classical music taught at State College of Music and Dance
c. late 1950s–mid-1980s	*Altan Üye* ('golden age') of Mongolian film music
1960	Construction began on the building of the Mongolian Film Archive
1961	Mongolia becomes a member of the United Nations
1962	Mongolia joins COMECON
1962	Mongolia becomes a member of UNESCO
1963	The Film Factory's first short film in colour, *Two Friends* (*Khoyor Naiz*)
1963	National Academic Drama Theatre established
1964	Eight Mongolian students (the first of many) sent by UNESCO to study at the University of Leeds
1964–82	Leonid Brezhnev is General Secretary of the CPSU
1966	Fifteenth Congress of MPRP: Mongolia is considered to have established socialism
1967	Mongolian National Broadcaster (state television) established
1971	First state rock band, Soyol Erdene (Cultural Treasure), officially founded
1973	The Film Factory's first full-length colour film, *New Acquaintances* (*Shine Taniluud*)
1974–84	Jambyn Batmönkh is Prime Minister of Mongolia
1982–84	Yuri Andropov is General Secretary of the CPSU
1984–85	Konstantin Chernenko is General Secretary of the CPSU
1984–90	Dumaagiin Sodnom is Prime Minister of Mongolia
1985–91	Mikhail Gorbachev is General Secretary of the CPSU
Mid- to late 1980s	Gorbachev instigates policies of glasnost and perestroika
Dec. 1990	First in a series of (largely) peaceful demonstrations in Ulaanbaatar
Jul. 1990	Democratic elections in Mongolia; MPRP wins majority
1990–92	Dash Byambasüren of the MPRP is Prime Minister of Mongolia
Dec. 1991	Dissolution of the Soviet Union
1992	Mongolian National Horse-Head Fiddle Ensemble officially established
1992–96	Puntsagiin Jasrai of the MPRP is Prime Minister of Mongolia
1996–2000	Five Mongolian Prime Ministers in turn, all from Democratic Union (not MPRP)

168 *Mongolian Film Music*

2000–2012 (except Aug. 2004 to Jan. 2006)	MPRP back in power
2006	Celebrations for the eight-hundredth anniversary of the Mongolian State
2006	*Ikh Türiin Golomt* is first Mongolian film to use surround sound
2008	Forty-metre high Chinggis Khaan equestrian statue constructed in Töv province

Bibliography

Aalto, P., 1962. Music of the Mongols: an introduction. In: Sinor, D. ed. 1962. *Aspects of Altaic civilization*. Uralic and Altaic Series 23. Bloomington: Indiana University Publications, pp. 59–65.

Anon., n.d., *The secret history of the Mongols*. Translated from Middle Mongol and ed. by F. W. Cleaves. 1982. Cambridge, MA: Harvard University Press.

——, 1968. Honorable duties of artists [editorial in Ünen]. Translated from Mongolian in: Joint Publications Research Service, 9 April 1969, *Translations on Mongolia no. 190*. p. 24

Aubert, L., 2007. *The music of the Other: new challenges for ethnomusicology in a global age*. Translated from French by C. Riberio. Aldershot: Ashgate.

Baabar, 1999. *History of Mongolia: from world power to Soviet satellite*. Translated from Mongolian by D. Sükhjargalmaa et al., ed. by C. Kaplonski. Cambridge: White Horse.

Badrakh, G., 1960. *Mongolyn khögjmiin tüükhees* [*The history of Mongolian music*]. Ulaanbaatar: Studia Ethnographica.

Barth, F., 1969. Introduction. In: Barth, F. ed. 1969. *Ethnic groups and boundaries: the social organization of culture difference*. London: George Allen & Unwin, pp. 9–38.

Bartig, K., 2013. *Composing for the red screen: Prokofiev and Soviet film*. New York: Oxford University Press.

Batbayar, Ts., 1999. Stalin's strategy in Mongolia, 1932–1936. *Mongolian Studies (Journal of the Mongolian Society)*, 22, pp. 1–30.

Bawden, C. R., 1962. The Mongol 'conversation song'. In: Sinor, D. ed. 1962. *Aspects of Altaic civilization*. Uralic and Altaic Series 23. Bloomington: Indiana University Publications, pp. 75–86.

——, 1968. *The modern history of Mongolia*. London: Weidenfeld & Nicolson.

Beliaev, V. M., 1962. *Central Asian music*. Translated from Russian and ed. by M. Slobin and G. Slobin. 1975. Middletown: Wesleyan University Press.

Biddle, I. and Knights, V. eds, 2007. *Music, national identity and the politics of location*. Aldershot: Ashgate.

Blacking, J., 1976. *How musical is man?* London: Faber & Faber.

Booth, G., 2009. *Behind the curtain: making music in Mumbai's film studios*. New York: Oxford University Press.

Bruun, O. and Narangoa, L. eds, 2006. *Mongols from country to city: floating boundaries, pastoralism and city life in the Mongol lands*. Copenhagen: Nordic Institute of Asian Studies.

Bryusova, N. 1918. Proletarian music. In: W. G. Rosenberg, ed. 1990. *Bolshevik visions: first phase of the Cultural Revolution in Soviet Russia*. 2nd ed. Ann Arbor: University of Michigan Press. pp. 252–5.

Bulag, Uradyn E., 1998. *Nationalism and hybridity in Mongolia*. Oxford: Clarendon Press.

Buyandelger, M., 2008. Tricky representations: Buddhism in the cinema during socialism in Mongolia. *Silk Road*, 6(1) (Summer), pp. 54–62.

Camman, S., 1962. Mongol costume: historical and recent. In: Sinor, D. ed. 1962. *Aspects of Altaic civilization*. Uralic and Altaic Series 23. Bloomington: Indiana University Publications, pp. 157–66.

Cassidy Jr, R. B., 1971. Mongolia: at plan's end. *Asian Survey*, 11(1), pp. 86–91.

Central Statistical Bureau of the Council of Ministers of the MPRP, 1977. *National economy of the MPRP in 1977: a compilation of statistics*. Translated from Mongolian in: Joint Publications Research Service, 30 May 1979.

——, 1981. *National economy of the MPRP in 1981: a compilation of statistics*. Translated from Mongolian in: Joint Publications Research Service, 27 January 1986.

Dambaasambuu, P., 1970. Clubs and recreation rooms are centers of cultural, educational work. Translated from Mongolian in: Joint Publications Research Service, 1971. *Translations on Mongolia*, 245 (4 June), pp. 37–43.

Dashdondog, S., 1964. Basic questions of arts and culture. Translated from Mongolian in: Joint Publications Research Service, 1965. *Translations on Mongolia*, 63 (12 January) pp. 25–30.

Davis, R., 2000. *Complete guide to film scoring*. Boston: Berklee Press.

Djumaev, A., 1993. Power structures, culture policy, and traditional music in Soviet Central Asia. *Yearbook for Traditional Music*, 25, pp. 43–50.

Dönmez-Colin, G., 2006. *Cinemas of the Other: a personal journey with filmmakers from the Middle East and Central Asia*. Bristol: Intellect.

Dorjgotov, D., 2006. *History and culture of the Mongols*. Translated from Mongolian by E. Thrift and J. Tsolmon, ed. by Canzhid. Ulaanbaatar: International Institute for the Study of Nomadic Civilizations.

Egorova, T. K., 1997. *Soviet film music: an historical survey*. Translated from Russian by T. Ganf and N. Egunova. Amsterdam: Harwood Academic.

Emsheimer, E., 1986. Earliest reports about the music of the Mongols. Translated from German by R. Carroll. *Asian Music*, 18(1), pp. 1–19.

Enkhtsetseg, D., 2007. *Khögjim öv sang* [*Music heritage treasury*]. Ulaanbaatar: MNB Art.

Enkhtüvshin, B. and Enebish, J., 2007. *The inner sense and understanding of the nomadic people's musical psychology*. Ulaanbaatar: International Institute for the Study of Nomadic Civilisations.

Frolova-Walker, M., 1998. 'National in form, socialist in content': musical nation-building in the Soviet republics. *Journal of the American Musicological Society*, 51(2) (Summer), pp. 331–71.

Bibliography 171

Gorbachev, M. S., 1987. *Perestroika: new thinking for our country and the world.* Translated from Russian. New York: Harper and Row.

Grivelet, S., 1995. Reintroducing the Uighur-Mongolian script in Mongolia today. *Mongolian Studies: Journal of the Mongolia Society*, 18, pp. 49–60.

Hangin, J. G. ed., 1998. *Mongolian folklore: a representative collection from the oral literary tradition.* Translated from Mongolian by J. G. Hangin. Bloomington, IN: The Mongolia Society Incorporation.

Heissig, W., 1966. *A lost civilization.* Translated from German by D. J. S. Thomson. London: Thames & Hudson.

Herndon, M. and McCleod, N., 1983. *Field manual for ethnomusicology.* Norwood, PA: Norwood Editions.

Hill, S. P., 1967. The Soviet film today. *Film Quarterly*, 20(4), pp. 33–52.

Humphrey, C., 1974a. Horse brands of the Mongolians: a system of signs in nomadic culture. *American Ethnologist*, 1(3), pp. 471–88.

——, 1974b. Inside a Mongolian tent. *New Society*, 31 (October), pp. 273–5.

——, 1981. Text and ritual for the libation of mare's milk. *Journal of the Anglo-Mongolian Society*, 7(2), pp. 78–96.

——, 1992. The moral authority of the past in post-Socialist Mongolia. *Religion, State and Society*, 20 (3–4), pp. 375–89.

——, 2002. *The unmaking of Soviet life: everyday economies after socialism.* Ithaca, NY: Cornell University Press.

Humphrey, C. and Sneath, D., 1999. *The end of nomadism?: society, state and the environment in Inner Asia.* Durham, NC: Duke University Press.

Hyer, P., 1996. The re-evaluation of Chinggis Khan: its role in the Sino-Soviet dispute. *Asian Survey*, 6(12), pp. 696–705.

Isono, F., 2010. Soviet Russia and the Mongolian revolution of 1921 [1976]. In: Sneath, D. and Kaplonski, C. eds. *The history of Mongolia.* Folkestone: Global Oriental, pp. 910–29.

Jagchid, S. and Hyer, P., 1979. *Mongolia's culture and society.* Boulder, CO: Westview Press.

Jarrett, K., 1988. Mongolia in 1987: out from the cold? *Asian Survey*, 28(1), pp. 78–85.

Jenkins, J. L., 1960. The morienhur: a Mongolian fiddle. *Man*, 60, pp. 129–30.

Jigjidsüren, G. and Tsetseg, D., 2005. *Mongol kinony nevterkhii toli [Encyclopaedia of Mongolian cinema].* 800th Anniversary Special Edition. Ulaanbaatar:

Kaplonski, C., 2010. Democracy comes to Mongolia [2004]. In: Sneath, D. and Kaplonski, C. eds. *The history of Mongolia.* Folkestone: Global Oriental. pp. 1,039–1,059

Kozlenko, W., 1937. Soviet music and musicians. *Musical Quarterly*, 23(3), pp. 295–305.

Krueger, J. R., 1959. The impact of Russian and Western literature on Mongolia. *The Slavic and East European Journal*, 3(1), pp. 25–34.

Lattimore, O., 1962. *Nomads and commissars: Mongolia revisited.* Oxford: Oxford University Press.

Lattimore, O. and Urgunge Onon, 1955. *Nationalism and revolution in Mongolia.* Leiden: E. J. Brill.

Levin, T., 1996. *The hundred thousand fools of God: musical travels in Central Asia.* Bloomington: Indiana University Press.

Lovell, S., 2009. *The Soviet Union: a very short introduction.* Oxford: Oxford University Press.

McGregor, J., 1993. Mongolia's lament: in the post-Soviet era, a nation of nomads wanders into oblivion. *The Mongolia Society Newsletter*, 14, pp. 44–6.

Mackerras, C., 1983. Traditional Mongolian performing arts in Inner Mongolia. *The Australian Journal of Chinese Affairs*, 10, pp. 17–38.

Malkov, N., 1927. Music and the Cultural Revolution. In: W. G. Rosenberg, ed. *Bolshevik visions: first phase of the Cultural Revolution in Soviet Russia.* 2nd ed. Ann Arbor: University of Michigan Press, pp. 264–8.

Man, J., 1999. *Gobi: tracking the desert.* New Haven, CT: Yale University Press.

Mandel, W., 1949. Outer Mongolia's five-year plan. *Far Eastern Survey*, 18(12), pp. 140–44.

Manuel, P., 1991. *Popular musics of the non-Western world: an introductory survey.* New York: Oxford University Press.

Marples, David R., 2004. *The collapse of the Soviet Union 1985–1991.* Harlow: Pearson Education Ltd.

Marsh, P. K., 2004. Of fiddles and violins: a folk fiddle-maker seeks to aid Mongolia's violinists. *Mongol Survey*, 14, pp. 14–16.

——, 2006. Beyond the Soviet houses of culture: rural responses to urban cultural policies in contemporary Mongolia. In: Brunn, O. and Naronga, L. eds. *Mongols from country to city: floating boundaries, pastoralism and city life in the Mongol lands.* Copenhagen: Nordic Institute of Asian Studies, pp. 290–304.

——, 2009. *The horse-head fiddle and the cosmopolitan reimagination of tradition in Mongolia.* New York: Routledge.

Mend-Ooyo, G., 2007. *Golden hill.* Translated from Mongolian by Simon Wickham-Smith. Ulaanbaatar: Mongolian Academy of Culture and Poetry.

Merriam, A. P., 1964. *The anthropology of music.* Evanston: University of Illinois Press.

Metternich, H. R., 1996. *Mongolian folk tales.* Boulder, CO: Avery Press.

Morcom, A., 2007. *Hindi film songs and the cinema.* Aldershot: Ashgate.

Moses, L. and Halkovic Jr, S. A., 1985. *Introduction to Mongolian history and culture.* Uralic and Altaic Series 149. Bloomington: Indiana University Publications

Nash, M., 1995. Performing arts in Mongolia: coping with transition. *Mongolia Survey*, 2, pp. 29–33.

National Statistical Office of Mongolia. 2011. *Mongolian national census 2010: provisional results.* Ulaanbaatar: National Statistical Office of Mongolia.

Nettl, B., 1985. *The Western impact on world music.* New York: Schirmer.

——, 2006. *The study of ethnomusicology: thirty-one issues and concepts,* 2nd edn. Urbana: University of Illinois Press.

Nordby, J., 1993. *Mongolia.* World Bibliographical Series 156. Oxford: Clio Press.

Pegg, C., 1991. The revival of ethnic and cultural identity in West Mongolia: the Altai Uriangkhai *tsuur*, Tuvan *shuur* and Kazakh *sybyzgy. Journal of the Anglo-Mongolian Society*, 12(1–2), pp. 71–84.

——, 1992. Mongolian conceptualizations of overtone singing (*xöömii*). *British Journal of Ethnomusicology*, 1, pp. 31–54.

——, 1995. Ritual, religion and magic in West Mongolian (*Oirad*) heroic epic performance. *British Journal of Ethnomusicology*, 4, pp. 77–99.

——, 2001. *Mongolian music, dance and oral narrative: performing diverse identities.* Seattle: University of Washington Press.

Pokrass, D. ed., 1942. *Red Army songs.* London: Workers' Music Association.

Prendergast, R. M., 1991. *Film music: a neglected art.* New York: W. W. Norton.

Ratchnevsky, P., 1993. *Genghis Khan: his life and legacy.* Hoboken: Wiley-Blackwell.

Rees, L. M., 2011. *Mongolian film music during the Socialist era (1921–1990) and its aftermath.* PhD thesis. University of Leeds.

Rice, T., 1994. *May it fill your soul: experiencing Bulgarian music.* Chicago: University of Chicago Press.

Rimberg, J., 1956. The Soviet film industry today. *The Quarterly of Film, Radio and Television*, 11(2), pp. 149–53.

Rona, J., 2001. *The reel world: scoring for pictures.* San Francisco: Miller Freeman.

Rosenberg, W. G. ed., 1990. *Bolshevik visions: first phase of the Cultural Revolution in Soviet Russia.* 2nd edn. Ann Arbor: University of Michigan Press.

Rossabi, M., 2005. *Modern Mongolia: from khans to commissars.* Berkeley: University of California Press.

Rupen, R. A., 1957. Outer Mongolia since 1955. *Pacific Affairs*, 30(4), pp. 342–57.

Sanders, A. J. K., 1996. The ethnic and political borders of Mongolia and the resurgence of Mongolian nationalism. *Papers for the British Association for Korean Studies*, 6, pp. 183–212.

Siemering, B., 2003. Radio in the Gobi. *Mongol Survey*, 11, pp. 17–18.

Sipos, J., 2001. *Kazakh folk songs: from the two ends of the steppe.* Budapest: Akadémiai Kiadó.

Slobin, M. ed., 2008. *Global soundtracks: worlds of film music.* Middletown, CT: Wesleyan University Press.

——, 2009. Central Asian film music as a subcultural system. *Ethnomusicology Forum*, 18(1), pp. 153–64.

——, 2011. *Folk music: a very short introduction.* Oxford: Oxford University Press.

Slonimsky, N., 1944. Soviet music and musicians. *Slavonic and East European Review American Series*, 3(4), pp. 1–18.

Sneath, D., 2005. The rural and the pastoral in Mongolia. In: Bruun, O. and Naronga, L. eds. 2006. *Mongols from country to city: floating boundaries, pastoralism and city life in the Mongol lands.* Copenhagen: Nordic Institute of Asian Studies. pp. 140–61.

Sneath, D. and Kaplonski, C. eds, 2010. *The history of Mongolia*. Folkstone: Global Oriental.

Soronzonbold, S., 2003. *Tsogt Taij kinony khögjimiin sudlal* [*A study of the film score to Tsogt Taij*]. Ulaanbaatar: Admon.

State Statistical Office of the MPRP. 1991. *National Economy of the MPRP 1921–1991*. Ulaanbaatar: State Statistical Office of the MPRP.

Strayer, R., 1998. *Why did the Soviet Union collapse?: understanding historical change*. New York: M. E. Sharpe.

Suvd, B., 2006. *Mongol costume*. Translated from Mongolian by R. Nyamjav. Ulaanbaatar: Mongol Costumes Ltd.

Trotsky, L., 1923. Vodka, the church and cinema. In: W. G. Rosenberg, ed. 1990. *Bolshevik visions: first phase of the Cultural Revolution in Soviet Russia*. 2nd ed. Ann Arbor: University of Michigan Press, pp. 106–109.

Tsolmon, D., 1995. *Mongol Kino*. Ulaanbaatar: Mongol Ulsyn Soyolyn Yaam.

Underdown, M., 1976. The Mongolian film industry. *Canada-Mongolia Review*, 2(1), pp. 47–50.

UNESCO. 1982. *Cultural policy in the Mongolian People's Republic: a study prepared under the auspices of the Mongolian National Commission for UNESCO*. Paris: UNESCO.

UNESCO. n.d. *Elements on the Lists of Intangible Cultural Heritage* [for Mongolia]. [online] Available at: <www.unesco.org/culture/ich/index.php?lg =en&pg=00311&topic=mp&cp=MN> [accessed 27 May 2015].

Vähi, P., 1992. Buddhist music of Mongolia. *Leonardo Music Journal*, 2(1), pp. 49–53.

Vargyas, L., 1968. Performing styles in Mongolian chant. *Journal of the International Folk Music Council*, 20, pp. 70–72.

Workers' Music Association. 1941. *Popular Soviet songs: words and music*. London: Workers' Music Association.

World Bank, 2012a. *Rural population (% of total population) in Mongolia*. [online] Available at: <www.tradingeconomics.com/mongolia/rural-population-percent-of-total-population-wb-data.html> [accessed 10 October 2013].

——, 2012b. *What's behind Mongolia's Economic Boom?*. [online] Available at: <www.worldbank.org/en/news/video/2012/02/28/what-behind-mongolia-economic-boom> [accessed 10 October 2013].

Zhukovskaya, N. L., 1991. The main directions of Soviet ethnographic research in Mongolia in the 1970s and 1980s. *Journal of the Anglo-Mongolian Society*, 13(1–2), pp. 93–104.

Interviews

Altan Urag (band members: Bolortungalag, Bürentögs, Chimedtogtokh, Erdenbat and Oyunbileg. 9 April 2008. Interpreter: Zulaa. Ulaanbaatar: National Academic Drama Theatre.

Amgalum. Apprentice shaman. 3 April 2009. Interpreter: Almagul. Ulaanbaatar: Zorigtbaatar's *ger*, Gandan District.

Angirmaa, B. Producer, composer and singer. 11 December 2008. Interpreter: Bekhbat. Ulaanbaatar: Brauhaus.

Ariunaa, Tserenpiliin. Executive Director of the Arts Council of Mongolia. 2 April 2008. Ulaanbaatar: Arts Council of Mongolia office.

Ariunbold, T. Director of Administration and International Co-operation, State College of Music and Dance. 17 December 2008. Interpreter: Bekhbat. Ulaanbaatar: State College of Music and Dance.

Baigalmaa. Director of the Mongolian Film Archive. 25 November 2008. Interpreter: Bekhbat. Ulaanbaatar: Mongolian Film Archive.

Balkhjav, Lkhagvadorj. General Director of UBS TV, film composer and songwriter. 14 January 2009. Interpreter: Bekhbat. Ulaanbaatar: UBS TV Studios.

Batchuluun, Tsendiin. Director of the Mongolian Horse-Head Fiddle Ensemble. 2 December 2008. Interpreter: Bekhbat. Ulaanbaatar: Central Palace of Culture.

Bayar, Jigmeddorj (Art Director), Gereltsetseg, Urgunkhuu. (Journalist) and Bayardelger, Mandakh. (Foreign Affairs Manager) of UBS TV. 21 April 2008. Interpreter: Bekhbat. Ulaanbaatar: UBS TV Studios.

Bayarkhüü. Tsaatan reindeer herder. 24 May 2009. Interpreter: Soyoloo. Khövsgol province: Bayarkhüü's tepee.

Bayirdak. *Dombra* player and singer. 16 April 2008. Interpreter: Bek. Bayan Ölgii province: Bayirdak's house, Ölgii.

Buyandelger, Tsorj. Buddhist abbot. 19 March 2009. Interpreter: Almagul. Ulaanbaatar: Dashchoilon Monastery.

Buyankhesheg. Music Editor at MNB Radio and former music theory teacher at the State College of Music and Dance, Ulaanbaatar. 6 February 2009. Interpreter: Bekhbat. Ulaanbaatar: Sakura Café.

Chinbat, Prof. Chuluuny. Director of Chamber Orchestra of the State College of Music and Dance. 7 April 2008. Interpreter: Bekhbat. Ulaanbaatar: State College of Music and Dance.

Dolgion, B. Producer, composer, journalist and head of the Pentatonic Academy. 9 April 2008. Interpreter: Bekhbat. Ulaanbaatar: Grand Khaan Irish Pub.

Enebish, J. Researcher of traditional music. 18 February 2009. Interpreter: Bekhbat. Ulaanbaatar: Modern Nomads Restaurant.

176 *Mongolian Film Music*

Enkhtsetseg, Danzangiin. Musicologist, music editor at MNB Television and *khuuchir* teacher. 15 January 2009. Interpreter: Bekhbat. Ulaanbaatar: MNB Cultural Department.

Feinsmith, Daniel David. Composer. 20 November 2007. E-mail interview.

Gansükh, Choijiljaviin, Colonel. Director of the Mongolian Military Song and Dance Academic Ensemble. 2 April 2009. Interpreter: Almagul. Ulaanbaatar: Military Song and Dance Academic Ensemble headquarters.

Jantsannorov, Natsagiin. Composer, musicologist and civil servant. 9 April 2008. Interpreter: Bekhbat. Ulaanbaatar: Khaan Brau.

Jigjidsüren, Gombojavyn. Film director of the Socialist era, television producer and co-author of *Mongol Kino Nevterkhii Toli* [*Encyclopaedia of Mongolian Cinema*]. 7 April 2008. Interpreter: Dolguun. Ulaanbaatar: MNB Studios.

Jumdaan, Choimbolyn. Film director and stunt co-ordinator. 18 November 2008. Ulaanbaatar: London Restaurant.

Karagaz, Almagul. Film translator (Kazakh and Mongolian). 2 April 2008. Ulaanbaatar: Golden Gobi Guesthouse.

Luvsansharav, Dagvyn. Composer. 22 April 2008. Interpreter: Bekhbat. Ulaanbaatar: Grand Khaan Irish Pub.

Mönkhbat. Horse-head fiddle teacher. 10 April 2008. Interpreter: Dolguun. Ulaanbaatar: National University of Mongolia, Department of Mongolian Language and Culture.

Myagmarsüren, Demchigsürengiin, Film researcher and screenplay writer. 17 March 2009. Interpreter: Almagul. Ulaanbaatar: Central Palace of Culture.

Nyamsüren. *Yoochin* player, Tümen Ekh traditional music and dance ensemble. 1 May 2009. Interpreter: Nansar. Ulaanbaatar: Tümen Ekh Theatre.

Odsüren. *Khöömii* teacher. 19 March 2009. Interpreter: Almagul. Ulaanbaatar: Mongolian University of Arts and Culture.

Ogii. Anthropologist and co-founder of Black Shaman Film Logistics. 4 December 2008. Ulaanbaatar: Winners Café.

Oralbek and Saikabek. *Dombra* players. 5 April 2008. Interpreter: Baska. Töv province: Saikabek's *ger*.

Pürevdorj, Geserjavyn. Composer. 16 March 2009. Interpreter: Almagul. Ulaanbaatar: Swiss Café.

Reed, Amy. Sound designer and music editor. 6 November 2007. E-mail interview.

Sharav, Byambasürengiin. Composer. 21 April 2008. Interpreter: Bekhbat. Ulaanbaatar: State Academic Drama Theatre.

Solongo, Jambyn. Director of Mongol Kino Corporation. 4 April 2008. Interpreter: Dolguun. Ulaanbaatar: University of Film Arts.

Soronzonbold, Sürengiin. Music lecturer, author of book on the music for *Tsogt Taij*. 26 March 2009. Interpreter: Almagul. Ulaanbaatar: Mongolian University of Arts and Culture.

Taraa, S. Composer. 2 April 2009. Interpreter: Almagul. Ulaanbaatar: Military Song and Dance Academic Ensemble headquarters.

Tomoo. Music technology teacher and sound engineer. 23 April 2008. Interpreter: Bekhbat. Ulaanbaatar: Mongol Kino Studio.

Tsagaan Nokhoi. Film technician and former mobile cinema projectionist. 31 March 2009. Interpreter: Almagul. Ulaanbaatar: C1 Television Studio.

Tsogt. Horseman and *urtyn duu* singer. 5 April 2008. Töv province: Zuunmod.

Tsogzol, Püreviin, former state film studio designer (1964–94), film director and teacher of film studies. 7 February 2009. Interpreter: Bekhbat. Ulaanbaatar: Staff room, University of Film Arts.

Ukhnaa, Danzanvaanchigiin. General Director of the Mongolian Philharmony. 22 April 2008. Interpreter: Bekhbat. Ulaanbaatar: Mongolian Philharmony, Central Palace of Culture.

Ulambayar, Doljinsürengiin. Horse-head fiddle maker and Director of Argasun Music. 19 November 2008. Interpreter: Bekhbat. Ulaanbaatar: Argasun Music instrument shop.

Urtnasan. Film buff. 27 November 2008. Ulaanbaatar: Michèle's Bakery.

Zorigtbaatar. Shaman. 3 April 2009. Interpreter: Almagul. Ulaanbaatar: Zorigtbaatar's *ger*, Gandan District.

Filmography

Alexander Nevsky (Aleksandr Nevskiy). 1938. Sergei Eisenstein, dir. Soviet Union: Mosfilm.

At the End of the Tale (Ülger Duussan Khoino). 1987. Nyamdavaa, dir. Mongolia: State Film Head Office (formerly Film Factory).

Aurora of Venus (Üüriin Tsolmon). 1979. Buntar, dir. Mongolia: Film Factory.

Awakening (Serelt). 1957. Genden, dir. Mongolia: Film Factory.

Bad Boy, The (Azjargal). 2007. Batbold, dir. Mongolia: Khangarid.

Balapan: Wings of Altai. 2005. Hamid Sardar-Afkhami, dir. France: Zed.

Battle, The (Temtsel). 1971. Jigjid, dir. Mongolia: Film Factory.

Before the Enthronement (Zereg Nemekhiin Ömnö). 1965. Chimed-Osor, dir. Mongolia: Film Factory.

Beloved, The (Khani). 1975. Sumkhüü, dir. Mongolia: Film Factory.

Big Family, A (Önör Bül). 1980. Jigjid, dir. Mongolia: Film Factory.

Bridegroom, The (Khürgen Khüü). 1970. Jigjid, dir. Mongolia: Film Factory.

Cave of the Yellow Dog, The. 2005. Davaa, dir. Germany: Schesch Filmproduktion. Hochschule für Fernsehen und Film München.

Champion Horse, The (Tod Magnai). 1990. Buntar, dir. Mongolia: State Film Head Office.

City Slicker (Niislel Khüü). 1968. Jamsran, dir. Mongolia: Film Factory.

Clear River Tamir, The (Tungalag Tamir). 1970–73. Dorjpalam, dir. Mongolia: Film Factory.

Clear River Tamir, The [the comedy musical] *(Tungalag Tamir)*. 2003. Ineedmiin Tüts Comedy Group, dirs. Mongolia: Mongol Film.

Downward Spiral (Jin Dungui). 1998. Namsrai, dir. Mongolia: (studio unknown).

East of Eden[1] *(Urga)*. 1991. Nikita Mikhalkov, dir. China: Aria et al.

End, The (Tögsgöl). 1967. Buntar and A. Bobrovsky, dirs. Mongolia and Soviet Union: Film Factory and Mosfilm.

Eternal Power of the Sky* *(Mönkh Tengeriin Khüchin Dor)*. 1992. Baljinnyam, dir. Mongolia: Chinggis Film.

Extended Summer, An (Ilüü Sartai Zun). 1987. Selengesüren, dir. Mongolia: Film Factory.

Eyes (Melmii). 2002. Mashbat, dir. Mongolia: Mongoljin.

First Step, The (Ankhny Alkham). 1970. Jigjidsüren, dir. Mongolia: Film Factory.

---

[1] Asterisked titles denote English international release titles. All other English titles translated by Lucy M. Rees and Tümenjiin Bekhbat (January 2009).

180 *Mongolian Film Music*

Five Fingers (Garyn Tavan Khuruu). 1983. Baljinnyam and Nyamgavaa, dirs. Mongolia: Film Factory.

Flood, The (Üyer). 1966. Jigjid, dir. Mongolia: Film Factory.

Footprints (Khünii Mör). 1965. Jigjid, dir. Mongolia: Film Factory.

Forgotten Tale, The (Martagdsan Duuli). 1989. Selengesüren, dir. Mongolia: State Film Head Office.

Future is Coming, The (Irj Yavaa Tsag). 1986. Buntar, dir. Mongolia: Film Factory.

Genghis Khan: A Proud Son of Heaven. 1998. Mailisi Saifu, dir. China: Inner Mongolia Film Studio.

Golden Palace (Altan Örgöö). 1961. Dorjpalam and Gottfried Kolditz dirs. Mongolia and Germany: Film Factory and DEFA Film.

Golden Resurrection (Alt Amilakh Tsagaar). 1993. Törbat, dir. Mongolia: Batkhaan.

Happiness Taken for Granted (Jargal Daakhgüin Zovlon). 1982. Jigjid, dir. Mongolia: Film Factory.

Harmonica, The (Aman Khuur). 1963. Jamsran, dir. Mongolia: Film Factory.

Hello, My Life (Sain Uu, Amidral Mini). 2008. (Director unknown.) Mongolia: Uran Büteeliin Negdügeer Negdel.

Khadak.* 2006. Peter Brosens and Jessica Woodworth, dirs. Belgium: Cinéart.

Khökhöö Almost Gets Married (Khökhöö Gerlekh Dökhlöö). 1962. Jamsran, dir. Mongolia: Film Factory.

Kiran Over Mongolia. 2005. Joseph Spaid, dir. USA: BULKFilms.

Lost Finds His Way, The (Töörsöör Töröldöö). 1966. Sumkhüü, dir. Mongolia: Film Factory.

Mandukhai the Wise Queen (Mandukhai Tsetsen Khatan). 1988. Baljinnyam, dir. Mongolia: State Film Head Office.

Maternal Bonding (Khüin Kholboo). 1992. Binder, dir. Mongolia: Orchlon Film.

Messenger of the People (Ardyn Elch). 1959. Jigjid, dir. Mongolia: Film Factory.

Mirage in the Gobi (Goviin Zereglee). 1980. Dorjpalam, dir. Mongolia: Film Factory.

Mongol: The Rise to Power of Genghis Khan. 2007. Sergei Bodrov, dir. Russia, Germany and Kazakhstan: Andreevsky Film Company, Kinofabrika and Kinokompaniya.

Mongolian Ping Pong.* 2004. Hao Ning, dir. China: Kunlun Brother Film.

Morning (Öglöö). 1968. Jigjid, dir. Mongolia: Film Factory.

Mujaan.* 2004. Chris McKee, dir. USA: Ragcha Media.

Music of Mongolia. 1993. Yves Billon and Henri Lecomte, dirs. France: Les Films du Village.

My Beautiful Jinjimaa* (Jinjimaa). 2002. Mashbat, dir. Mongolia: Mongoljin.

My Mother Appears in My Dreams (Züüdend Irsen Khongorkhon Ijii). 2000. Mashbat, dir. Mongolia: Mongoljin.

Naidan the Shepherd (Khonichin Naidan). 1979. Nyamdavaa, dir. Mongolia: Film Factory.

Norjmaa's Way (Norjmaagiin Zam). 1938. Natsagdorj, dir. Mongolia: Film Factory.

Filmography 181

Not Yet Married (*Gerlej Amjaagüi Yavna*). 1981. Buntar, dir. Mongolia: Film Factory.

Obstacles We Confront, The (*Bidend Yuu Saad Bolj Baina*). 1956. Dorjpalam, dir. Mongolia: Film Factory.

Oh, Those Ladies! (*Ene Khüükhnüüd Üü?*). 1963. Dorjpalam, dir. Mongolia: Film Factory.

One of the Ten Thousand (*Tümnii Neg*). 1962. Jigjid, dir. Mongolia: Film Factory.

Our Melody (*Manai Ayalguu*). 1956. Oyuun, dir. Mongolia: Film Factory.

Poor Suffer, The (*Yaduugiin Zovlon*). 2005. Khüselbaatar, dir. Mongolia: Altain Büshig.

Prayer for the Broad Steppe (*Saruul Talyn Yerööl*). 1984. Dorjpalam, dir. Mongolia: Film Factory.

Quick-Witted Man, The (*Adtai Damshig*). 2007. Altan-Ölzii, dir. Mongolia: Orchlon Film.

Red Forest (*Ulaan Oi*). 2006. Ian Allardyce, dir. Mongolia: C1.

Respected Mother (*Öndör Eej*). 1968. Dorjpalam, dir. Mongolia: Film Factory.

Scent of the Land (*Gazryn Üner*). 1978. Damdin, dir. Mongolia: Film Factory.

Secret of the Cave, The (*Aguin Nuuts*). 1969. Sumkhüü, dir. Mongolia: Film Factory.

Slave's Contract, The (*Boolyn Geree*). 2008. Khürelkhüü, dir. Mongolia: Comedy Art.

Son of Mongolia (*Mongol Khüü*). 1936. I. Z. Trauberg, dir. Soviet Union: Lenfilm.

Start of the Journey, The (*Ikh Zamyn Ekhend*). 1978. Sumkhüü, dir. Mongolia: Film Factory.

*Storm over Asia** (*Potomok Chingis Khana*) 1928. Vsevolod Pudovkin, dir. Soviet Union: Mezhrabpomfilm.

Story of Bushkhüü, The (*Bushkhüügiin Ülger*). 1979. Tsogzol, dir. Mongolia: Film Factory.

Story of the Weeping Camel, The. 2003. Davaa and Luigi Falorni, dirs. Germany: Hochschule für Fernsehen und Film München.

Stranger, The (*Khünii Khün*). 1987. Jumdaan, dir. Mongolia: State Film Head Office.

Sükhbaatar. 1942. A. G. Zarkhi and I. Z. Trauberg, dirs. Soviet Union: Lenfilm.

Sükhbaatar [the comedy musical]. 2003. Ineedmiin Tüts Comedy Group, dirs. Mongolia: Mongol Film.

Tales of First Love (*Ankhny Khariyn Duuli*). 1975. Sumkhüü, dir. Mongolia: Film Factory.

*Tracking the White Reindeer.** 2008. Hamid Sardar-Afkhami, dir. France: Zed.

Tsogt Taij. 1945. Tarich Yuri, dir. Mongolia: Film Factory.

Unforgettable Autumn, An (*Martagdashgüi Namar*). 1975. Damdin, dir. Mongolia: Film Factory.

Unfortunate Fate (*Kheltgii Zayaa*). 1993. Gankhuyag, dir. Mongolia: Khangarid.

Wall, The (*Khana*). 2006. Ochbayar, dir. Mongolia: KUDS and ZDS.

Whirlpool (*Ergüüleg*). 1989. Jumdaan, dir. Mongolia: State Film Head Office.

Wings of the Land (*Gazryn Jigüür*). 1978. Jigjid, dir. Mongolia: Film Factory.

Wooden Snake, The (*Modon Mogoi*). 1991. Nyamdavaa, dir. Mongolia: Mongol Kino.
Wrestler, The (*Garid Magnai*). 1983. Buntar, dir. Mongolia: Film Factory.

Index

Page numbers in **bold** refer to figures. Page numbers in *italics* refer to music examples. Page numbers followed by the letter n refer to footnotes.

1921 Revolution
  anniversaries of 56, 62, 74, 75, 76, 94
  as beginning of modern Mongolian
    history 1, 22
  events of 7, 36
  films about 7, 36, 55, 56, 61, 70, 76, 142
    Clear River Tamir, The 11, 62, 76,
      78, 79, 85, 92, 94
    other specific films 37, 61, 62, 70,
      71, 72, 76, 78
    Jigjid 57, 70, 71, 76, 78
    Luvsansharav 72, 74
    Sumkhüü 70, 72

accordion
  composers learning to play 67, 98
  in film soundtracks 1, 35, 77, 83, 88,
    90, 143–4
  origin of 35n
Alexandrov Ensemble 30
Altan Urag 129–31, 136
Altankhuyag 96, 107, 108, 111–13, see
  also *Whirlpool*
Alexander Nevsky 48
Angirmaa 107, 124
Archer, The 99, 127
archery 4, 18
At the End of the Tale 111
Aurora of Venus 62
Awakening 58, 61, 70

Bach 121, 130
Baljinnyam 99, 101, 108, 113
Balkhjav 107, 128
bassoon 86, 87
Batsükh 73
Battle, The 56, 61, 62, 71–2, 76, 78

Bayan Ölgii 4, 41n, 134, 135, 136, *see also*
  Kazakhs
Bayasgalan 67, 68
Beatles, The 106, 111, 120
Beloved, The 72–3, 77, 95
Birvaa 50, 51
bishgüür
  Altan Urag 130
  definition 16
  in film soundtracks 45, 71, 73, 91, 144
  Luvsansharav learning to play 67
  in traditional-instrument orchestras 24
black and white film 62, 73, 77, 121, 122
Bogd Khan 6, 7, 30, 37, 71, 79, 80, 81
Bolshevism 7, 79, 80, 82, 87
Bömbögör Nogoon theatre 23, 78
Bridegroom, The 76, 78
Buddhism
  before 1921 5, 6, 29, 38
  in films 7, 9, 17, 29, 35, 61, 77
    Battle, The 71–2
    Clear River Tamir, The 75, 77,
      80–81, 82, 83, 86–7, 88, 90
    Naidan the Shepherd 96
    Tsogt Taij 38–9
  Luvsansharav 66, 67
  music (other than in films) 14, 17, 27,
    29, 66, 143
    instruments 15, 16–17, 29, 39, 83,
      90
    vocal music 17, 29
  purges 9, 38, 39, 90
  revival after 1990 5, 10, 29, 120
  suppression during Socialist era 5, 20,
    27, 29, 47, 67

capitalism 52, 82, 106, 107, 111, 137

Cave of the Yellow Dog, The 131, 132, 136, 146
celebrity, concept of 57, 119
censorship, *see also* propagandists, professional
    of films 55, 60, 62, 63, 76, 84
    government policies 9, 20
    relaxation of 108, 119, 145
    in the Soviet Union 34, 108
Central Palace of Culture 23, 65
Champion Horse 99, 127
children's films 56, 62, 74, 77, 78, 107
Chinese films 137
Chinggis Khaan (band) 108
Chinggis Khaan (historical figure)
    absent from films of Socialist era 6, 36, 39–40, 52, 105
    celebrations in 2006 123–4, **123**
    films about, after 1990 6, 122–3, 124, 127, 130, 137
    films featuring, before 1990 34, 101, 105
    as national icon 6, 10, 123, 127, 147
    songs about 40, 116
Chinzorig 109
Choibalsan 6, 8–9, 38, 60, 145
Choidog 50
chorus 30, 45, 69, 72, 77, 102
Chuluun 50, 51
cinemas
    makeshift 122
    in mines and factories 63
    mobile 8, 57, 63–5
    permanent 8, 33, 57, 63, 64, 65, 99, 122
    in red corners 36
    Stalin's private cinema 34
City Slicker 61, 72n, 76, 107
Clear River Tamir, The (film)
    case study 75–94
    characterisations 56, 62, 79, 81–3, 87–8, 93–4, 95
    cinematographer 108
    comparisons to *Mandukhai the Wise Queen* 99, 103, 104
    portrayal of Mongolian traditions 82, 85, 88–90, 91–3, 103, 144, 145
    the score 11, 76, 83–94, **85**, **89**, *93*,104, 144, 145

Clear River Tamir, The (novel) 76, 77, 78, 81, 106
climate, Mongolian 4, 133
Clockwork Orange, A 112
Cold War 95, 97, 142
colour film 61, 62, 73
COMECON 9–10, 61, 140
comedies
    about collectivisation 76
    Harmonica, The 61, 68–9, **69**, 145
    music, use of 68–9, 84–5, 86, 145
    Oh, Those Ladies! 61, 78
    popular genre 36, 61, 74, 122
    Tales of First Love 73
communism 8, 51, 58, 140
composers, formal training of
    after 1990 3, 118, 119, 124, 127, 128
    Altankhuyag 108
    benefits of 22, 56,138
    content of training 30, 31, 98
        symphonic music 2, 21, 41, 42, 45
        Western staff notation 26, 41, 63, 90
    and development of professional music 2, 10, 42–3, 141, 143
    Duragjav 20
    from ethnic minorities 28
    Gonchigsumlaa 45, 127
    government support of 19, 31, 42, 45–6, 106
    Jantsannorov 98, 104, 113
    Luvsansharav 67, 68, 73, 78
    by other Mongolian composers 23, 48, 127
    Namsraijav 77, 78, 79, 90, 92
    replacing traditional oral learning 21, 24, 26
    on returning to Mongolia 22, 31, 51, 53
    Sharav 127
    at Soviet conservatoires 1, 2, 21, 23, 41, 48, 49, 113, 140–41
        additional learning and experiences 22, 31, 95
        Kiev Conservatoire 104
        political motives 2, 140–41
        Sofia Conservatoire, Bulgaria 108
        Tchaikovsky College of Music and Dance, Ulan-Ude 124

Tchaikovsky Conservatoire
    Moscow 41n, 67, 78
  in Ulaanbaatar 21, 23, 48, 119, 138
  by visiting Soviet experts 20, 26, 33,
    41, 55
composers, status of 2, 10, 47–9, 52, 53
costume, traditional Mongolian
  and 1990 demonstrations 116
  deel 5, 133
  deel in films 80, 112
  ethnic groups and societies 5, 14
  in films 38, 99, 146
  in performances 98
cultural centres 23, 30, *see also* cultural
    clubs; red corners; red *ger*s
cultural clubs 23, 24, 27, 64, 67, 71, 73, *see*
    also cultural centres; red corners;
    red *ger*s
Cultural Leap Forward, *see under* cultural
    revolution
cultural revolution
  Cultural Leap Forward (1959) 20, 21, 65
  Great Leap Forward (1929–32) 20, 81
  in Soviet Union (1928–31) 20n, 34

Damdinsüren 26, 38, 47, 48–9, 50, 96
Dashnamjil, *see under* Sükhbaatar
Davaa 131–3, 135
Democratic Revolution (1990) 1, 3, 7, 95,
    115–16, 117, 121, 145–7
Dew, 99
diegetic music, *see also* semidiegetic music
  definition 37
  in film soundtracks 51, 142, 144
    Clear River Tamir, The 83, 88–90, **89**
    Harmonica, The 61, 68
    Mandukhai the Wise Queen 102
    Morning 71
    post-1990 films 132, 133, 136
    Tsogt Taij 39, **39**, *40*
    Whirlpool 109–111
dombra 134, **135**, 136
domestic music 15, 16, 27, 41, 67, 68
Dolgion 107, 124
Dorjpalam
  Clear River Tamir, The 77–9, 81, 83,
    86, 88–90, 94

  collaborations with composers 51, 77,
    78n, 79, 88–90, 94
  Obstacles We Confront, The 58, 60,
    77, 94
  training in Moscow 77, 108
Drums
  Buddhist 29, 71
  drum kit 30, 72, 106, 107, 111, 130, 136
  frame drum 136
  in *Secret History of the Mongols, The*
    105
  shamans' 15, 17, 29, 71, 102, 103
  snare 71, 74
  timpani 71, 102, 105
Duragjav 20

economy, Mongolian 1, 4, 7, 9, 20, 117–18,
    125, 146
Eisenstein, Sergei 34, 38, 48
electric organ 66, 72, 73, *see also* keyboard
End, The 61
Enemy of the State 124, 126
Eternal Power of the Sky 122
ethnic groups, *see* Kazakhs; Khalkha;
    Tsaatan

fanfares 39, 71, 104, *105*
Feinsmith, Daniel David 133
feudalism
  eradication during Socialist era 6, 19,
    27, 139, 140
  portrayal in films 55, 76, 89, 90, 144
Film Factory, *see* state film studio,
    founding of
film posters 64
film scores, handwritten 3n, 26, 38, 63, 66,
    90, 128
films for children, *see* children's films
First Step, The 62
Five Colours of the Rainbow 56
Five Fingers 96, 99
five-year plan 9, 21, 56, 74, 76, 122, 139, 143
Flood, The 61, 78
flute (orchestral) 30, 39, 45, 88, 91, 92
flute (traditional Mongolian), see *gyaling*;
    limbe; *sybyzgy*; *tsuur*
folk music, definitions 13–15

Footprints 61, 78–9, 94
Forgotten Tale, The 96, 127
French horn 46, 59, 92
funding after 1990
    for films about Chinggis Khaan 122,
       123, 124, 127
    for films, lack of 3, 118, 121, 124, 128,
       129
    for music, lack of 3, 118, 119, 120,
       124, 128, 129
    in rural areas, lack of 119, 134
    Soviet aid, withdrawal of 118, 119, 137
    for television, lack of 122
funding before 1990
    for films about 1921 Revolution 37, 40,
       71, 77
    for new music 8, 19, 106
    for state film studio 19, 35, 53, 63, 66

Gandan monastery 39, 116
Genghis Khan, *see* Chinggis Khaan
ger, definition 4, 5
glasnost, *see also* Gorbachev, Mikhail;
      perestroika
    definition 97
    and perestroika 7, 10, 11, 95, 96, 97,
      115, 145
    and Soviet Black Wave 108
golden age of Mongolian film music 10,
      49–52, 53, 96, 128, 138
Golden Palace 6, 77
Gonchigsumlaa 41n, 45, 48, 50, 127, 140
Gorbachev, Mikhail
    and the dissolution of the Soviet Union
      117
    glasnost and perestroika 7, 10, 95, 96,
      97, 110, 113, 115
Great Leap Forward, *see under* cultural
      revolution
guitar 14, 72, 73, 106, 107, 134
gyaling 16, 29

handwritten film scores, *see* film scores,
      handwritten
harmonica 61, 68–9, 145
Harmonica, The 61, 68–70, **69**, 145
harmonising folk melodies

in film soundtracks 39, 45, 46, 91, 92,
      103, 132
    pentatonic scales 39, 45, 46, 103, 132,
      144
    professional music, early development
      of 26, 39, 44, 48, 143, 144
    in Soviet Central Asian Republics 26,
      143
harp 88, 91
heavy metal 3, 119, 126, 146
Hello, My Life 124
Heritage of the Great Leader, The 123
hip-hop 3, 119, 125, 126, 128, 133, 138,
      146
hit-points, matching of 84–5, **85**, 145
Hollywood
    after 1990 in Mongolia 122, 138
    film scoring conventions 37, 70–71,
      83, 84, 86, 87, 128
    Soviet film influenced by 34
Hong Kong films 122, 124, 126, 138
horse-head fiddle
    Altan Urag 129–30, 131
    bowing techniques 21, 144
    celebrations in 2006 for Chinggis
      Khaan 123
    construction of **17**, 25, 121
    as cultural icon 5, 10, 16, 18, 120–21
    definition 16
    in film soundtracks after 1990 129,
      130, 132
    in film soundtracks before 1990 38, 79,
      94, 102, 112, 70, 144
      Clear River Tamir, The 84, 85, 88,
        91, 92
    Horse-Head Fiddle Ensemble 23, 121
    origin 17
    repertoire 16, 19, 29, 44, 59
    tuning 25, 104
    Ulambayar 16, 120–21, 147
    violoncello, comparison to 21, 24, 70,
      130, 144
horse racing 4, 5
horses, songs about 5, 16, 59, 88

I Love You 99
ikh büree 29, 67, 71

ikh khuur 25, 129, 132
Inadequate Fate 127
Ivan the Terrible 38

Janchiv 50, 51, 107
Jantsannorov
    background and training 41n, 42, 98–9,
        104, 113, 115, 141
    as civil servant 95, 96, 98–9, 113
    commercialisation 102, 147
    compositional techniques 45, 101–5,
        106, 114, 141, 144
    concert music 121
    film scores other than *Mandukhai the*
        Wise Queen 99, 122, 127
    Mandukhai the Wise Queen 96,
        99–105, **103**, *105*, 108, 113, 114
    perestroika, influence of 95, 101–2,
        113, 145
    "the pinnacle of professional music"
        46, 104
    preservation of traditional music 98,
        103, 105, 146
    prolific composer 50, 96, 126
Japanese films 122, 124, 137
jaw harp 16, 29, 99
Jigjid
    as cinematographer 70
    collaborations with composers 51, 70,
        71, 73, 78
    films about 1921 Revolution 57, 70,
        71, 76, 78
    minor characters praising socialism 70,
        71, 74, 83
Jigjidsüren 51, 132
Jumdaan 95, 99, 108–13, 114, 115, 145,
    see also *Whirlpool*

Kazakhs 4, 5, 14, 28, 134–6, *see also*
    Bayan Ölgii
keyboard 35, 107, 111, 112, 113, 128, *see*
    also electric organ
Khaar Torgon Khamjaar 112
Khadak 129, 130, 131, 136
Khalkha
    costume, traditional 5
    folk music modified during Socialist
        era 4, 14, 15, 19, 27, 28, 134

government support of 31, 19, 28, 144
    music in films 27, 28, 88, 91
    musical characteristics 14, 15, 26, 44, 91
    population 4
Khangal 50, 51, 107
Khökhöö Almost Gets Married 76
Khokhny Duu 115
Khonk 108, 115
khöömii
    Altan Urag 130, 131
    definition and technique 17–18
    in film soundtracks 18, 19, 25, 102–3,
        130, 133, 134
    traditional performance contexts 18,
        25, 29
Khrushchev, Nikita 7n, 9
Khrushchev Thaw 9, 60, 145
khuuchir 16, 17, 24, 27, 102, 132
Kiran Over Mongolia 135–6
Korean films 122, 124, 126, 128, 136–7, 138

Lenin, Vladimir 33, 37, 60, 75, 76, 97, 105;
    see also Marxist-Leninist ideology
limbe
    definition 16
    in film soundtracks 45, 84, 85, 91, 92,
        102, 132
    played by herders 41
    in traditional-instrument orchestras 24
Live from UB 133
Lodoidamba 76, 77, 78, 81, 83, 106
long-song, *see also* short-song
    celebrations in 2006 for Chinggis
        Khaan 123
    definition 18
    in films 18–19, 38, 85, 102, 103, 112, 133
    Jantsannorov 98, 102
    Luvsansharav 67
    performance contexts 18–19, 41, 67
    in *Three Dramatic Characters* 26
Lost Finds His Way, The 61, 68, 70–71
Luvsansharav
    artistic freedom 63, 68, 140
    background and training 41n, 66–8, 73,
        74, 78, 141
    case study 66–74
    collaborations with directors 51, 63,
        70–74

Harmonica, The 61, 68–70
popular music, desire to listen to 106, 125, 140
professional music 66, 70, 73–4
prolific composer 11, 50, 55, 66, 74, 96

Mandukhai the Wise Queen, see also
Jantsannorov
case study 99–105
celebrating lost traditions 100, **103**, 105, 109, 113–14, 116, 137, 146
Jantsannorov, composer of 96, 98, 99, 108
Jumdaan, stunt team leader 108, 109
perestroika, influence of 95, 101, 145
production of 38, 99, 100, 101, 108, 113, 115
the score 90n, 101–5, *105*, 113, 114, 122, 127
Marxist-Leninist ideology 1, 55, 97, 140, 141
Maternal Bonding 127
mergejliin khögjim, see professional music
Messenger of the People 44, 45, 61, 70, 78
military music, *see also* revolutionary
songs
Alexandrov Ensemble 30
in film soundtracks 1, 30–31, 35, 69, 104, 106, 111
Clear River Tamir, The 77, 78, 79, 83, 92
Luvsansharav's scores 71, 73
military brass bands 1, 8, 30, 71, 83, 92, 143
military music ensemble 23, 24, 30
Mongolian Military Song and Dance
Academic Ensemble 30, 71, 120
Red Army Choir 30
symphonic music inspired by 30, 69, 71, 83
Minister of Culture 76, 106, *see also*
Lodoidamba
Ministry of Culture 49, 96, 98, 101, 106
Ministry of Internal Affairs 113
Ministry of Public Education 33
mobile cinemas, *see under* cinemas; *see also* Tsagaan Nokhoi
Mongol 129, 130–131, 136
Mongol Empire 6, 17, 52, 98, 123, 124

Mongol Kino, *see* state film studio
renamed Mongol Kino
Mongolian Arts Committee 98
Mongolian Association of Musicians 99
Mongolian Bling 133
Mongolian Composers' Union
control over music-making 26, 27, 46, 53, 106
establishment of 20
and film composers 49, 53, 96, 117–18, 119
Mongolian Film Archive 3n, 63, 65–6, 122
Mongolian Military Song and Dance
Academic Ensemble, *see under*
military music
Mongolian National Song and Dance
Academic Ensemble 23, 24, 120, 134, *see also* Mongolian People's
Song and Dance Ensemble
Mongolian People's Party, founding of 6
Mongolian People's Party renamed
Mongolian People's Revolutionary
Party 7
Mongolian People's Revolutionary Party
after 1990 7, 116, 118, 146
Mongolian People's Revolutionary Party,
only party until 1990 7, 81
Mongolian People's Song and Dance
Ensemble 23n, 67, *see also*
Mongolian National Song and
Dance Academic Ensemble
Mongolian Philharmony 3n, 23, 24, 46, 64, 65, 73, 89n, 106
Mongolian Writers' Union 56–7, 62, 63
Mördorj
blending traditional and symphonic
music 45, 46, 59, 141
collaborations with directors 51
film scores 36, 38, 44, 45, 46, 58
prolific composer 45, 48, 50, 59, 96
state medals 48–9
training 41n
Morning 56, 61, 71–2, 76, 78, 87
Mozart 111, 120, 121
MPRP, *see* Mongolian People's
Revolutionary Party after 1990;
Mongolian People's Revolutionary
Party, only party until 1990

Mujaan 131, 132–3, 135, 136
musicals 36, see also *Our Melody*
Myagmarsüren 60, 99, 102

Naadam
    festival 4, 5, 18, 99, 105, 120
    portrayal in films 19, 144, 145
        Clear River Tamir, The 80, 81, 90, 92
        Mandukhai the Wise Queen 104
        Messenger of the People 44
Naidan the Shepherd 96
Namsraijav 41n, 50, 78–9, 84–6, 88–94,
    104, 145, see also *Clear River*
    Tamir, The (film)
National Academic Drama Theatre 23
national anthem 49
"national in form and socialist in content"
    20, *see also* Stalin, Joseph
National University of Mongolia 115
Natsagdorj 50, 126
New Acquaintances 62
New Babylon, The 48
New Year, Mongolian, see *Tsagaan Sar*
Nineteen Twenty-One Revolution, *see*
    1921 Revolution
Norjmaa's Way 35
Norovbanzad 102
Not Yet Married 96

Obstacles We Confront, The 45, 46, 55,
    58–60, 77, 94, 145
October Revolution (1917, Soviet Union) 97
Oh, Those Ladies! 61, 78
One of the Ten Thousand 61, 78
organ, *see* electric organ
Our Melody 28, 36, 45, 60, 134, 140, 145,
    see also musicals
overtone singing, see *khöömii*

palace music 15, 27, 34, 37, 39, 103
party newspaper, see *Pravda*; *Ünen* (party
    newspaper)
pentatonic scale
    in film soundtracks 44–5
    of the Socialist era 39, 46, 59, 68,
        70, 73, 91–2
    after 1990 132
    harmonising of 39, 45, 46, 103, 132, 144

pre-1921 folk music 14, 26
post-1921 tuning 26, 44, 103
perestroika, *see also* glasnost; Gorbachev,
    Mikhail
    definition 97
    and glasnost 7, 10, 11, 95, 96, 97, 115, 145
    Jantsannorov, influenced by 95, 101–2,
        113, 145
    Jumdaan, influenced by 95, 109, 110
    and Soviet Black Wave 109
    Zorig, influenced by 115
Pink Floyd 107, 111
Pioneers 22, 140, 144, *see also*
    Revolutionary League of Youth
popular music after 1990
    Altan Urag 129–31, 136
    "bad influence" 132
    Dolgion 107, 124
    from foreign countries 10, 120, 122,
        126, 146
    immediately after 1990 119–20, 121,
        128, 138, 145
    Kiran Over Mongolia 135
    Mongolian compositions 124, 125,
        126, 128, 133, 137, 146, 147
popular music before 1990
    in film soundtracks 2, 107, 109
        Whirlpool 11, 108, 110, 111, 113,
        114
    introduced to Mongolia 106–8, 143
    Khonkh and *Khonkhny Duu* 115
    Luvsansharav, desire to listen to 106,
        125, 140
    Soyol Erdene 23, 46, 106–7
    underground scene 107, 108, 119
Pravda 7, 8, 23, 47
professional music
    and composers, formal training of 2,
        10, 42–3, 141, 143
    definitions 2, 10, 46–7, 103
    early development of 41–7, 53, 141,
        143, 147
    in film soundtracks 111, 128, 141, 142,
        144
        Clear River Tamir, The 83, 85,
        91–3, **93**, 144
        Mandukhai the Wise Queen 11,
        103, 104, **105**, 127

Obstacles We Confront, The 46, 59
Tsogt Taij 39, **39**, *40*, 44, 46
Jantsannorov 11, 103, 104, 127, 147
"the pinnacle of professional
music" 46, 104
Luvsansharav 66, 70, 73–4
state support for 26, 45–6, 106, 143, 144
Prokofiev, Sergei 38n, 41, 48
propagandists, professional 9, 56, *see also*
censorship
public song 27, 34, 37, 51, 67, 79
Pürevdorj 128–9
purges 8, 9, 38, 66, 83, 90, 100, *see also
under* Buddhism; shamanism

Red Army Choir 30
red corners 23, 36, 64, 140, *see also* cultural
centres; cultural clubs; red *gers*
red *gers* 22, 30, *see also* cultural centres;
cultural clubs; red corners
religion, *see* Buddhism; shamanism
Revolutionary League of Youth 22, 140,
144, *see also* Pioneers
revolutionary songs, *see also* military
music
fanfares 104
in film soundtracks 1–2, 22, 28, 72, 78,
125, 143–4
Battle, The 71
Clear River Tamir, The 83, 88, 90
Harmonica, The 69
Morning 71
Sükhbaatar 37
performance contexts 22
Rinchen 27, 38
rock music, *see* popular music after 1990;
popular music before 1990

saxophone 30, 72, 107
Scent of the Land, The 62, 76
Secret History of the Mongols, The 6, 105
semidiegetic music 37, 44, 88, 89, 90, *see
also* diegetic music
semidocumentaries 59, 131–3, 134–6, 137
shamanism
before 1921 5, 6, 29
in films 9, 17, 29
Khadak 130

specific films of Socialist era 38,
58, 71, 72, 102, 103, 105
music (other than in films) 14, 15, 17,
27, 29, 143
purges 9
revival after 1990 5, 29, 120
suppression during Socialist era 5, 20,
105
shanz
concerto 121
definition 16
in film soundtracks 71, 73, 89, 90, 92,
144
origin 17
Sharav 41n, 42, 48, 50, 121, 126, 127, 141
short-song 19, 67, 71, *see also* long-song
Shostakovich, Dmitri 42, 46, 48
shudraga, see *shanz*
Slave's Contract, The 124
Smirnov, Boris 25, 26, 38
socialist realism, *see under* Soviet cinema
Solongo 46
Son of Mongolia 34–5
Sosorbaram 116
Sound of a Bell, The, see *Khonkhny Duu*
Soviet cinema
birth of Soviet film industry 33–4
films 33, 37, 38, 48, 57, 108
Hollywood influence 34
screened in Mongolia 33, 37, 64
socialist realism 34, 58n, 108
Soviet Black Wave 108–9
music 2, 8, 36, 37, 39, 52, 107–8, 143
policies 8
Soviet Union, dissolution of 8, 11, 95, 97,
115, 116–17, 118, 127
Soviet Union as elder brother to Mongolia
7–8, 20, 21, 35, 56, 97, 117,
139–40
Soyol Erdene 23, 46, 106–7
Spaid, Joseph 135, 136
spotting 38, 85–6
Stalin, Joseph 9, 20, 34, 38, 60, 116, 145
State Big Band 46, 73
State College of Music and Dance
founding of 21
staff 13, 21, 22, 42, 44, 48, 128
students 22, 45, 48, 109, 120

Index

191

state film studio, founding of 1, 10, 23, 33
state film studio renamed Mongol Kino 35n, 66, 118, 121
State Opera and Ballet Theatre 23, 24
state rock band, *see* Soyol Erdene
State Symphony Orchestra 3n, 23, 42, 64, 65, 106, 120, 143
Storm Over Asia 34
Story of Büshkhüü, The 78
Story of the Weeping Camel, The 131–2, 135, 146
Stranger, The 109
Sükhbaatar
 films about 36–7, 40, 56, 113, 144
  Battle, The 56, 71
  Clear River Tamir, The 75, 77, 79–81, 83, 86, 87, 88, 89, 91
  Dashnamjil 56, 71, 87
  Lost Finds His Way, The 70
  Messenger of the People 44, 45
  minor characters praising 60, 61, 70, 71, 77, 80, 83
  Morning 56, 61, 71
  Sükhbaatar 37, 40, 52
 as military leader of 1921 Revolution 6, 7, 79
 as new national hero 33, 36, 38, 40, 52, 105, 108, 123
 portrayal as national hero in films 7, 33, 37, 61, 91, 123, 142
 renaming of capital city to Ulaanbaatar 7, 36, 81
Sükhbaatar, character in *Mujaan* 132–3
Sükhbaatar Square, Ulaanbaatar 23, 36, 115, 116, 123, **123**
Sumkhüü 51, 70, 72, 73
surround sound 123, 126
Suvd, Namsrain 99, **103**
sybyzgy 134, 136

Tales of First Love 72, 73, 95
Tchaikovsky, Pyotr 41, 46
Teachers' [training] College 98
temperature in Mongolia 4, 133
Three Dramatic Characters 26, 47
Three Friends 78
'three manly sports' 4, 5, 99, 127, *see also* archery; horse racing; wrestling

throat singing, see *khöömii*
timpani, *see under* drums
Toroi Bandi 82, 91, 92
traditional-instrument orchestras 17, 23, 24, 73, 103
training of composers, *see* composers, training of
Tsaatan 60, 134
Tsagaan Nokhoi 64–5
Tsagaan Sar 4–5, 52, 64, 100, 120
Tsogt Taij
 DVD release 38n, 61
 Jigjid as cinematographer 70
 narrator 58
 patriotism 38, 100, 145
 score 36n, 38–40, *39*, **40**, 44, 46, 145
 score, handwritten 66
Tsogzol 56, 57, 63, 68, 78, 79, 108
tsuur 16, 17

Ukhnaa 65, 89n
Ulaanbaatar, naming of 7, 36, 81
Ulambayar, *see under* horse-head fiddle
Ulan Bator, *see* Ulaanbaatar, naming of
underscoring 37, 39, 44, 69, 83, 86, 90, 102
Ünen (opera) 48
Ünen (party newspaper) 2, 7, 8, 23, 58, 65, 110, 142
UNESCO 4, 8, 18
Unforgettable Autumn, An 76, 107
Ungern-Sternberg, Baron 7
University of Film Arts in Ulaanbaatar 3n, 30n, 57, 60n, 66, 131
urban drama films
 during the 1980s 62, 70, 77, 96, 101, 106, 126
 after 1990 122, 126, 131–2, 133, 137
uukhai
 definition 18
 in film soundtracks 19, 38, 105
 in *Naadam* scenes 44, 90, 92, 144, 145
Uyakhan Zambutiviin Naran 102

vibraphone 66, 72, 74, 109
vocal music, traditional, see *khöömii*; long-song; short-song; *uukhai*

Whirlpool 95, 96, 108–13, 114, 137, 142, 145, *see also* Altankhuyag; Jumdaan

widescreen 77

Wings of the Land 73, 74, 77

Wrestler, The 99, 100, 101, 127

wrestling 4, 34, 44, 72, 73, 92, 127

xylophone 86, 102

yatga 16, 17, 73, 91, 102, 104–5, 132

Yeltsin, Boris 117

yoochin
 Altan Urag 130, 131
 concerto 121
 definition 16
 in film soundtracks 102, 103, 130, 132
 Tümen Ekh ensemble 27, 120

yurt, see *ger*, definition

Zorig 115, 117